Barbara Rose was an instructor in English at Tsuda College, Japan. She currently lives in Newfoundland.

D1714371

Tsuda Umeko and Women's *Education in Japan*

Barbara Rose

Tsuda Umeko and Women's Education in Japan

Yale University Press
New Haven & London

LA
2383
.J32
T787
1992

Copyright © 1992 by Yale University. All rights reserved. This book may not be reproduced, in whole or in part, including illustrations, in any form (beyond that copying permitted by Sections 107 and 108 of the U.S. Copyright Law and except by reviewers for the public press), without written permission from the publishers.

Set in Joanna type by Compset Inc., Beverly, Massachusetts. Printed in the United States of America by Vail-Ballou Press, Binghamton, New York.

Library of Congress Cataloging-in-Publication Data
Rose, Barbara, 1958–
Tsuda Umeko and women's education in Japan / Barbara Rose.
p. cm.
Includes bibliographical references and index.
ISBN 0-300-05177-8 (alk. paper)
1. Tsuda, Umeko 1864–1929. 2. Women educators—Japan—Biography. 3. Women—Education (Higher)—Japan—History. I. Title
LA2383.J32T787 1992
376'.952—dc20 91-784
CIP

The paper in this book meets the guidelines for permanence and durability of the Committee on Production Guidelines for Book Longevity of the Council on Library Resources.

10 9 8 7 6 5 4 3 2 1

"Someday, when I am older, will I be able to get rid of this impulse, this wanting to be a 'good wife,' without feeling lost? Would I then be able to write my own story? I don't wish not to be a woman, but I'd certainly like to be a woman whose sense of purpose comes from within."

—Uno Chiyo, *A Genius of Imitation*
(*Mohō no Tensai*, 1936, translated by Yukiko Tanaka)

Contents

Preface

Writing a life of Tsuda Umeko presents an opportunity to examine the intersection of two cultures: post-restoration Japan of the Meiji and Taishō eras (1868–1926), and the United States of the late nineteenth and early twentieth centuries. More specifically, the values that underlay one of the contentious debates of the period—women's higher education—are represented in Tsuda's life, work, and person. New nations often regard female education as critical to their security, placing a special emphasis on the capacity of women as mothers to raise loyal and obedient citizens. Thus Tsuda was sent by the government of her newly created nation to study the essentials of "woman's sphere" in another recently formed nation. She returned to Japan over a decade later thoroughly steeped in the standards of the Western domestic ideal, standards that she regarded as the elements of civilization. How these ideas were received in Japan, which was just then articulating its ideal of domesticity, *ryōsai kembo* (good wife and wise mother), and how Tsuda appealed to both the American and the Japanese versions of the domestic ideal to establish herself as an authority on female education are the focus of this biography.

Most of the source material I have used is in English. Tsuda College Library holds over thirty years' worth of Tsuda Umeko's letters to Charles and Adeline Lanman, her American guardians, as well as letters to and from the individuals and organizations in the United States that offered her support. The speeches and public addresses Tsuda gave in Tokyo, and even the letters she wrote to members of her family, are also in English. These papers, as well as the previously published collection of some of her letters, journals, and essays, provide a rich source of materials that offer a look at Meiji and Taishō Japan as experienced by a Western-educated daughter of the samurai class. These documents are described more fully in the bibliography.

Writing a woman's life offers specific challenges. Biographies are monuments to their subjects: we expect an extraordinary life or at least an exemplary life lived during extraordinary times. Biographies, in other words, are about heroes. But a biography of a woman tends to pull against or run into the central assumptions of the genre. If we celebrate elite women who have gained privilege in a world of male power or lionize strong women who have struggled in a world of oppression, we present them as exceptional, the tokens that prove the rule. These women, in the words of Adrienne Rich, are offered as "honorary men."[1]

Writing the biography of a woman involved in the struggle for women's higher education raises other problems. Tsuda Umeko is customarily presented as a "pioneer" of Japanese women's education, a characterization based on the assumptions of tokenism, for the word is loaded with associations of conquest and exploitation. Once again we confront an honorary man. The compelling features of rugged individualism, moreover, obscure the presence of various groups whose efforts to promote women's rights offered instrumental support to these pioneers. We lack a vocabulary to describe such lives as unexceptional, as the lives of ordinary human beings, neither saints nor deviants.

And indeed Tsuda's life was in many ways unexceptional. Although much of her experience reflects the political and social currents of Meiji and Taishō Japan, her story also dramatizes issues that remain fundamental to women's higher education. This raises another problem: a biography of an advocate of women's education must confront the class-based assumptions that often lie behind efforts to educate the daughters of "good" families. Issues of class and race are interwoven with the history of female schools: higher education for women, as Florence Howe has observed, does not necessarily raise women's status in relation to men—it raises women's status in relation to other women.[2]

Thus I do not regard Tsuda's achievements in women's education and her social-reform efforts as unambiguous triumphs. Her advantage lay in her ability to expand women's opportunities without challenging the status quo, a success achieved by rooting her program in the compelling American ideology of domesticity and the equally powerful Japanese ideology of ryōsai kembo. There is another side to her achievements. Domesticity, though empowering, was finally limiting: it proved to be a restrictive ideology that held women to a life within the imposed boundaries of woman's proper place. In concerning herself only with the daughters of privilege, moreover, Tsuda helped to create an elite who received a small share within the established system of power. Her life is typical of the contradictions of nineteenth-century feminism in both Japan and the United States, contradictions that revolve around issues of women's difference and universal equality.

To this day the domestic ideal remains the influential model of womanhood in Japan. Tsuda Umeko's vision of the educated wife and efficient mother is still promoted at institutions of higher learning for women, where it is assumed that graduates will find their identity through marriage and motherhood. What this means for contemporary Japanese women and their society is an issue beyond the scope of this book.

A note on the Japanese names in this study: personal names are presented in the Japanese order—that is, the family name comes first, followed by the given name(s). In some citations, however, individual authors' given names are followed by their surnames.

Tsuda Umeko's spelling of Japanese names and words has been standardized (Stematz, for example, becomes Sutematsu), but her English has been reproduced exactly as it appears in her writings.

It is a pleasure to thank the people who assisted me in writing this book. The project began as a collaboration with Professor Furuki Yoshiko of Tsuda College. Differences in method and interpretation, however, have made separate biographies necessary. I am grateful to

Professor Furuki for letting me read the notes she took from the two Japanese biographies of Tsuda Umeko and for reading the earliest drafts of my chapters 2 and 3. Rebecca Copeland, Bill Steele, Clair Hughes, and George Hughes read the entire manuscript and offered valuable criticism. Margaret Mitsutani and Hiroko McDermott gave encouraging support; Mary Harada and Martha Toccu also showed an interest in the project. To Nakano Takako, a model research assistant, I am also indebted.

I am grateful to Tsuda College for permission to quote from Tsuda Umeko's letters and papers, and especially to the archivist of Tsuda College Library, Hirata Yasuko, for her patient assistance. Caroline Rittenhouse, of the archives at Bryn Mawr College, readily made available all of Byrn Mawr's materials related to Tsuda. The intelligent help of Sakurai Yoshiyuki of International Christian University Library was also indispensable.

To Gladys Topkis of Yale University Press, for having confidence in my work and being so supportive of it, I am deeply grateful. Special thanks to William Schipper and Adam, to whom I dedicate this book.

Chronology

1868	Meiji Restoration
1871	Iwakura mission leaves Japan
1879	Great Principles of Education issued
1886	Japan Women's Temperance Association (Kyōfukai) established
1889	Meiji Constitution promulgated
1890	Police Security Regulations issued
	Imperial Rescript on Education issued
	First Diet convened
1894–1895	Sino-Japanese War
1898	Meiji Civil Code promulgated
1899	Girls' Higher School Law issued
1901	Japan Women's Patriotic Association (Aikoku Fujinkai) established
1904–1905	Russo-Japanese War
1910	Korea annexed
1912	Death of Meiji emperor; succeeded by Taishō emperor
1920	New Women's Association (Shin Fujin Kyōkai) established

1921	Red Wave Society (Sekirankai) established
1923	Great Kantō Earthquake
1925	Universal Male Suffrage Act passed Women's Suffrage League established
1926	Death of Taishō emperor; succeeded by Shōwa emperor
1931	Great Japan Federated Women's Association (Dai Nihon Rengō Fujinkai) established
1932	Manchukuo (puppet state in Manchuria) established Great Japan National Defense Women's Association (Dai Nihon Kokubō Fujinkai) founded
1933	Japan secedes from League of Nations
1936	Anti-Comintern Pact (Germany-Japan) signed
1940	Tripartite Pact (Germany-Italy-Japan) signed
1941–1945	Pacific War
1942	Great Japan Women's Association (Dai Nihon Fujinkai) established
1945–1952	American Occupation

Tsuda Umeko and *Women's* Education in Japan

Chapter One

Introduction: The Old Life & the New

In the summer of 1853 Commodore Matthew Perry of the United States Navy anchored his four ships off Uraga at the mouth of Edo Bay and delivered a letter to the shōgun from President Millard Fillmore requesting that Japan open trade relations with the United States. Accompanying the president's letter was another written by Perry: it informed the Japanese envoys that he would return for an official answer the following year, but this time with more ships, effectively presenting the Tokugawa government with an ultimatum to open the country. The threat was underscored two days later, when Perry sailed two of his ships further up the bay to within sight of Edo.[1]

Perry was not the first representative of a Western power to demand that Japan begin relations with the West. In 1846 an American naval officer had been sent to Japan to investigate the opening of negotiations, without success; three years later the USS *Preble* was ordered to Nagasaki, and although the commander was able to secure the release of shipwrecked American sailors held there, he was unable to establish a consul in Japan. The ships of other countries had also appeared in Japanese waters. In 1808 a British frigate entered Nagasaki harbor and seized supplies. After Britain acquired Hong Kong at the end of the Opium War with China in 1842, the Royal Navy conducted a lengthy survey of the Ryukyu Islands, to the south of Japan. In August 1845 another British survey ship arrived in Nagasaki with a request for supplies; before leaving, it surveyed the harbor. Four years later the HMS *Mariner* also attempted a survey, this time of the strategic approaches to Edo. Russia, too, attempted contact with its Asian neighbor and in 1804 sent a ship to Japan in a fruitless effort to establish relations. Growing colonization of Siberia and vital interests in northeast Asia made Russia wary of British and American overtures to Japan, and news of Perry's squadron prompted another Russian expedition to Japan. Admiral Putyatin's ships arrived one month after Perry's.

Commodore Perry represented an external threat to a country already destabilized by internal strife. The arrival of the Americans in Uraga had come as no surprise: the government in Edo had been forewarned of Perry's expedition but was unable to deal decisively with the crisis. In an effort to buy time, the authorities accepted Fillmore's letter at a solemn ceremony on shore watched by five thousand Japanese troops and within firing range of two of Perry's ships. This was certainly a sign of the Tokugawa shōgun's weakness, for the "barbarian-suppressing great general" (the meaning of his title) was no longer able to keep the barbarians from Japan's shores.

In 1603 Tokugawa Ieyasu had become shōgun—the military deputy of the emperor, but de facto ruler of Japan—and established his headquarters in Edo (now Tokyo) on the Kantō plain, leaving the imperial court in Kyoto virtually powerless. The Tokugawa administration in Edo elaborated a system of government generally characterized as centralized feudalism—a rule that extended to the Meiji Restoration of 1868. Owning over 25 percent of all land, the Tokugawa family allotted the rest to feudal lords (*daimyō*), who presided over their own domains. To assert its control, the central administration frequently increased, decreased, and even transferred the domains; especially difficult feudal lords were eliminated. The Tokugawa regime also maintained control through the alternate attendance system: feudal lords were required to spend six months of each year in Edo, and their wives and children were forced to live permanently in the city as virtual hostages.

Attempts at social control were made through the codification of a strict class system. The warrior class, or *samurai*, were at the top of the hierarchy, followed by farmers and artisans, and next merchants, with the *hinin* and *eta*, social pariahs, at the bottom. The appearance, manner, and residence of each class were restricted, and the duties and privileges of each regulated. Within each class there were further gradations of distinction, but in principle people could not rise above the class in which they were born. Because the aristocracy presiding at the imperial court in Kyoto was outside the class system, the samurai class was the ruling class: from it came the feudal lords and shōgun. The strictures of these social and political hierarchies were buttressed by a neo-Confucian ideology that emphasized loyalty, obligation, and obedience to authority.

The family system was another hierarchy underpinned by neo-Confucian thought, and although this structure was originally confined to the samurai, it was later adopted by other classes eager to imitate their social superiors. All members of the family were subordinate to the welfare and safe continuity of the family line, a subordination supported by the strictures of filial piety. At the head of the family was the patriarch, followed by the eldest son; beneath them were the younger sons, whose status was also ranked by age, the youngest sometimes suffering extreme hardship. Younger sons of the samurai class were commonly adopted into another family, a practice that allowed them to avoid poverty and sometimes offered opportunities for advancement.

The main duty of the women was to continue the family, and the supreme task of a wife was to give birth to a son. The keeping of concubines to increase the chances of begetting an heir was allowed, for the bloodline was traced through the father. A wife of the samurai class led a fairly secluded existence, as the meaning of her title, *okusan*, suggests: the *oku* were the innermost sections of the house. Pleasure trips were denied her and temple visits were discouraged until she reached forty. The wife was to devote all her energies to the household; she had no time for pleasure or learning. This seclusion extended to daughters of the samurai class: ethical treatises recommended the segregation of girls and boys after age seven. Because daughters were not considered part of the bloodline, their main function was to marry (between the ages of thirteen and sixteen) and produce a son, thereby assuring the succession of some other family. Marriages furthered the interests of the families concerned and were arranged by their heads.

Japan's policy of seclusion, begun in the 1630s, was another method of social and political control, and for a while at least, the country enjoyed relative peace. During these years of calm the samurai changed from an unlettered warrior caste into educated administrators and bureaucrats. They traditionally held land in their lord's domain, but this gradually gave way to stipends paid from the domain's granary, which forced them to live on fixed incomes during times of economic growth. Many samurai and their lords thus found themselves in constant debt to merchant brokers, who converted their rice income into cash in the developing commodities markets. Periods of rampant inflation left many impoverished.

By the nineteenth century changes in the Japanese social structure were apparent. Wealthy merchant families, whose position at the bottom of the social scale was meant to curtail their potential power, were able to climb the social ladder. Prosperous farming families assumed some of the local administrative posts normally held by their social superiors, while managerial farmers took advantage of growing commercialization and developing transit routes to ship their produce to the great urban centers. Increasingly, many samurai found their status unequal to their income: some turned to farming, while others took the more drastic measure of selling their hereditary status.

As Tokugawa hegemony weakened during the nineteenth century, Japanese society was punctuated more and more by upheaval. A series of poor harvests, for example, meant famine and farmer rebellions. Revolt was also apparent in other quarters. The growing rate of male literacy strained the ability of the authorities to control what they regarded as subversive thought. A new awareness of Japan's precarious position in a world apparently presided over by the European colonial powers was gradually felt, and a marked sense of urgency characterized many divergent opinions on how to meet that ominous threat. China's defeat in the Opium War in 1842 dealt a serious blow to the official worldview. China no longer held the position of cultural supremacy when Western superiority in military technology became obvious. The government in Edo began to promote studies of the West for strategic reasons, but official encouragement could change to alarm: scholars came under suspicion of political subversion, and some were executed.

Erratic government policy indicated the Tokugawa regime's inability to maintain control. Unable to respond effectively to Perry and other intrusions from the West, the government agreed in 1854 to sign a treaty with the United States which opened the ports of Nagasaki, Hakodate, and Shimoda. It also agreed to the establishment of an American consular official, Townsend Harris, in Shimoda. Other Western powers soon signed their own treaties with Japan opening other ports, and all of the agreements had come into force by 1859. These unequal treaties specified most-favored-nation status, and they contained extraterritorial clauses that placed foreign residents under the jurisdiction of their own governments and tariff clauses that restricted import and export duties. Many samurai had been politicized by the crisis brought by Perry's ships, and the humiliation symbolized by these treaties seriously damaged the shōgun's legitimacy to rule in the name of the emperor. Impatient samurai, especially those from the lower ranks, began to question the feudal bonds of loyalty and obedience. Others began to speculate about new forms of social organization and political institutions.

The 1860s were a decade of increasing violence, culminating in a brief civil war that resulted in a move from military rule to a civil and bureaucratic form of government. The assassination of a central government leader left the Tokugawa administration rudderless: antiforeign sentiment ran high, and renegade samurai were attacking foreigners, causing the Tokugawa regime much embarrassment and hardening Western attitudes against Japan. The leaders of two of the most powerful domains, Satsuma and Chōshū, condemning the government's failure to solve the country's problems with the West, challenged Tokugawa authority by arming themselves with imported weapons. Allying themselves with the hitherto powerless imperial court, and soon joined by four other domains, they sought to overthrow the Tokugawa and restore the emperor to his former glory. On 3 January 1868 a palace coup ended the rule of the last Tokugawa shōgun.

During these decades of political crisis and social upheaval new criteria of individual merit were being formulated: knowledge and ability began to replace rank and hereditary privilege. The meaning of the title given to the newly restored emperor's reign, *Meiji* (enlightened rule), seemed to signify a move to a system freed from the restrictions of centralized feudalism. Men of ability, not men of rank, were needed to unite the country into one nation under imperial rule—a goal met largely through military conscription and a nationwide system of public education.

In December 1871 the Iwakura mission set sail from Yokohama for the United States and Europe to study both the forms and the sources of Western power. The delegation, led by Prince Iwakura Tomomi, included almost half of Japan's political leaders; also on board the *America* was a large contingent of students going to study abroad. Hoping to "catch up" with the West as rapidly and efficiently as possible, the Meiji government was beginning an extensive scheme of sending students to the industrialized nations of the West to gain the knowledge and skills most needed for Japan's modernization.

Among these students were five girls ranging in age from six to fourteen,[2] also being sent abroad to acquire knowledge deemed beneficial for an industrialized nation: while the male students were charged with the task of learning specific technologies, the female students were given the duty of studying what the Bluestocking Hannah More, in *Strictures on the Modern System of Female Education* (1799), had described as "the profession of ladies." The five were to be trained in the diffuse lore of domesticity, the "natural" role of women, which nevertheless required preparation and instruction.[3] Their participation in so important a mission and the imperial sanction it received indicated that the domestic realm was acquiring new importance for public welfare. Since the new nation of Japan depended for its survival on an obedient populace educated in the virtues of patriotism and hard work, attention was focused on women as caretakers of the family. The government saw the social value and political utility of training girls and women in a state-defined ideal of motherhood, and it intended these five, after ten years of American education and life, to return to Japan to teach other girls the standards of domesticity.

Tsuda Umeko, the youngest of the group, fulfilled her assignment and returned to Japan with her own mission. Envisioning a special calling, she was determined on her return to elevate the status of Japanese women and expand their influence in society. Essentially a social conservative, Tsuda sought to create a place for women within the existing order by offering them a substantial education, but one that was bound by the conventions of domesticity and limited by notions of class propriety. Tsuda was moreover able to capitalize on the domestic ideal to further her own career. In widening the sphere of Japanese women, she hoped to widen her own. With the transformation of society begun by the decline and collapse of Tokugawa feudal rule, a new generation of leaders familiar with the West was emerging, and with her foreign education and modern ways, Tsuda intended to achieve a position of authority in the new Japan.

Chapter Two

To Study for the Good of Our Countrywomen, 1871–1882

What began as a vague scheme had far-reaching consequences. Kuroda Kiyotaka, then deputy head of the recently established Hokkaido Colonization Board, had come to the United States in 1871 to engage American experts as special advisers for the development of northern Japan. Impressed with American women, he was told that their "happy lot" was because they "were educated, treated with the highest consideration, and regarded [as] equal to men in all the higher qualities of humanity." Like many people on both sides of the globe, Kuroda assumed that one key to Western success was its "home life," and that Japan's lack of progress could thus be explained in part by its low estimation of women. In a memorandum to his government on the subject of women's education, Kuroda suggested sending a group of school-age girls to be educated in the United States. His flattered hosts applauded the proposal: self-assured American opinion held that Japan would be civilized only when Japanese women were accorded the status of Western ladies. As one American traveler to Japan put it: "We do not look to see women receive, even in Europe, much less in the East, such chivalric deference and respect as are shown to them in America, but the nearer any people imitate us in this respect, the more advanced will they be found in the other refined amenities of social life."[1]

Japan was eager to appear civilized. One of the major obstacles to revision of the humiliating treaties the Tokugawa regime had signed with the major Western nations was Japan's image as a backward country ruled by barbaric laws and customs. It was no accident that five girls accompanied the Iwakura mission, one of whose unofficial tasks was to see about negotiating treaty revision. Ōkuma Shigenobu, a chief architect of the mission, regarded it as a goodwill and propaganda tour: Europe and America, he hoped, would learn more of Japan's indigenous ways and would then no longer consider the nation uncivilized. The five girls were thus a token of the government's good intentions, and for years to come, in articles and speeches aimed at a Western audience, they continued to be used as proof of Meiji Japan's sincere efforts to elevate the status of women.[2]

While in Washington, Kuroda discussed his ideas with Mori Arinori, leader of the Japanese legation in the United States, and the direction of their conversation reveals Meiji views of women, their place, and their utility to the state. Mori, though hardly enthusiastic, agreed with Kuroda's plans, and their conversation then turned to the topic of interracial marriage. Kuroda may have been joking when he suggested that Mori marry an American woman—if many Japanese were to marry people of what were considered the more enlightened foreign countries, Japan would quickly become an advanced nation.[3] Yet Mori took him seriously. The *New York Times* reported that he was looking for an American wife, and in 1872 he was approached by a certain Miss Loring, who proposed to him. Interested yet perplexed, he sent two of his secretaries, Takagi Saburō and Magome Tamesuke, to ask his American secretary, Charles Lanman, if it was an American custom for a woman to ask a man to marry her. If so, Takagi and Magome would advise Mori to accept, as he wanted an American wife.[4]

Mori's interest stemmed from the belief that Westerners were racially superior and that children from Japanese marriages with Western women would strengthen Japan. In order to "advance our country to the heights of civilization and enlightenment," he told a group of Japanese students in New York, "the first requirement is to improve the race. It will be necessary for Japanese in the future, therefore, to marry with Westerners. You fellows should associate with American girls during your studies here, marry them, and take them home with you."[5] In their biological role as mothers, Mori and others believed, women could act as conduits of "civilized blood" that would facilitate Japan's transformation.

In Japan, meanwhile, Kuroda's memorandum was fairly well received. In an imperial message to the aristocracy in October of the same year, 1871, the Meiji emperor acknowledged the lack of formal education for females: "Due to the inadequate provisions for the education of women in our country, most of them are not able to understand the meaning of civilization." Therefore, he urged, "it is obviously desirable for men who go abroad to take their wives and sisters with them" so that these women might learn the "essentials of civilization and methods of child rearing" in Western countries. At the same time, David Murray of Rutgers University, when asked by Mori for advice on the development of Japan's new public education system, stressed that female education was necessary for the country's future. Even though the "employments of woman do not carry her into the same" sphere as man, he wrote, "she is equally important." Because the "comfort and happiness of home depend largely upon her" and the "care and supervision of children fall into her hands during their most impressionable years," the "guardians of the future men and women of a nation ought, in common prudence," Murray stressed, "to be well educated."[6]

This idea of education as a means of training future wives and mothers underlies all the arguments for Japanese women's education. It would be for the future good of the country. While men were to build the nation, both economically and militarily, women were to nurture the children, who, as workers and soldiers, would fortify the state's power. In terms of Meiji ideology, the nation, as one harmonious family, would work together to attain the goal of *fukoku kyōhei* (wealthy nation and strong army). Women's education was thus tied to their biological function.

Behind Kuroda's memorandum was a more immediate concern: the Hokkaido Colonization Board was established shortly after the Meiji Restoration to develop northern Japan politically and militarily. Under Kuroda it concentrated on developing such natural resources as coal, minerals, timber, and fishing, as well as Western-style farming and railways. After abolishing the feudal domains in 1871, the new government encouraged immigration to and reclamation of new areas in the northern island by impoverished samurai; at the same time the government wanted a sizable population in Hokkaido to "assimilate" the native Ainu. These modern farmers therefore would need wives with some knowledge of recent Western technology as well as such domestic skills in self-sufficiency as sewing, nutrition, and hygiene. Thus Kuroda connected the development of Hokkaido with the development of women. Productive expansion, he argued, requires knowledgeable men, and capable men are raised by educated mothers: schools for girls must therefore be founded.[7] The women needed to run these schools, Kuroda reasoned, could be educated in a country that was also expanding control of its own perceived frontiers, the United States. If foreign wives would be a national asset, these educated Japanese women would be another natural resource. In associating motherhood with race, civilization, colonization, and national strength, Kuroda indicated the main elements of the emerging rationale for educating women.[8]

Iwakura Tomomi, whose position was equivalent to that of prime minister, supported the proposal, and Kuroda's department promptly began to recruit applicants. The notices, however, went mostly unheeded. In spite of two recruitment drives and an attractive offer—a ten-year stay in the United States with free tuition, travel, room and board, and eight hundred dollars pocket money—just five applied: Yoshimasu Ryōko, age fourteen; Ueda Teiko, also fourteen; Yamakawa Sutematsu, age eleven; Nagai Shigeko, seven; and Tsuda Ume, six years old.[9] All five were of the samurai class, and all five came from families connected with the former Tokugawa regime. Although they were not the first Japanese students to study abroad—in 1862 and 1865 the Tokugawa government had sent sons of high-ranking vassals abroad, and the southwestern domains of Chōshū and Satsuma had secretly, in violation of Tokugawa isolationist law, sent groups of young samurai (including such future leaders as Mori Arinori, Itō Hirobumi, and Inoue Kaoru) to such Western centers as London—they were the first, and for a good while the last, females to receive a foreign education.

This indifference to female education is in direct contrast to the "education furor" that characterized much of the 1870s and later. The Meiji emperor's Charter Oath of 1868, an official statement of the new government's intentions, offered a largely egalitarian promise of social mobility, and self-advancement through education was further emphasized in the Education Act of 1872. Learning, this code declared, was the way to success in life, and individual advancement meant national progress. Overseas study, moreover, was actively promoted by the government. The Ministry of Education increasingly sent students abroad to be trained as competent teachers of specific fields in the extensive nationwide educational system then being created. In Western countries, according to one government document, these students could "master the character, government, customs and nature of the people there. . . . This will help the Japanese people to advance and will aid in the development of a civilized Japan, so that the country can prosper."[10]

The promise of individual advancement through education may help to explain why the families of these five girls decided to send them to the United States. Their fathers and some of their brothers were former government officials, and all came from feudal domains that were on the losing side of the imperial restoration because of their support for the Tokugawa regime. Having their children receive a Western education was one way to ensure their survival in a politically uncertain world.

This was certainly the case with Yamakawa Sutematsu. Born in 1860, she was the youngest daughter of Yamakawa Hisae, a senior retainer of the domain of Aizu.[11] During the last years of Tokugawa rule, Aizu, whose feudal lord was related to the Tokugawa family, was one of the government's strongest supporters, and in May 1868, with the support of an alliance of northeastern domains, Aizu became a focus of resistance to the imperial forces. The castle at Wakamatsu was marked for ruthless military retaliation, and, when surrounded by the imperial army in August, it was the scene of a bloody battle followed by gruesome defeat. After the Meiji Restoration, when the domain was destroyed through division, the Yamakawa family fell into disfavor and became destitute. Sutematsu's family, however, had always appreciated the benefits of education and understood how it could be translated into personal success. Her older brother Kenjirō used his studies at Rutgers and Yale (also sponsored by the Hokkaido Colonization Board) to further his career, later becoming president of Tokyo Imperial University.[12] Education, and especially a Western one, was a means for the Yamakawa family to regain its authority.

Nagai Shigeko's guardians also regarded the chance to study in the United States as a route to advancement. Her father's career in government service had been disrupted by the imperial restoration, and her oldest brother, Masuda Takashi, who had had a checkered career as cavalry officer, worker in the government's mint, and office boy at the U.S. legation in Edo, saw a Western education as a source of financial security. Having learned English at the American legation, Masuda was ordered to accompany a mission to the United States and France, where he furthered his knowledge of foreign languages and ways. Masuda was just then embarking on his career with the Mitsui trading house, a powerful business enterprise that had backed the new Meiji government financially, and his background in Western knowledge proved lucrative for the foreign trading end of the family business. Masuda, "a merchant to the marrow," as one American later said of him, understood that an American education was a sound investment that could be converted to various advantages.[13]

Tsuda Ume, her parents' second child and second daughter, was clearly an unwelcome child to her father. At her birth on 31 December 1864, Tsuda Sen stormed out of the house in a rage. By the seventh day, when the baby customarily receives a name, Ume's father had still not returned, and her mother, Hatsuko, named her *ume* after the bonsai plum tree that stood by her bed. A common name for samurai women, *ume* represented strength, perseverance, and resilience, for the plum tree blooms in late winter, often in the snow.

Tsuda Sen's aspirations, coupled with his belief in the strategic nature of Western knowledge, suggest why he filed an application for his daughter to go to the United States. Restless, enterprising, and above all ambitious, Sen quickly recognized that a Western education could be a ticket to personal advancement. Born in 1837, he was the fourth son and the eighth child of Ojima Zenemon Yoshichika, a retainer of the feudal lord of Sakura in Shimōsa province, a small but important domain, where Ojima was the head of the treasury. As the child of a high retainer, Sen witnessed a world of prestige, but as the fourth son he had no certain future in a strict hereditary system, for he had little chance of succeeding his father and taking over the prerogatives connected with his father's rank and position. Thus, at age fourteen he was adopted by another family of the domain, the Sakurai.

The policies of Sakura's feudal lord, Hotta Masayoshi, suggested possibilities to such discontented young samurai as Tsuda Sen. From one of the four families that normally supplied the *tairō*, the shōgun's highest official, Hotta held important offices in the Tokugawa administration. In 1856 he attempted to initiate fresh discussion of foreign policy: Japan, he argued, needed foreign trade and armaments, alliances, and the adoption of selected foreign ways. Believing it impossible to keep the country closed, in 1858 he negotiated a commercial treaty with the American consul, Townsend Harris, provoking a crisis for which he was eventually put under house arrest. Hotta also devoted his energies to reforming his own domain, to which he brought scholars of both Eastern and Western learning. The famous Confucian scholar Yasui Sokken taught at the domain school, and Satō Taizen, a well-known scholar of *Rangaku* (Dutch studies, or more generally, Western learning), started his school, Wada Juku, in Sakura and later, at the invitation of Hotta, established Japan's first private hospital, Juntendō, where he practiced surgery. Hotta's encouragement of Western studies earned him the nickname *Rampeki* (Dutch maniac).[14]

Sen therefore grew to maturity in an environment that emphasized the new learning as well as the old. At the domain school, he received the usual education for a retainer's child: the Chinese classics—the Confucian *Four Books* and *Five Classics* were typically the center of the curriculum at most domain schools—as well as the martial skills of riding, archery, jūjutsu, kendō, and fencing. The competitive spirit of this school must have encouraged and at the same time exacerbated the hopes of an ambitious younger son. The teaching methods of domain schools imbued a spirit of self-assertion in their pupils. The young samurai trained in single combat and studied the glorious deeds of the illustrious men of history and legend, a practice that could only foster dreams of individual honor and glory.[15]

In 1853 Sen was one of the samurai of the domains surrounding Edo sent to join the artillery guarding the coast of the shōgun's city. That July he watched Perry's squadron sail into Edo Bay. Impressed with the technological might the steamships embodied, the sixteen-year-old Sen decided to learn more about the West: a mastery of Western technology, and especially military techniques, would soon be in high demand. Like other young samurai who began flocking to the Western-studies schools after the coming of Perry, Sen envisioned a prestigious career for himself.[16] With an expertise in Western knowledge, he believed he could overcome the feudal restrictions of rank by using his knowledge as a way to a government appointment and a position in society.

In 1856 Sen used the death of his adoptive mother as an opportunity to dissolve his unpromising connection to the Sakurai family, and left for Edo. The weakening of feudal ties allowed for increased migration between the provinces and major urban centers, and Sakura, like many other small domains in the Kantō area, was beginning a slow decline. Edo acted as a magnet for the disaffected and ambitious.[17]

Sen studied Dutch and later English in various Edo private schools, and his fractured but nonetheless energetic studies finally brought success in 1858 when, at age twenty-one, he was appointed interpreter in the Foreign Office, to help in treaty negotiation. His good fortune was furthered two years later with his marriage to Tsuda Hatsuko and adoption into her family, retainers of the Tayasu family, one of the branch houses of the Tokugawa. As a government official and a member of a locally prominent family, Sen had arrived.

In January 1867, in the month of the Meiji emperor's enthronement and one year before the palace coup and brief civil war destroyed Tokugawa rule, Sen was ordered to accompany a delegation to the United States to see about the delayed delivery of a purchased warship and to acquire rifles for the army. In the United States Sen was again impressed by American technology, and he used the opportunity to buy books, especially reference books and manuals of information—valuable sources back in Edo.[18] Sen also performed an act that proclaimed his pro-Western sympathies: in San Francisco he cut off his *chonmage* (topknot), a distinguishing feature of a samurai, and sent it home to Hatsuko. The act cannot have been too provocative—Sen was promoted to the position of government interpreter and instructor of English at the Niigata office shortly after his return. But the turbulent fall of the Tokugawa regime soon convinced him to sever all ties with the government.

Sen's connections to the Tokugawa both by employment and by feudal ties—links he had worked hard to forge—had become a liability. Amid political turmoil he was forced to scramble for another career, once again relying on his knowledge of the West. The thirty-one-year-old samurai decided to become a hotelier. In autumn 1868, the start of the new Meiji era, Japan's first Western-style hotel opened in the foreign settlement in the Edo harbor district of Tsukiji. Characterized by an eclectic mixture of architectural styles that seemed to suggest Japan's new openness to foreign cultures, the Tsukiji Hoterukan (as it was known to the locals; foreigners called it the Edo Hotel) instilled pride in the citizens of the newly named capital, Tokyo. Epitomizing the new Meiji slogan of *bunmei kaika* (civilization and enlightenment), it was instantly famous and attracted mobs of Japanese sightseers. The hotel's ambience of confident optimism—it was built at great expense, for a reported $100,000—made it an exciting symbol of the aspirations of the new Japan.[19]

On the strength of his English-language skills, Sen joined the hotel's management in 1869, but the venture soon turned to disaster. The newly cleared Tsukiji settlement, created by the authorities to protect (or segregate) foreign residents, was exceedingly ugly: it had the ramshackle appearance of a muddy frontier town. Many foreigners preferred to live in the central areas of Tokyo, but those who did decide to reside in the hotel—described by one inhabitant as an "*apology* for a hotel"—found it unbearable.[20] The guests were confronted by a virtual monopoly of tradesmen and merchants who, by making it impossible for outside shopkeepers to send purchases to the hotel, were able to charge exorbitant prices for their services and goods. The food was also a problem—owing to a lack of Western foodstuffs the guests found the meals inedible—and the hotel workers could also be awful. By 1870 the hotel was already semi-deserted, and in 1871 it was temporarily closed. That January Sen quit.

With two promising careers that had ended in failure, a growing family—two daughters, two sons, and a wife pregnant with twins—Sen must have welcomed the opportunity to send a daughter abroad. In this patriarchal family system Ume was superfluous, and thus her father's action may have been a benign form of *mabiki* (infanticide—literally, weeding out). As her mother wrote in 1872 to Ume's American guardians: "It is fortunate for Ume that she is in her present position, because, with so many brothers and sisters as she has, she would have much less attention paid to her in Japan."[21]

Expendability may also have been a deciding factor for the families of the other four girls. (Sutematsu's mother feared she would never see her daughter again. She renamed her Sutematsu, "thrown-away pine," shortly before the departure of the Iwakura mission.) Each family faced an uncertain future, and the more weather-wise among them may have taken the dissolution of the feudal domains in 1871 as a portent of the coming abolition of the hereditary status and prerogatives of the samurai class in 1873. Their daughters' foreign education, should it prove advantageous, could reverse the families' fortunes. An overseas education was becoming more and more a mark of status—many in the new Meiji leadership had been educated abroad—and so each daughter might yet bring honor and prestige, if not material wealth, to her family. Certainly Sen still nurtured aspirations for his family: he named the twin boys born shortly before Ume's departure Kingo and Gingo (literally, my gold and my silver).

In December 1871 Ume and the four others had an audience with the Empress Haruko—the first time, Ume later recalled with pride, "that the Empress ever had received in audience the daughters of Samurai." The privilege of kneeling before "a heavy hanging screen, through which we could see nothing, even if we had dared to raise our bowed heads, but behind which we knew was seated the sacred presence," was a clear indication of imperial authorization for the role of women in the modernization of the new nation. After the empress urged the group to be model students in the United States, she gave each girl a length of red silk, a "quantity of wonderful court cake" so sacred that it could cure all sickness, and, "most precious of all," a document bidding them to go abroad "to study for the good of our countrywomen."[22]

On 23 December 1871, one week before Ume's seventh birthday, the five girls left Yokohama in a small skiff for the *America*, anchored in Tokyo Bay. They had received little preparation for what lay ahead of them (the Iwakura mission, in fact, was not finalized until September or October and not officially announced until late November).[23] Ume's older sister Koto was originally to have gone, but Koto balked at the idea, as Ume wrote in one of her earliest English compositions: "My sister was appointed to come instead of me but she would not come and so I came as she did not like to come so far from home." Consequently there was little time to prepare Ume: she left Japan equipped with a red shawl, the only article of foreign clothing her father could obtain for her; paper, ink, and brushes for letters home; illustrated history books of Japan; a small dictionary, an English primer, and "a knowledge of English limited to 'yes,' 'no' and 'thank you.'" Although she was as frightened as her sister at the prospect of leaving Japan, her curiosity was stronger: "Neither did I like to leave my mother and father but I wanted to come," she wrote in the same composition. After a nineteen-gun salute from the Japanese warships anchored nearby, the *America* lifted anchor and Ume, standing on the ship's deck, watched the coast of Japan slowly disappear. "How my heart beat, when I saw the distant land fading away," she wrote. "I tried not to think about it."[24]

The voyage was rough. The weather was so stormy one night that the ship was almost wrecked, but because many of the mission were miserably ill with seasickness, Ume recalled, nobody seemed to care. The five girls were wretched: crowded into a single cabin, bewildered, and seasick. They also had a language barrier between them and their stewardess to overcome. Although she knew a few Japanese words, communication was difficult. Even asking for food was a problem.

To add to their misery, Yoshimasu Ryōko was sexually molested by an attendant of the mission, an event whose aftermath reveals the emptiness of their largely symbolic role in the Iwakura mission. One of the American ship's officers warned that legal action was necessary if Japan was to appear civilized, so a hearing, chaired by Vice Ambassador Itō Hirobumi, was opened. The meeting, however, deteriorated into a kangaroo court, only further humiliating Yoshimasu.[25]

After nearly four long weeks the *America* arrived in San Francisco Bay, and Ume, glad to see land, took heart in the fact that Americans also lived in houses. On disembarking, however, they were overwhelmed by a throng of people: "crowds upon crowds of people were at the wharf, and I remember going through a narrow passageway made among the sight-seers." The newspapers had impressed upon the Americans the importance of the visit, and although the Iwakura mission was not the first embassy from Japan to the United States, its Japanese members were still a sensation. "Once," Ume wrote, "when two of us were in the hall [of the San Francisco Grand Hotel], a party of ladies with children took us by the hand and led us into their room, talked to us in language, not one word of which we could understand, looked at us all over, handled us, showed us toys and pictures, and then, after what seemed like hours of suspense—for we did not know what was going to happen to us—we were led safely back again to our own rooms." On the evening of January 16, one day after the mission's arrival, forty thousand San Franciscans filled the square and streets surrounding the hotel, shouting "loud cries of welcome."[26] Overwhelmed by their sudden celebrity status, the five hardly dared venture from their rooms.

Everywhere they went crowds gathered to catch sight of the "princesses," as the press had mistakenly described them, in their bright costumes.[27] The woman who escorted them to Washington, D.C., Mrs. Charles E. DeLong, wife of the American minister to Japan, had agreed to see that the five girls were outfitted in Western clothes as soon as they arrived in California, but Mrs. DeLong was thrilled with the attention the kimono-clad girls attracted and so refused to get them new clothing. Ume recalled the suffering this publicity caused in a composition written a few months after landing:

> Once on a time five girls left yedo in steamer America for Sanfrancisco their names were Tei and Rio and stemats and shige and mume. Tei was sixteen Rio fifteen and stemats thirteen and shige eleven and mume eight, a lady named Mrs. delong took care of them, first all the girls think her very kind then she went to sanfrancisco . . . and stayed three ore for weeks then she went to saltlake there was much snow and the cars can not go. and stay long time, Rio eyes were much hurt by the snow and a she put a green shade over them
>
> there her dress is a Japanese dress and all the girls dont like it ask Mrs delong to buy american dress but she dont like the American dress and the Mrs delong was not kind first the girls was very nice but last was not kind

Not until nearly two months later, after repeated requests, did the girls receive Western dresses.

America and the Americans were bewildering to the girls. On board ship, Ume later wrote, they had "gazed with awe at the tall American officers and the sailors." She was particularly afraid of the black hotel waiters, a fear that was only increased when she was taken to see a minstrel show. American food was also a mystery. Once, not knowing what was put before them, they each helped themselves to a spoonful of butter, which they found to be revolting. All, however, was not threatening: while their train was snowbound in Omaha, a group of smiling schoolgirls came to the train, clapped their hands, and blew kisses at the Japanese girls. This, Ume recalled, "we thought was very polite and kind."[28]

Finally, on 29 February 1872, they arrived in Washington during a snowstorm wearing ill-fitting American clothes. There they were formally placed in the care of Mori Arinori, the Japanese minister to the United States and their legal guardian. On the same day each was settled with an American family while it was decided what to do with them. Kuroda Kiyotaka may have planned for them to be sent to the United States, but, apart from some vague notions of education, there his plans ended. The unprepared Mori (who complained: "What am I to do? They have sent me a baby"), in turn, gave all five into the care of Charles Lanman, a secretary at the Japanese legation, and Ume and Yoshimasu Ryōko were temporarily placed in his home.[29]

Soon, however, it was decided to move all five to a rented house at 826 Connecticut Street and to provide a governess who would teach and care for them. They led a happy life together in the capital but were not progressing in English. Niijima Jō, an associate of Tsuda Sen who had smuggled himself out of Japan in 1864, lived close by and often acted as interpreter of American culture for them. "They don't understand what the ladies in the families speak to them," he wrote. "When I go there to see them, they are delighted to see me, and ask me ever so many questions." The girls were not learning English because their household, Ume later recalled, had become "more Japanese than American, and the five children combined were more than any one American woman could influence or hold in hand. . . . Our governess could not manage us as she might have done had we understood English."[30]

After six months and two governesses, the five were again split up. Yoshimasu Ryōko and Ueda Teiko, the two oldest of the group, returned to Japan: Ryōko's eyes had been damaged by snowblindness while in Omaha, and Teiko was homesick. Yamakawa Sutematsu was sent to the family of the Rev. Leonard Bacon in New Haven, and Nagai Shigeko went to the family of the Rev. John Abbott in Fair Haven, Connecticut. Ume, however, returned to the Georgetown house of Charles Lanman because his wife, Adeline, had become especially fond of her.

The Lanmans' residence, according to a petition written years later to save it from demolition, was "a rare collection of literary and artistic works," one of a superb pair of brick houses at 120 West Street given to Adeline Lanman by her New Englander merchant father, Francis Dodge, as a wedding present. An energetic though thoroughly conventional woman, Adeline was in striking contrast to Tsuda Hatsuko, a worn-out and unhappy woman in whom all emotions had been repressed.[31] Charles Lanman was equally active. A grandson of Senator James Lanman of Connecticut, he was a diversely talented man: an explorer and outdoorsman (he was one of the first to popularize the canoe), a painter, and a prolific writer with at least twenty-five books to his credit. Although he began his career as a journalist, he worked for much of his life as a librarian, first at the War Department, then at the Interior Department, at the House of Representatives, and finally at the Washington City Library. (Charles expected to be made librarian of the Library of Congress and was bitterly disappointed when he was refused the post.) He also served as secretary to Daniel Webster and later the Japanese legation. In addition to Charles's full and varied career, the Lanmans led a busy social life: friends with such men of letters as John Whittier and Washington Irving, they were pleased also to have known such celebrities as Longfellow and Dickens, whom Charles entertained during his American tour.

The Lanmans, being childless, welcomed Ume, and the presence of "this waif-child," Charles Lanman wrote, "made it indeed a sunny and happy home." Ume readily returned their affection. In a note written a month or so after her arrival in 1872, she told Adeline Lanman: "I am very happy. I gave you this to make a presant for you. I hope you would like it. I think your very nice lady. I think you like me. I love you better then you love me. good bye you friend Mume." And in another note at about the same time, addressed to "My Dear american mother" and signed "Your affectionate Japan daughter," she told her, "You are a very nice woman you are kind to me you love me." Some time during that same year Ume also constructed a small book from an exercise tablet in which she described the ocean voyage and train journey across the United States. Complete with her illustrations of the ship, the Grand Hotel, a bird, and a final flourish, it was intended as a surprise gift: "Tise is mume fixt to herself and give to Mr Lamman Mrs Lamman helf too. I show to Mr Lamman so prise."

Because she was so young, the Lanmans decided against the East Coast boarding school Ume's Japanese guardians apparently had in mind and instead sent her to local schools, where she received the education typical of a middle-class American girl. She went first to the Georgetown Collegiate Institute, run by Lucy Stephenson, and impressed everyone with her progress. "She is spoken of as remarkably bright," the *Georgetown Courier* reported, "and is a great favorite among her young fellow students." Ume accepted Stephenson's praise for her good work but, when also praised for her good conduct, refused the commendation. Good manners, Ume told Lucy Stephenson, come from birth and breeding and therefore deserve no special credit. Ume took pride in her successes and at an early age showed her growing sense of independence. While working on her compositions, Charles Lanman wrote, "her habit was to inquire from others about the spelling of certain words," but "she always decidedly objected to being interfered with by the offer of outside suggestions." On her graduation from the Collegiate Institute in 1874, the *Georgetown Courier* observed, with some condescension, that "there is a live Yankee element in the Oriental mind."[32]

Having proved herself to be more than capable in American schools, Ume entered the Archer Institute in Washington, a school of about one hundred students, many of them the daughters of politicians and local bureaucrats. There she studied the standard curriculum for a girls' school and became something of a celebrity—she played the piano at one graduation ceremony when the diplomas were given out by Lucy Webb Hayes, wife of the president—and Miss Archer, the school's principal, was especially proud of "her Japanese girl."

Ume further demonstrated her strong desire to fit into her surroundings by asking, in the summer of 1873, to be baptized. Although Charles Lanman wrote that she had decided "without a word of advice from any one," the pious, regular churchgoing household of the Lanmans must have made Ume feel out of place. The Lanmans, themselves Episcopalians, believed she would be best baptized in a nonsectarian rite and decided on the Old Swedes Church in Bridgeport, Pennsylvania, then under Octavius Perinchief (whom Mori had also asked for advice on Japan's new public education system). The church, with its own charter and constitution, was purely evangelical. When Perinchief suggested a ceremony with simplified responses, Ume, determined to belong to her surroundings and probably offended, refused the offer of special treatment and demanded a regular baptism.

Her assimilation into American life, however, had its disadvantages, for she was rapidly forgetting her Japanese. At the end of 1872, Charles Lanman asked a sixteen-year-old boy studying in Michigan, Kawamura Kiyo, to live with the Lanmans and Ume in Georgetown. Kawamura's family, also connected to the former Tokugawa regime, had sent him to receive an education in the United States, but he wanted to be an artist, and because Charles Lanman was a distinguished amateur painter (he had studied with Asher Durand of the Hudson River School) the Japanese legation in Washington asked for Lanman's help. It was decided that if Kawamura would give Ume Japanese lessons, Charles would help him with his English and, more to the point, teach him Western techniques of sketching and oil painting, which he also taught Ume. Although the Japanese lessons, if they ever took place, never helped her, Kawamura's example did—he returned to Japan to become an expert teacher in Western methods.

Tsuda Sen during these years was also becoming an authority on Western technology. The failure of the Tsukiji hotel, especially its problems with food, set his enterprising mind to work. With Western dress and hairstyles being promoted as the proper accoutrements of a civilized nation, surely a Western diet would follow? If he were to grow Western fruits and vegetables, Sen would have—for a while at least—a monopoly of the Tokyo market. So, with the help of a borrowed encyclopedia he began to cultivate first asparagus, which sold well, and then such foreign edibles as eggplant, figs, gooseberries, and strawberries from Holland. He also nurtured the sapling of an apple tree taken from the grounds of the German legation. After the success of these experiments, Sen bought a farm in the Furukawa district of Azabu, then on the outskirts of Tokyo, where he applied Western methods to the cultivation of indigenous and foreign produce.

His experiments received a boost from the government: the land tax reform, said by some historians to be the most important reform of the Meiji Restoration, gave farmers a strong incentive to increase the productivity of their land by investing more time and money in new methods of cultivation. The government encouraged innovative techniques of horticulture and experiments with new crops, established research stations to develop new seed strains, and created information networks to provide the more remote regions of the country with information about new farming techniques. Because at this time about 80 percent of Japan's work force farmed and most tax revenues consequently came from direct taxes on the agricultural sector (77 percent between 1878 and 1882), Sen's new profession as an expert in agriculture seemed to offer both status and security.[33]

With a growing reputation as an authority on Western agriculture, Sen was appointed to a mission dispatched to the Vienna Exposition of 1873. There he met Daniel Hooibrenk, a Dutch agronomist responsible for the care and propagation of the Japanese specimens that had been taken to Europe from Nagasaki by Philipp Franz von Siebold in 1830. Sen studied horticulture with Hooibrenk for six months and, after returning to Japan, in 1874 published his *Nōgyō Sanji* (Three matters of agriculture), a description of Hooibrenk's methods for propagating grains, nourishing fruit trees, and enriching soil. That year he tried the first method at his Azabu farm: to stimulate the pollenization of rice and barley artificially, Sen took a woolen rope, painted it with honey, and brushed it four or five times against the ears of grain when they were about to flower. The experiment was a success: both crops increased in quality as well as volume.

These promising results led Sen to market the *Tsuda nawa* (Tsuda rope). It was an instant success. By 1877 he had a factory of two hundred hands producing a thousand ropes a day. At the peak of the demand, the Tsuda family could not obtain enough wool in Japan so they purchased ready-made woolen mufflers and unraveled them. So proud was Sen of his rope that in 1877 he took one to the palace to show the emperor. But like most overnight successes, the popularity of the Tsuda rope soon sharply declined, and the family was left with a large unsalable supply. Auspicious beginnings ended in failure—a pattern that was becoming a distinctive feature of Tsuda Sen's life.

At the peak of his success, in January 1876, and probably with the money earned from the Tsuda nawa, he opened an agricultural school, the Nōgakkō, at the Azabu experimental farm. The school fostered Sen's brand of civilization and enlightenment: Western techniques of agriculture informed by the reforming spirit of evangelical Christianity, for he had converted in 1875. Taking as its motto George Washington's saying "Agriculture is the most healthful, most useful, and most noble employment of Man," the Nōgakkō attracted many students eager for exposure to Western enlightenment and for a time ranked as one of Meiji Japan's leading Western schools. Sen also began publishing the *Nōgyō Zasshi* (Agriculture journal) to improve Japanese methods of farming and to promote Christian ideals, and he founded a society for agricultural studies, the Nōgakusha.

Because of his association with Western technology, in 1874 Sen was able to join the Meirokusha, a distinguished society of intellectuals modeled after the literary and scientific societies of the West and founded by Mori Arinori, with Fukuzawa Yukichi and Nishimura Shigeki, after Mori's return to Tokyo in 1873. The society's objective was the promotion of civilization and enlightenment, and its members dealt in their writings and lectures with such diverse themes as the separation of church and state, economic policy, chemistry, and language reform, as well as the status of women. To disseminate new ideas it published a journal, the *Meiroku Zasshi* (the Meiji six journal, so called because the Meirokusha began in the sixth year of the Meiji era). Written in clear, easy to read prose, its translations of Western texts and original articles played an important role in introducing Western thought to the intellectual elite of Japan. The society's members, including Sen, advocated science and scientific methods, an attitude that not only looked to the future but also symbolized a break with the antiquated feudal past.[34]

Sen described his experiment with Hooibrenk's method of pollenization in the August 1875 issue of the *Meiroku Zasshi*, but the article was to be his only contribution to the influential journal. One month later, in September 1875, the Meirokusha voted to cease publication because of newly enacted libel laws and newspaper regulations. Intended to stifle opposition to the government, these ordinances held editors accountable for the material they published, and it was clear to members of the Meirokusha that the journal could avoid neither discussion of government policies nor political debate. That December the *Meiroku Zasshi* folded.[35]

Tsuda Sen's desire to achieve a position of intellectual authority, a standing he lost with the dissolution of the Meirokusha, is also apparent in his conversion (with Hatsuko) in 1875 by an American Methodist missionary named Junius Soper. While in Vienna, Sen had seen an exhibit of hundreds of translations of the Bible. Impressed by the sheer bulk of the display, he associated Christianity with progress and power—so many translations must have suggested a strong colonizing force. His conversion was not an uncommon decision.

As it became increasingly obvious that Western knowledge was a means to advancement, former samurai began flocking to the mostly American missionaries converging on Japan in the 1870s. These ambitious men sought Western languages and technology to maintain or even recapture their lost status in the uncertain climate of the early Meiji years. The circumstances of the conversion of Uemura Masahisa, later a prominent Christian, are typical: having been told that Western learning was "the best way to rise in the world," his mother secured for him a Western education. Often the only available source of such knowledge, missionaries led many of their followers to believe that the source of Western strength lay in Christianity. Many students of the West, indeed, viewed civilization and Christianity as virtually synonymous. Regarding Christianity as a direct route to civilization and enlightenment, they hoped their conversion would improve their position in society. Not surprisingly, many converts came from the pro-Tokugawa domains that had been defeated with the imperial restoration. Like Sen, almost all were raised in provincial centers and came to the capital in search of advancement, and many Christian ex-samurai were eager to form the elite of an emerging urban and educated middle class.[36]

Channeling much of his energies into Christian causes, Sen as well as Hatsuko, and soon their children, certainly became devout. Many Meiji intellectuals felt that the new Japan, in breaking with its feudal past, needed spiritual regeneration. Eager, in his words, to "root out all our old habits and plant anew the true Gospel seed," Sen typified evangelism's zeal for charitable works and social reform.[37] When Niijima Jō returned from America, Sen helped him in his Christian work, and in 1875, with Nakamura Masanao and Kishida Ginko, Sen founded the Rakugenkai—the Tokyo School for the Blind and Dumb—and later became active in such social reform efforts as the temperance cause.

In the United States, Ume did her best to adjust to American society, but she was intensely conscious of being Japanese. She wrote in June 1883, shortly after her return to Japan: "Many times I have felt that I was of different race & blood, that there were none whose blood was kin to mine, who had the characteristics of our race. And in many ways, I was an oriental. . . . For I am different, I know." Having taken the empress's words to heart, as a loyal samurai daughter ready to serve her nation, she considered herself a representative of her country. She realized that only while living abroad had she gained a strong belief in Japan as a nation.

Although Ume's deep awareness of her Japanese identity naturally resulted from her sense of being in a unique position, American racism may also have played a role. When she attended the Collegiate Institute, she walked to school each day with a friend, three months her senior, who tried to protect her from other children who pulled her long black hair. And in Washington she was once chased by a gang of boys yelling, "Chinamen eat rats!" Racist insults had also been hurled at other Japanese. In 1860, for example, when the first Japanese envoys arrived in Washington, their carriages were surrounded by a mob. "One burly fellow," the *New York Illustrated News* recorded, "swore that all they wanted was to have a little more crinoline and be right out decent looking nigger wenches." At the close of their visit to Congress, the envoys were "followed, of course, by a loud laugh from the representatives and by a wild mob rush of men and women from the galleries, which were left nearly empty."[38]

When not overtly racist, Americans could be insufferably condescending. Fukuzawa Yukichi, an attendant to this first mission, recalled in his autobiography that his American hosts expected the Japanese to be surprised by each new device of modern engineering they were shown. Many inventions they were taken to see, such as the telegraph, were nothing new to the Japanese—such innovations could be read about at government institutes in Edo. And even when they approved of the Japanese, Americans did so in essentially racist terms. The press hailed the Japanese as "the British of Asia" and found them to have "elements of the Anglo-Saxon mind." One young man was described as "almost Caucasian in his complexion." Newspapers were also eager to distinguish the Japanese from the people the Americans had particular contempt for, the Chinese.[39]

Ume had arrived in Washington in the optimistic early years of Reconstruction, when openly racist behavior was by then, presumably, frowned upon. The Iwakura mission was generally well received in Washington, and Japan's resolution to "civilize" itself was warmly encouraged. The United States, a young nation, had revolted against European despotism; Japan similarly had recently broken from its feudal past—or so the Americans viewed it. In identifying with Japan, America assumed the role of big brother: it would teach

Japan. The condescending attitude became a patronizing one. Secretary of State Hamilton Fish, for example, took an avuncular attitude toward Mori Arinori, instructing him in the most elementary arts of diplomacy as well as in the everyday business of running a legation. And openly racist remarks were quite common. Charles Lanman's book *The Japanese in America*, first published in 1872, is implicitly directed at those who were contemptuous of the Japanese. A narration of incidents about and collection of essays by some of the Japanese men then living in the United States, it sets forth "good examples" of their adaptation to American life to "prove conclusively that the sons of Japan are quite equal to those of America in their intellectual progress, their morals, and general good conduct. . . . And these," Lanman exclaims, "are the people whom some of the fools of America would treat with ridicule!"[40]

America's role as Japan's teacher was also apparent in the Lanman household. Ume acquired their middle-class values of self-help and enterprise, tempered by the ideals of charity and selflessness. Life with the Lanmans instilled in her a strong sense of self-worth and personal dignity that fostered her growing spirit of independence. Charles and Adeline Lanman also displayed a combination of refinement and piety typical of their class: Ume was fond of reading, but consumed only "poetry and the better class of novels," Charles was quick to note. Charles, more than Ume, was proud of her acquaintance with such men as Longfellow and Perinchief, as well as his physicist friend Joseph Henry, director of the Smithsonian Institution.

Learning was thus highly valued. Annual summer excursions, for instance, were not merely for pleasure. The Lanmans, taking seriously their duty to provide Ume with an American education, wanted Ume to see as much as possible of the country and its culture. During school vacations they took her to the Allegheny and White mountains, the Berkshires, the coasts of Maine, Rhode Island, New Jersey, and all through Massachusetts, Connecticut, and New York, with special emphasis on the northern cities, not omitting Niagara Falls. Being Easterners, they thought little of the American West and chose instead to travel to Quebec and the Atlantic provinces of Canada. Ume's education, however, was not the simple gathering of empty knowledge: it was character formation, for in the Lanman household learning was not true education unless imbued with a strong sense of morality. Like religion, it was meant to impart a system of ethics.

Some American values echoed Japanese ethics. Ume's sense of duty, for example, while strengthened during her years in the United States, was rooted in the Confucian stress on filial piety and the samurai values of loyalty and service. Self-help was similar to *risshin shusse*, "rising in the world," and in Meiji ideology personal success and material improvement were defined in terms of national progress. Other values, especially the notions of separate spheres and the exaltation of domestic virtue, would be very suitable to Meiji Japan. Mori Arinori, as the legal guardian of the five girls, "would, in the first place," according to an approving Charles Lanman, "have them made fully acquainted with the blessings of *home life* in the United States; and, in the second place, he would have their minds fully stored with all those kinds of information which will make them true ladies." Home life and the education that produced true ladies—"intellectual and physical, religious, moral and polite"—were the cornerstones of the American cult of domesticity.[41]

Ume formed her perspective on womanhood when Catharine Beecher, a central advocate of domestic virtue, was at the height of her career. Because women had a "natural" capacity for exerting a civilizing influence, Beecher wrote in *A Treatise on Domestic Economy* (1841), their education was crucial for the future of America and, by extension, the democratic and Christian West: "Let the women of a country be made virtuous and intelligent, and the men will certainly be the same. The proper education of a man decides the welfare of an individual; but educate a woman, and the interests of a whole family are secured. If this be so, as none will deny, then to American women, more than to any others on earth, is committed the exalted privilege of extending over the world those blessed influences, that are to renovate degraded man."[42] Though innovative in many ways, Beecher's ideas were profoundly conservative. Unlike her contemporaries the Grimké sisters, Sarah and Angelina, whose arguments extended to women Enlightenment ideas of the natural rights of man, Beecher's argument gave women a secure place within the social order by maintaining hierarchical authority.

Domesticity was grounded in the concept of separate spheres: while men exercised power in the public world of commerce and politics, women held sway in the private domain of the home; men went out to work to provide financial support for their family while women stayed in the home to manage the household, to teach their children to live virtuous lives, and to provide emotional support for their family. Women were thought by nature to be morally superior to men, and their "blessed influences" within the home would improve their family and consequently society as a whole. This certainty of woman's sacred mission led Beecher to extend her argument for women's higher education to their participation in the teaching profession: women, she argued, should permeate the country with their special character and natural capacity for nurturing and benevolence through their influence as teachers in public schools. Women thus had a civilizing mission. By restraining the supposed innate brutishness of their husbands, by molding their children into sociable beings, and by bringing their young pupils to enlightenment, women were to be the agents of modernity.

Other advocates of women's unique capacity for influence offered similar arguments that linked female education to the well-being of society—arguments whose note of urgency were later repeated by Ume. In 1787 Benjamin Rush spoke of women's role as mothers of the new republic's future male citizens in a public address inaugurating the opening of the Philadelphia Young Ladies Academy. Hannah Mather Crocker, writing in 1818 on the "real rights of women," voiced similar ideas: "It is woman's appropriate duty and particular privilege to . . . implant in the juvenile breast the first seed of virtue, the love of God, and their country, with all the other virtues that shall prepare them to shine as statesmen, soldiers, philosophers and christians." Similarly, Emma Willard, who established Troy Female Seminary in 1821, maintained that the success of the nation lay in the proper education of women. Like other such female educators as Catharine Beecher and Mary Lyon, she extended women's moral mission from the private sphere of the home to the schoolroom, arguing that female teachers could foster future generations of virtuous pupils, male and female. Believing that a greater influence could be wielded by women teachers from the middle class, Mary Lyon established Mount Holyoke Female Seminary in 1837, a school "based entirely on Christian principles," which recruited girls "from the middle walks of life." She raised funds from middle-class women, observing that "this work of supplying teachers is a great work, and it must be done, or our country is lost, and the world will remain unconverted."[43]

Teacher-training gradually ceased to be the central justification for women's education—although teaching remained the common profession for educated women—and by the time Ume and the other four Japanese girls arrived in the United States, higher education for women was gaining acceptance. State colleges and some universities in the western states began accepting women students in the 1860s. Vassar College opened in 1865, Smith and Wellesley colleges in the 1870s, Bryn Mawr in 1884, and Radcliffe College in 1894.

While Ume was attending school in Washington a vision of woman's role in society more radical than the domestic ideal was becoming increasingly visible through the growing woman suffrage movement. From 1871 the National Woman Suffrage Association held annual conventions in Washington, where it maintained an office to lobby for a federal amendment granting women the vote. Because of the publicity given to these meetings, to the suffrage petitions presented to Congress, and to the testimonies offered by individual suffragists to various House and Senate committees, Ume was probably aware of the controversial ideas and combative image of such women's rights activists as Elizabeth Cady Stanton. Ume may also have learned of the scandal that surrounded such notorious suffragists as Victoria Woodhull, who was reputed to be an advocate of "free love."

Ume, Sutematsu, and Shigeko were steeped in the ideas of Beecher and other prominent advocates of woman's special mandate. Domesticity, by now the cornerstone of female education in the United States, not only pervaded much of their schooling but was absorbed through their involvement in women's clubs and improvement societies as well as their participation in charitable organizations. In New Haven, Sutematsu and very likely Shigeko, too, belonged to a women's club named Our Society, and Ume learned the particulars of fund-raising through her early involvement in charities.

They also assimilated the standards of the domestic ideal in the homes of their guardians. The Beecher family was associated with the family of Leonard Bacon, Sutematsu's guardians: both were prominent New England families in the Congregational church.

Catharine Beecher had tried to vindicate her friend Delia Bacon, Leonard's sister and a former student at Beecher's Hartford Female Seminary, after Delia had claimed that her relationship with a young minister amounted to an engagement—a claim the man denied, forcing the Bacon family to demand a clerical trial to clear Delia's name. Using her notes taken at the hearing, Beecher published a defense of Delia Bacon, *Truth Stranger Than Fiction*, in 1850. Like Beecher, the Rev. John Abbott, Shigeko's guardian, was a major spokesman for woman's supremacy in the domestic sphere. His 1833 book, *The Mother at Home, or The Principles of Maternal Duty*, became a bestseller in the United States and in Europe, where it was translated into several languages. "Mothers," he wrote, "have as powerful an influence over the welfare of future generations, as all other earthly causes combined. . . . When our land is filled with pious and patriotic mothers, then will it be filled with virtuous and patriotic men. The world's redeeming influence . . . must come from a mother's lips." John Abbott and his brothers Jacob and Gorham—both supporters of Catharine Beecher's educational efforts—put his ideas into practice in their New York seminary for fashionable young ladies, the Abbott's Institution.[44]

This American ideal of domesticity dovetailed with its Japanese counterpart, then being elaborated by both the state and its critics. Before it ceased publication, the *Meiroku Zasshi* provided the forum for a lively debate about the role of women in the new Japan. An important and innovative idea regarding woman's place, first proposed by the Meirokusha, was proffered by Sen's friend and associate Nakamura Masanao. A Confucian and Western scholar who became a Methodist in 1874, Nakamura translated a number of influential English works, such as John Stuart Mill's *On Liberty*. His most famous translation was of Samuel Smiles's *Self-Help*, said to be one of the "holy books" of Meiji Japan. So popular was this gospel of "rising in the world" that people lined up and even camped out overnight to purchase copies of *Saikoku Risshi Hen*, as Nakamura's translation was titled.[45] The work preached that character, rather than hereditary privilege, was the basis of both individual and social progress. National prosperity, in the words of Smiles, was "the sum of individual industry, energy, and uprightness, as national decay is of individual idleness, selfishness, and vice." The linchpin of material and spiritual progress was the home: "The Home is the crystal of society—the very nucleus of national character; and from that source, be it pure or tainted, issue the habits, principles and maxims, which govern public as well as private life. The nation comes from the nursery; public opinion itself is for the most part the outgrowth of the home; and the best philanthropy comes from the fireside."[46]

Following Smiles, Nakamura identified women in their maternal role as a prime source of national strength, and he coined the slogan that came to be used by both conservatives and liberals alike: *ryōsai kembo*, "good wife and wise mother." Like Beecher, he believed that properly educated women would be a transforming force for society. "We must invariably have fine mothers," he argued, "if we want effectively to advance the people to the area of enlightenment and to alter their customs and conditions for the good. If the mothers are superb, they can have superb children, and Japan can become a splendid country in later generations. We can have people trained in religious and moral education as well as in the sciences and arts whose intellects are advanced, whose minds are elevated, and whose conduct is high." In order "to develop fine mothers," he reasoned, "there is nothing better than to educate daughters."[47]

The appeal of Nakamura's argument was the civilized and civilizing cast it gave to this new ideal of modern womanhood, a view that was a far cry from the traditional notion of women. In Tokugawa thought a woman was nothing more than a "borrowed womb," a passive incubator of the active seed that perpetuated the all-important family. She was not only inferior but inherently irrational. According to Kaibara Ekken, an influential neo-Confucian authority on female education, a woman "merely follows instinct and not reason; so she cannot educate [her children] properly"—a view that reflected women's status as nonpersons under Tokugawa law.[48] In Nakamura's vision a woman was now accorded an active role as moral guardian of her children (though still within the confines of the largely unaltered family), a position that undercut the traditional principle of *danson johi* (respect the male, despise the female). Women now had a vocation as mothers.

Nakamura's ideas were particularly suited to the family-state ideology that was emerging in the tumultuous opening decades of Meiji Japan. Just as Beecher's ideas, spawned during America's troubles with popular democracy and growing abolitionism, offered the promise of social stability, so too preserving the sexual hierarchy within the Japanese family acted as a unifying force at a time when the distinctions among the traditional hierarchies of class and profession had been largely demolished. As gender boundaries were an essential element of the old order, their preservation in the new order offered security. With the emphasis on domesticity and especially on maternal responsibility, women were required to be upholders of tradition; one historian has noted how Japanese women in the 1870s were held to be the repositories of a nostalgic and often sentimentalized past.[49] Buttressed by the ideology of ryōsai kembo, the family became a "home," a retreat from the unstable world of competition—for with the abolition of hereditary privilege one had to struggle to stay on top—nurtured by a familiar and unthreatening wife and mother. At the state level, women would aid the struggle for survival in their dual roles as mothers and teachers, neatly cemented in the ryōsai kembo slogan. By fostering obedience and patriotism in their sons, who would honor their country and its patriarch, the emperor, while preserving the nation's unique character, women would be the mainstay of the family-state.

American domesticity was but one expression of the enthusiasm of nineteenth-century evangelism for social reform. Behind the vision of Victorian womanhood held by such champions of domestic virtue as Catharine Beecher was the heritage of republican womanhood: the "daughters of liberty," in their commitment to the American Revolution, saw themselves as actively involved in the creation of a new nation. Although in the mid-1760s they offered profuse apologies whenever they ventured to discuss politics, by the 1780s the women of the Republic were reading all kinds of political literature, publishing their opinions while engaging in debates over public policy, and eagerly promoting the war effort in a variety of ways. Women, they realized, had a role in the context of society as a whole, and they not only could but should contribute to their world through their individual and collective behavior: because the women of the Republic believed in the meliorative capacities of their action, feminine influence became a duty. Abigail Adams, for example, in a letter of 1778, described her "satisfaction in the Consciousness of having discharged my duty to the publick."[50]

This legacy of republican womanhood influenced Ume. The Lanmans, proud to be descended from the Adams family, took it for granted that Ume, as well as Sutematsu and Shigeko, would actively share in the creation of a new, postrevolutionary Meiji Japan. Others were also convinced that Ume would make a serious contribution to her country: when Charles Lanman wanted to write her biography, most of his Washington friends thought he was being too hasty.

During their years in the United States the three Japanese young women saw each other regularly, and together they planned their future contribution to Japan: with the help of Alice Bacon, Sutematsu's foster-sister and closest friend, they would operate a school for girls to provide them with the benefits of their American education. From 1878 to 1881, Shigeko had been a special student at Vassar College, where she studied music. Sutematsu also attended Vassar, and the yearbook of 1882 hopefully predicted that she would become the principal of a famous girls' school in Japan.[51] Shigeko almost scuttled the scheme, however, when she returned to Japan immediately after her graduation to prepare for her marriage to Uryū Sotokichi, a young naval officer studying at Annapolis. The overall plan, however, remained: Sutematsu was to be principal of a school, and Ume and Alice would assist her.

Convinced of her duty to Japanese women and seeing herself in a future role as an authority on female education, Ume felt it was her special obligation to share her advantages: "I feel I must be of use, not because I know much, but because I am a *Japanese* woman with an *education*," she wrote in a letter to Adeline Lanman in December 1882. "Truly there is much to be done for the women of Japan." Believing that the Meiji government would carry out Kuroda's vague notions of a girls' school, run by Sutematsu and herself, Ume naturally assumed that after eleven years of preparation in the United States she would be expected to participate fully in the building of a new nation.

In October 1882, seventeen-year-old Ume and Sutematsu set out for Japan. Having come with one mission, they were leaving with another of their own, but this time they were better prepared. As farewell presents the Lanmans gave Ume over a hundred reference books with which to start a library of Western knowledge and, what would be a rarity and status symbol in Japan, a piano. Both were necessities of female education.

In San Francisco the two young women boarded the *Arabic* and, Ume wrote in her journal, "said good bye to America and American ways." Again standing on deck, this time "watching & watching the last of America," she became depressed. "For nothing in particular am I blue but that my spirits are low & I have been thinking of America & the many many weary days between me & my friends. . . . my sad feeling, doubts & fears, & foreboding for the future might make me want to weep my woes out." Eleven years earlier she had left her family to live in an unknown country; now, excited but anxious, she had left her second family to return to an equally unknown country. "In heart," Ume wrote, "I am as true a Japanese as ever was, and love & feel proud of my country which will be my country whatever comes, & wherever I go." But her knowledge of Japan had become superficial, for she believed that her repatriation would involve merely matters of appearance: "I confess many of my ways are American & my ways of thinking also, but the ways in Japan that are good I shall adopt very soon—that is the manners, customs, and dress." Such reassurances, however, were not enough to overcome her apprehension. "Every throb of this great boat brings me nearer Father, Mother, & all at home, and this gloomy time is only the passage between the old life & the new, which begins when I touch the shores of Japan."

Chapter Three

My Right, & My Place, 1882–1889

By the 1880s Japan had acquired many of the institutions and technologies needed to transform itself into a "civilized" nation. A centralized administrative system was in place, and government ministries, experimenting with Western models, laid the groundwork for the transition from an economy based on agriculture to one based on industry. A national army and navy, law courts, a nationwide police network, and a public school system were among the new institutions created. New legal codes were planned and different public educational systems tried. A postal system and telegraph offices were established, and the number of newspapers and publishing houses increased. A national railway network was being created, and factories, supported by new banks and chambers of commerce, were being built. The goal of nation building—the transformation of a conglomeration of feudal domains into a strong nation—was rapidly being achieved under the rule of the Meiji emperor.

Nowhere was the sense of nation more strongly conditioned than in the primary schools of the new public education system, where school attendance was compulsory for children of both sexes. Public education, however, was neither universal nor egalitarian. After primary school, the end of formal education for most Japanese, public education became more competitive and elitist: boys and girls were separated, and boys advanced to middle schools. From there, after entrance examinations, they could advance to the higher schools, which were essentially preparatory schools for the imperial universities. The few girls who received a public education beyond the elementary level attended middle schools called "girls' higher schools" (*kōtō jogakkō*), which, aside from Japan's two normal schools for women, marked the end of the female educational track in the public system. By 1890 the structure of the educational route for advancement into the elite sectors of society was firmly in place.

From the social and political ferment of the first decades of the Meiji era an urban educated middle class was emerging. Composed of people with diverse occupations and levels of income, many of them former samurai, this group placed a high value on education and the social mobility it offered. Traditional morality had been undermined but by no means rejected, allowing this class to pursue new standards of individual worth and new forms of civilized behavior. Individuals such as Tsuda Sen and Tsuda Ume hoped to achieve positions of leadership in this new middle class by appealing to the need to establish an enlightened social morality.

As an important Christian educator, Sen became involved in the establishment of a variety of institutions and social movements. He either helped found or was connected to the founders of a number of mission schools, charitable hospitals, and shelters for the disabled. He was most prominently involved during these years with the *Rikugo Zasshi* (Cosmos journal) and the public lectures sponsored by the Tokyo Young Men's Christian Association, which this journal published. Started in 1880 by Sen, Uchimura Kanzō, Kozaki Hiromichi, and other leading Christians, the *Rikugo Zasshi* was an important voice in the political and social debates of the decade. Discussing religion, philosophy, politics, and the sciences in their connection to Japan's modernization, the journal looked to the urban intelligentsia, both Christian and non-Christian, for its audience. Like the leading intellectual journal of the previous decade, the *Meiroku Zasshi*, this journal took as its central concern the future of Japan; by filling the gap left by its defunct predecessor, the *Rikugo Zasshi* assumed the mantle of intellectual authority. As an editorial in its first issue declared: "We have learned about Christianity and confirmed that it is the spirit of civilization. We have planned therefore to interpret and circulate the doctrine to the world." Concerned by the social unrest of the time, the journal's editors argued for the establishment of a new order, their order. "Unless we devise some Way," the inaugural issue warned, "there will be no order, our nation will become a political debating society."[1]

Among the men behind the *Rikugo Zasshi*, Sen was a lesser light. Although he had hoped once again for a lasting position of intellectual leadership, he was outshone by such fellow editorial board members as Tokutomi Sohō, Uemura Masahisa, and Niijima Jō. Sen's gamble with Ume's American education, however, provided some compensation. During the years when Japan was rushing to catch up with the West, foreign education was the royal road to a distinguished career either in the government bureaucracy or in a government-sponsored undertaking, and Sen, as the father of one of these noteworthy students, lost no opportunity to bask in some of this prestigious luster. In 1879, while delivering a speech at the opening of Dōninsha Jogakkō, a girls' school begun by Nakamura Masanao, he reminded his audience of Ume when he likened the need for women's education to the cultivation of a healthy *ume* tree: "While Japan is educating her young men so finely, let her not forget the women, else she will be like a lopsided plum tree, one side tall, shapely, and blooming with fair promise of abundant fruit, the other deformed and barren. Let both grow together into a tree which shall delight the eyes of all beholders."[2] Sen also enjoyed displaying his daughter's easy familiarity with Western ways. He took her to foreign restaurants—nonchalantly eating beef in public indicated one's state of enlightenment—and to the meetings of such scholarly groups as the Japan Asiatic Society, where some of his Meirokusha and *Rikugo Zasshi* associates were sure to be present. At a meeting of the Romajikai, a society that wanted to replace Chinese characters and the Japanese syllabary with a romanized script, Ume was asked to play the piano: not many men could boast of a foreign-educated daughter who could speak English and play Mendelssohn.

On her return to Japan in November 1882, Ume was naively optimistic about the important place in society she believed would soon come to her thanks to her Western education. Certain that all she need do was wait for the government's summons, in the meantime she would refresh her knowledge of Japanese life. Convinced that her adaptation to Japan involved merely a facile reacquaintance with different kinds of food and clothing, she declared in her journal on the day of her landing: "Henceforth I am totally Japanese except in remembrances." Yet she was unprepared to relinquish her foreign ways. She was pleased, for instance, with the Westernized features of the Azabu house, proudly describing her Western-style bedroom in a letter to the Lanmans and assuring them that her family used a parlor, took their meals sitting at a table, and always ate at least one Western food, usually bread, at each meal. "It is so nice to have a Christian home to come to," she wrote that same month. Any adoption of Western things was to her a comforting sign of progress.

Yet during this exuberant period of adaptation and reform most Japanese remained as insular as they had been in Tokugawa times. Opening the country did not guarantee instant cosmopolitanism. The Western world was still galaxies away. An entry in the diary of Meiji Japan's foremost woman writer, Higuchi Ichiyō, with its rigid oppositions and strict categorizations that attempt to show "what makes Londoners different from Parisians," indicates the difficulty many experienced in trying to comprehend other cultures: "Parisians walk on the right side of the street; Londoners, on the left. In Paris, several families live in one building, like a barracks; in London, they live one family to a house. Parisians gather in cafés, Londoners prefer private clubs. Parisians sleep along the wall; Londoners sleep in the middle of the room. Parisians eat twice a day; Londoners three or four times. Parisians have long bread; Londoners, square. Parisians drink coffee; Londoners drink tea. In Paris, they talk incessantly during meals; in London, they don't talk at all."[3] Higuchi's disquisition, it should be noted, was not written in the early years of the Meiji era, nor was it the result of youthful ignorance—she probably gleaned her information from a newspaper.

Except to a very few, the West remained a distant, though intriguing, place. Like the realm of myth and legend, it was a land "over there."[4] Ume again found herself treated as an exotic creature. Her Western clothes and hairstyle, for example, attracted great curiosity. Visitors to the house—calling ostensibly to congratulate her on her safe return but more likely to watch and take note—asked to see her dresses, hats, and ribbons. They "have been showed over & over again," Ume complained in a letter to Adeline Lanman written the month of her return. While visiting her mother's sister, Takeko, who served at the residence of Tokugawa Yoshiyori, Ume let the attendants examine her hat and was asked to stand up and turn around slowly. Even hairpins were fascinating. Once, while she was making a purchase, a crowd formed around Ume to watch—an occurrence she calmly described in another letter as typical of her shopping expeditions—and a pickpocket used the opportunity of the pressing crowd to steal her purse. Her foreign clothes made her an easy mark: one Sunday, when walking to church, she was accosted by a drunk who asked in English for her parasol. After Ume, dumbfounded, gave it to him, he pulled a cat from his pocket, handed it to her, and left. He knew her name but she did not know his.

As in America, Ume was extremely conscious of being different from others. She decided to wear Japanese clothing as often as possible, she told Adeline Lanman in September 1883, "to experience for once in my life the feeling of looking like those around me, & of not being the one to be stared at." Her initial attempts at the kimono, however, were far from successful. She refused to give up foreign underwear, probably because it symbolized for her civilized femininity, and the layers of corset, camisole, stockings, garters, knickers, and petticoats beneath her kimono made her look ridiculous. Most humiliating was her family's laughter which greeted these first experiments.

Many Japanese customs proved more difficult, if not more shocking, than she had assumed they would be. Removing her shoes before entering the house was particularly annoying: "It is the greatest nuisance to have to button and unbutton every time you go anywhere." A number of Japanese ways, moreover, initially offended her Protestant sensibilities. Giving gifts was "a dreadful custom," she told Adeline Lanman, because it seemed an extravagant waste. And although she disliked sitting on the floor, she accepted it. But Ume was astounded by public breastfeeding and scandalized when people spoke openly of pregnancy or asked to use the toilet.[5]

The overwhelming restrictions on women's behavior made her feel very constricted. "Japanese ways & customs are so different," she confided to the Lanmans on her return in November, "that I long to jump around, rush wildly about & yet not have it thought strange. . . .

Japanese ways are so strange. In America at home there is no formality, as one goes away in the morning, they remark good bye, or I must be off or else they can go without a word. But here even when I go on a call or to shop, all the people of the house go to door, & bow & say sayonara." Ume did not realize the special honor her family was showing her, for such ceremonious behavior was normally reserved for men.

She especially enjoyed visiting Shigeko's house, Ume wrote a month later, because there she and Sutematsu could "talk, eat, rush around & do what we want, without having it thought strange or outlandish. We feel so free and easy. . . . It is well I have a happy disposition," she observed, "because I see much unpleasant." Japanese life, she was beginning to realize, was not merely an Asian version of American life. Her painful adjustments taught her caution: she learned to suppress her liveliness, becoming a reserved, serious, and sometimes dour, woman.

Once the excitement of her return had faded, Ume's first year in Japan was isolated and lonely. She felt disoriented and even alienated. "Though many things come back to me," she wrote, "still it does not seem natural at all. I still feel in a dream and would not be surprised at awakening. I feel constantly as if I was not to stay but more as if I were visiting . . . and often feel strange and lonely." Even though Ume insisted on her Japanese identity, she frequently felt different from, if not superior to, the Japanese: "I truly think that the climate affects the Japanese disposition," she noted, "they are a slow, languid, putting off lazy race"—a charge often made against black people in the United States. Not understanding the language, moreover, and not being understood by others isolated her by turning her into a foreigner among her own people: "My language is unknown to these people," she wrote. Even though Ume began at once to learn Japanese, she was distressed by her inability to talk to her mother. Sen and Ume's older sister Koto (who had attended and later taught at a mission school) could speak English reasonably well and translated for her at mealtimes; but Ume hated having to rely on them. After a few months of study she was still frustrated: "To my own mother I can only say so little, ask her if I can help, or inquire how she is, or any little thing like that." "I am blue often," she confessed to Adeline Lanman, "& feel that perhaps it were just as well if I had never gone to America."[6]

Ume was equally isolated from the foreign community in Tokyo. Her only foreign friend was Clara Whitney, daughter of American lay missionaries in Tokyo, but she was put off by the fervent religion of Clara and her father, Dr. William Whitney. "I think them both a little peculiar," she confided in one letter. Although she enjoyed the relative freedom she experienced in their company, she nevertheless often found foreigners dull and tedious: "The foreigners are pretty nice, but they are *monotonous*, that is the very word, *monotonous*. Is it because they are all missionaries? I think so." Though she supported mission schools, especially their work in education, Ume was nonetheless suspicious of them precisely because of the female education they offered, which she saw as potential competition to the Western education she had received. Many of the missionaries she considered narrow-minded and intolerant, and their petty sectarian squabbles only hardened the Japanese against them. Their bigotry, moreover, was galling: discussing "the higher, educated class" of Japanese, Ume wrote that some missionaries "call these great minds heathen, half civilized." Even William Whitney warned her about becoming "too Japanese." Assimilation meant apostasy. American missionaries, according to Ume, were the worst. "It is their excessive narrow mindedness," she explained, "& their want of appreciation of anything whatever good in Japan or anywhere outside of America & American ways. . . . They truly look down on us, & it makes me very furious. . . . I have no friends among them." Equally obnoxious was the degree of comfort they lived in compared to the squalor of their schools: "Are their consciences, so tender in talking religion, & distributing tracts, hard on this? Are they blind?" Nor was she being overly sensitive; many foreign visitors to Tokyo had observed the hypocrisy. In *Eight Years in Japan, 1873–1881*, E. G. Holtham noted in his description of the foreign settlement in Tokyo: "With the exception of the American Legation, one mercantile establishment, and a miserable hotel [the Tsukiji Hoterukan], the only buildings in Tsukiji concession were the residences, schools, or churches of the foreign missionaries: the residences being extremely comfortable, and the schools and churches (always excepting those under the Catholic missionaries) being a set of mean little conventicles."[7] Yet Ume, if she wanted English-speaking friends, was in a bind, for most foreigners in Japan were missionaries. (It was with a group of missionaries, for example, that she was unabashedly able to display her brisk energy when, in July 1883, she climbed to the summit of Mount Fuji, making Ume one of the first women, she claimed, to do so.)

Criticizing Americans was also a way of reassuring herself that she belonged to Japan. "If you were Japanese," she asked Adeline Lanman, "would you not think American way funny, American people rough, boisterous, & rather pushing?" "As a rule, though I don't feel so," she hastened to assure her, "I can see just how foreign manners strike the mind of the quiet, polite, self depreciating, retiring Japanese, & I am trying to soften down my own rough ways according to Japanese standard. But it does seem difficult." Still, when Ume met an old friend from Washington who had just returned to Japan, she found him "refreshingly American in his manners towards women." She could not wholly convince herself of her happiness in Japan, for she talked often with Sutematsu about returning to the United States. Yet her sense of obligation always overcame the temptation: "I would not come back to America, even if I could because this is my country and home and duty keeps me here." She would feel "like a coward and deserter" if she left Japan. "The thought of the weary, sad, women here would rise up."[8]

While in the United States Ume considered herself well informed about the condition of women in Asia. On the ship home to Japan she had met a Chinese woman who was "like a baby, really." "It is marvelous to see how a little education, even a very little, makes [a difference] in one's looks, and O how much greater in the mind. This woman cannot read or do anything hardly," she wrote in her journal. "Woman in the east," she concluded, "in the higher class is a play thing, a toy, in the lower, a servant. Nothing more." Feeling superior to such women and the culture that shaped them, Ume intoned against universal ignorance: "Let those who scoff at woman's education, and at missionaries' work, but look at her & then at the fair daughters of their own land, and keep silent." Blithely confident in the reason and righteousness of her mission, Ume foresaw few obstacles to her future career.

Her reaction to the everyday life of Japanese women was one of shock. Two weeks after her arrival she wrote the Lanmans that women "have the hardest part of life to bear in more ways than one. Even in America I often wished I were a man. O how much more so in Japan. Poor poor women how I long to do something to better your position." Any American woman, she stressed, should be grateful for her lot: "Thankful for her strong mind, ideas, strength of decision, and the kindnesses she receives, and her position, socially." What distressed Ume was the complete dependence—both material and psychological—of Japanese women. "When I returned home after my first visit to America," she later recalled, "I was especially struck with the great difference between men and women, and the absolute power which the men held. The women were entirely dependent, having no means of self-support, since no employment or occupation was open to them, except that of teaching, and few were trained for teaching or were capable of it. A woman could hold no property in her own name, and her identity was merged in that of father, husband, or some male relative. Hence there was an utter lack of independent spirit." Shocked by the extent of women's subordination in all areas of life, she was also angered by the general contempt shown for females within the family. When Shigeko gave birth to a girl and family and friends commiserated, Ume, who knew of her father's rage at her own birth, was indignant: "In the breath of all Japan, everyone wants boy children, not girls & it makes Sutematsu & I so mad for we do stand up for our own sex." Later that year, when two imperial princesses died, she reported the common sentiment: "'But girls are nothing, only a lot of bother.'"[9]

Japanese views of marriage also outraged Ume. Arranged marriages offended her American ideal of a companionate marriage, with the husband and wife as the core of the family. That the Japanese bride was often barely past adolescence made such marriages seem a brutal interruption of girlhood. Describing an evening in January 1883 at the house of Kanda Naibu, a Japanese man who had also studied in the United States, she noted in her letter that one of the "wives there was a little bit of a thing, a mere girl fifteen or sixteen Japanese age, equal to thirteen or fourteen your way of counting." "Why, Mrs Lanman," Ume exclaimed, "most all the women are married before or at my age. It is dreadful." Such marriages, she believed, could lead only to a life of ignorance. "How can they study or learn anything if they are married at fourteen?" "Most wives," she wrote in another letter, "are truly good for little else than to keep house, wait on husbands & sew clothes." A restricted mind, Ume thought, creates self-delusion: a woman "believes herself perfectly happy if she has a house, a husband and children."[10]

Ume held that such practices would stop if women were better educated, but the only school then offering higher education for women was the Tokyo Women's Normal School, which was, in Ume's words, "no good." "It is in the control of people who know nothing of education." The mission schools, according to Ume, were equally bad because "only poorer classes attend," and "no one of any rank would send a daughter" to them. Social reform, she believed, could come only from the new middle and upper middle classes—her people, the educated and mainly former samurai. As she told Sutematsu's American foster-sister Alice Bacon nearly ten years later, "Today the great work of bringing the country out of the middle ages into the nineteenth century is being performed by the samurai more than by any other class."[11]

Revealing her rooted sense of bourgeois respectability, Ume regarded the upper classes as immoral. At a summer party at the country house of Saigō Tsugumichi, a state councillor who held a number of government posts, she considered all the men disgraceful because they drank. The reliance of the upper class on the concubine system to ensure male heirs was also deeply offensive to Ume. She described it euphemistically in a letter of March 1883: "It is considered all right not the slightest wrong for a daimyō or anyone like a prince or for the Emperor to have many in their homes & palaces who are not real wives . . . the heir apparent is what you would call illegitimate." In this, if nothing else, "the lower classes are morally better than any of the higher."

She was scandalized to learn that many men of the political elite were married to former geisha. "I think Mrs. Saigō very pleasant," she wrote, "though I cannot talk to her. She is the only one . . . whose past can bear inspection, for she came from a good family . . . and was not a *geisha*, a dancing girl, a singing woman like Mrs. Yoshida, Mrs. Inoue and the rest." Even though she hailed these marriages as "love-matches" and therefore civilized, she was disturbed by them. Such women, she believed, were disreputable and had no place in the upper classes. Their careers were supposed to move in a downward direction, a speedy and painful process of physical and moral decline into misery, poverty, and disease. The social standing of these women threw some of her standards into confusion: in Victorian Anglo-American society they would be classified as prostitutes or, more vaguely, as "fallen women," and would thus be placed at the bottom of the social hierarchy, among the "dangerous classes."

But these women were obviously neither vicious nor wicked, nor were they helpless victims who had been led astray. Ume's notions of class-specific behavior could not reconcile their previous profession with their present social position. "I cannot get over the fact," she wrote in January 1883.[12]

Because of the social prominence of these individual geisha, the entire profession clearly challenged Ume's notions of respectability. Such women, she believed, should not be in positions of leadership. In March 1887 she informed Adeline Lanman about an anti-geisha society she hoped to form (which never materialized):

> You know there has been a great deal of talk in Japan, in the paper and every where about women—women's sphere, women's education, and the position of women in Japan, dress, manners and etc. There have been also in the newspapers a great deal about these women of doubtful reputation, the singing and dancing girls. . . .
>
> Sutematsu and I talked the matter over, & thought it was a perfect shame that these women did all the entertaining, leaving nothing to the ladies to do in reality, & by their appearing in society and mingling with the men, they become first the mistresses and finally the true wives of the finest and highest ranked gentlemen. . . .
>
> There is this to say in excuse, that the young ladies have been until now most stupid and least to be desired as wives—and so it was natural that men chose the bright geishas. But now everything is different, and so this customs ought to be changed. Sutematsu and I decided that we would form a society if we could an anti geisha society.

Failing to comprehend that the sexual exploitation of geisha, as well as prostitution and the concubine system, was part of the social structure, Ume assumed that if ordinary women were trained in conversation and other social graces, geisha would soon disappear.

She was not alone in this assumption. Many Christian educators believed that a wife accomplished in the social arts would be able to keep her husband happy, entertained, and content in his home, safe from the lures of geisha and drinking establishments. Years later Charlotte DeForest, an American missionary and president of a women's school, believed that a "constructive way to meet the *geisha* problem is recognized to be that of creating homes that furnish intellectual companionship and recreative charms. The educated wife, and all the home adjuncts of civilization—rational diet, well-ordered house-keeping, the piano or organ or victrola, the day's books and magazines . . . the modern *geisha* will be driven to the wall as these multiply." Similarly, Allen Faust, principal of another mission school for girls, stressed the need to educate young women in such accomplishments as Western music, to arm them in the battle (his metaphor) against the geisha. Men, he suggested, would be drawn to "the beautiful strains of Beethoven or Chopin, played on a piano by a pure young girl." The sheer size of the piano, moreover, made it a valuable weapon in this war: "The piano will always remain in the home of the young woman, because it is too heavy to be moved at will. The friends of the young musician—girls and boys—if they wish to enjoy the music, will have to come to her home. In due time there will be young men who come to hear the music and also to associate with the girl making the music. In this will be, it is hoped, the beginning of a new social world for the young Japanese people."[13]

To ensure that women of her own class would occupy positions of social authority, Ume felt it necessary to establish a school in which respectable girls could be "fitted," in her words, "to be wives of great men." The education she envisioned, vaguely centered around English literature, would transform the students into cultivated young ladies who would then be able to overcome the traditions that segregated men and women. "How can love matches be made," she wrote, "when gentlemen never call on ladies, & there is so little society when the men & women mingle? . . . Talk of reform in society, men and women must be most educated, cultivated, & be better, to mingle, especially with the women." After becoming the wives of great men, moreover, women who were versed in the standards of Western genteel ladyhood could use their social influence to promote civilization and enlightenment: "What Christianity leaves undone in the higher classes is done by foreignized ideas."[14]

Although Ume's early views on education were limited to the formation of ladies and gentlemen, she held that proper education was not superficial. Learning developed character. Thus, in March 1883, Ume obliquely criticized the assumptions underlying the official view of women's education. She remarked in a letter that some women "are treated much better than ten years ago & now they are getting educated too," but noted that this education came only after marriage. These women were educated merely because of their husband's high positions. They were fitted, in other words, to appear at official functions as wives of great men. "Do you see," she wrote, "this is not right." True education of women, Ume believed, entailed more than their appearance at social functions dressed in Western clothes. Her belief that education was for the sake of the individual and not the state ran counter to the government's position.

After haphazard educational experiments in the 1870s, the government had become less than enthusiastic about women's education. Having been sent at government expense to study abroad, Ume naturally assumed that the Ministry of Education would employ her after she returned. Most overseas students, in fact, were obligated to work for the government on their return, usually as low-level bureaucrats or language teachers. Many rose quickly in their careers, however, to occupy important posts in both the public and private sectors, for with Japan's modernization, new and important jobs were always opening up, and those who had studied abroad were often the only ones sufficiently competent for the position. Ume was at first frustrated and then despondent when her letters to the Ministry of Education announcing her return were consistently ignored. Similarly, she and Sutematsu prepared themselves at considerable expense for presentation at court, but the event never took place. "We have come home at a bad time," she told the Lanmans in March 1883.

By the opening of the decade, feminism in general, and women's education in particular, had become a major source of political dissent in the eyes of the authorities. Numerous works discussing sexual equality were published in the 1880s, and the debate had begun in earnest with the publication in 1876 of *Great Civilized Learning for Women*, Dohi Kōka's influential meditation on Mill's *Subjection of Women*. In October 1883, shortly after Ume's return, a twenty-year-old member of the Jiyū Minken Undō (Movement for Freedom and People's Rights), Kishida Toshiko, delivered a riveting speech in Ōtsu attacking the family system and stressing the need to educate women. Real parents, she argued, "are people who open the doors of knowledge to their daughters and give them appropriate tools for managing their lives. Heaven has given freedom to daughters; this is an age that demands that they develop a thorough knowledge of the world around them." Kishida's ideas were too radical for the authorities: the police interrupted her speech, arrested her, and broke up the crowd. The government, which had faced its last major armed rebellion in 1877, was now intent on silencing political opposition, and in the increasingly violent politics of the early 1880s it enacted severe laws that restricted public assembly, further stifled freedom of speech for the press, and prohibited specific groups from joining or attending the meetings of political organizations. In the interests of "family harmony" the authorities further reduced the legitimate political activity of women by adding them to the list of those forbidden political participation.[15]

With the increasing restraints imposed by the Public Meetings Act of 1880, the political allegiances of schoolteachers came under scrutiny, and the authorities dealt harshly with those who introduced their students to political theory and feminist issues. In 1882 the Ministry of Education stated that it was dissatisfied with the people involved in female education, complaining that many of them "have a wrong view of girls' education." Government-sponsored newspapers criticized women's education, charging that its proponents neglected "traditional womanly pastimes." Mission schools were often faced with the charge that "your girls walk like men," and the president of a women's college that had evolved from one of these small mission schools later recalled that at a "commencement in the early eighties it was decided that it was altogether too forward for a student to read a graduating essay facing the audience; to read it herself was almost too much; but a compromise was found in her reading it with her back to her listeners." Such schools as the one for working girls and women begun by the feminist Fukuda (Kageyama) Hideko, another popular-rights activist directly inspired by Kishida's speeches, were closed by the authorities.[16] Women's education became closely associated with the sources of political dissent in the official mind; with her foreign education Ume was thus unwelcome as a teacher in a state institution.

A conservative reaction that would climax in the 1890s also began in the 1880s. After a giddy period of indiscriminate borrowing from the West, Japan was beginning to react against perceived Western excesses, and anti-foreign sentiment and attacks on the corrupting influence of Western thought were already apparent in the field of education. Foreign-educated and Americanized Ume would not be chosen to teach: "There is but little hope of that now much to my disgust. You see the whole tide of affairs has turned against foreigners, foreign languages, anything progressive, & they will want no English & foreign notions now," she wrote in October 1883. At the beginning of the decade, the government began to reassert central control over the nation's public school system by redirecting the educational goals and content of the curricula from the excesses of the educational experiments of the 1870s. Regulations enacted in 1881 redefined the curriculum of the middle schools by emphasizing traditional subjects over foreign languages. Whereas several subjects had been taught in English, courses were now to be taught in Japanese by Japanese instructors.[17] Ume was fluent in English but incompetent in Japanese. Like her father before her, she had arrived too late.

Ume also represented a deep-seated fear: to many eyes she was no longer "pure" Japanese. Because of her foreign upbringing and education, she had lost the "unique spirit" that many believed set Japan apart. Fearing that their country was losing its identity, many Japanese felt that they were in danger of becoming "second-rate Westerners." In the 1880s numerous societies were established, in a direct inversion of the ideals of the defunct Meirokusha, to counter the pernicious effects of modernization and to promote Japanese traditions. *Nihonjin* (The Japanese), the bimonthly journal of one such society, the Seikyōsha, was dedicated to "the preservation of the national essence"; the Kairansha (Turning the Tide Society), begun at the end of the decade, aimed at upholding the Japanese spirit against indiscriminate Westernization. Another magazine, published by the adherents of a Shintō group, criticized the advocates of Western ideas: although such people "were registered as Japanese, their minds had undergone a change and they could no longer be considered pure men of the Land of the Gods."[18] Ume was more than a curiosity in her native land; she was an alien.

Regarding the conservative reaction as merely superficial and temporary, she failed to understand how entrenched it was becoming. Nor did she realize that women's education would be one of the first areas affected by a conservative backlash. When Ume heard in October 1883 that the Tokyo Women's Normal School was discarding its Western furniture and fixtures and thoroughly refurbishing in the Japanese style, she considered it childish: "Well, they are fools because in a year or so they will buy them all back again, & keep on piling up the expenses in their changeable fickle ways, and why, when they take a step forward, need they take a half one back." Not recognizing the symbolic meaning of such actions, she regarded such people as *baka*, fools.

By 1886, however, the Tokyo Women's Normal School was directly administered by the Ministry of Education, with Mori Arinori as its minister and a curriculum oriented toward inculcating in the students the state's definition of the ryōsai kembo ideal of a good wife and wise mother. Women's education, according to Mori, was a pillar of the state: from patriotic mothers come patriotic children. "The foundations of national prosperity," he declared in 1887, "rest upon education; the foundations of education upon women's education. We must remember that the safety or peril of the state are related to the success or failure of women's education. It is extremely important to foster the spirit of thinking of the nation in our education of women."[19] State-directed women's education was a form of insurance. If girls were inculcated with such virtues as obedience to authority, then their children would be raised as loyal subjects obedient to the state.

The change in educational policy went beyond the mere replacement of school equipment. The Great Principles of Education (*Kyōgaku Taishi*), issued in 1879 as an imperial rescript, expressed the emperor's views and bore the characters *seishi* to emphasize that it embodied his "sacred will." Written by Motoda Eifu, the emperor's Confucian tutor, the rescript deplored the confusion brought about by the introduction of Western thought and the loss of Japanese tradition. Education based on Western models, it said, "reduced benevolence, justice, loyalty, and filial piety to a secondary position. The danger of indiscriminate emulation of Western ways is that in the end our people will forget the great principles governing the relations between ruler and subject, and father and son." The Great Principles of Education promoted traditional ethics as a solution to what Motoda and others saw as the degeneration of Japanese society, an ethics based on the teachings of the sages: "For morality, the study of Confucius is the best guide." Motoda also suggested that each classroom display "portraits of loyal subjects, righteous warriors, filial children, and virtuous women . . . so that when the pupils enter the school, they will immediately feel in their hearts the significance of loyalty and filial piety."[20]

This criticism had far-reaching results. The government, already abandoning the American system of education, was about to adopt the Prussian model, strengthening central-government control of education. The system, moreover, was based on the principle of *seikyō itchi*, "unity of government and education," for the emperor, according to Motoda, had a "heavenly calling as both ruler and teacher." With education subordinate to political objectives, Western ethics texts were banned, and traditional ethics were moved from the bottom of the curriculum to the top.[21] Ethics education for girls was to be devoted to the emulation of Motoda's "virtuous women."

A major prescriptive source for the education of this traditional ideal of womanhood was the neo-Confucian *Onna Daigaku* (Greater learning for women), a seventeenth-century compilation of writings by Kaibara Ekken, whose precepts formed the basis of the education of samurai women so that it became a sort of catechism for every daughter of a samurai family. As her sole vocation was marriage and motherhood and her only role was service, Kaibara emphasizes, all a woman needs to learn are her proper duties to the family, duties fulfilled in following the "three obediences": while "it is the chief duty of a girl living in the parental house to practice filial piety towards her father and mother," after marriage "her chief duty is to honor her father-in-law and mother-in-law." Following her husband's death, her "chief duty" is then to her son.[22]

As a being who has no existence outside of service to others, a woman, according to the *Onna Daigaku*, is not even a member of society:

> A woman has no master but her husband whom she should serve with respect and humility, never with a light attitude and disrespect. In a word, the way of woman is obedience. To her husband she should be submissive and harmonious, serving him with gentle and humble expression of the face and speech. Never should she be impatient and willful, proud and impertinent. This is her first duty. She should absolutely follow the husband's teaching and wait for his direction in everything of which she is not sure. If the husband puts a question to her, she should

> answer in the correct manner. An incomplete answer is a piece of incivility not to be excused. If the husband gets angry and acts accordingly, she should fear and be ruled by him; never contradict him. The husband is Heaven to the wife. Disobeying Heaven only incurs righteous punishment. . . .
>
> The common evil natures of woman are: (a) to be willful, (b) to be offended easily, (c) to be inclined to abuse others, (d) to be jealous, (e) to be shallow-witted. Seven or eight out of every ten women have all these five sins. This is what makes woman inferior to man. She should know herself and conquer her weaknesses. Above all, shallowness of mind is her worst fault and is the cause of all the other evils. Woman is the negative principle, like night and darkness. Therefore woman is ignorant and does not foresee anything; does not know what is despicable to the eye of others; what is a hindrance to her husband and her children. Her ignorance is even such that she reproves and bears ill-will toward those who have no cause for being reproached and cannot tell her who are her true enemies. In bringing up her children, she merely follows instinct and not reason; so she cannot educate them properly. Utterly devoid of wisdom, she should humbly follow her husband in everything.

Kaibara's conclusion praises "the custom of the ancients," which required that a newborn girl "be laid for three days under the house floor. This is because man symbolizes Heaven and woman, Earth." If the infant survived she would have received her first lesson in submission and humility.[23] "Women," as the saying went, "have no place of their own anywhere in the world."

With the Meiji Restoration such attitudes were seemingly scrutinized anew. Many, like Mori Arinori, deplored the situation of women in Japan, yet little changed. The members of the first Tokugawa mission to the United States, for instance, recorded in their journals their shock at the appalling freedom of American women. Eleven years later, the Iwakura mission, whose members were from the Meiji elite, paid lip-service to the idea of women's improvement; Iwakura Tomomi, at least, had agreed to the education of the five Japanese girls in America. But the journals of members of the second embassy are as contemptuous of women as those from the first.

A national system of compulsory elementary education, the Meiji leaders knew, was needed to create a unified nation state with an obedient citizenry. In feudal times Japan was a country but not a nation—membership and loyalty were tied to one's domain—so a unified school system offering universal education was required to strengthen the modern state. Thus the Meiji emperor's Charter Oath of April 1868 contained a plea for national unity and an encouragement of seeking knowledge in order "to strengthen the foundations of Imperial Rule." Yet even though the Charter Oath encouraged education, almost nothing was done about women's education. Girls' schools were left mainly to foreign missionaries, and by 1894, twenty-six years after the Restoration, there were only thirteen public middle schools for girls, with a mere two thousand students, in the entire country. Nor were parents eager to send their daughters to school. In Akita prefecture, for example, school attendance of girls stood at only 3.1 percent in 1875.[24] Although four (later six) years of elementary schooling were compulsory, girls' attendance was clearly not considered worth enforcing.

The opponents of women's education argued that it would spoil women for their roles as wife and mother—the very roles for which others believed women needed to be educated. They would fail to marry and have children, becoming "tutors and old maids as in the West," thereby ultimately weakening the nation. As late as 1910, newspapers warned that those who attended female higher schools would lose their femininity and consequently their marriageability.[25]

Similar arguments had received prominence in the West and were probably known in Japan. Herbert Spencer, whose writings were widely translated into Japanese, argued that "absolute or relative infertility is generally produced in women by mental labor carried to excess." In 1873, when the Harvard Corporation agreed to a request from the Women's Educational Association of Boston that women be allowed to sit for examinations, a Harvard professor, Edward Clarke, published *Sex in Education*. A discussion of the deleterious physiological effects of higher education on women, Clarke's book claimed that a great number of women had been reproductively disabled by the demands of rigorous study. These were the "mannish maidens" who "graduated from school or college excellent scholars, but with undeveloped ovaries. Later they married and were sterile." The next year, 1874, another professor of medicine, Henry Maudsley, published his influential work, "Sex in Mind and in Education," in the English *Fortnightly Review.* Beginning with the premise that "the period of the real educational strain will commence about the time when, by the development of the sexual system, a great revolution takes place in the body and mind, and an extraordinary expenditure of vital energy is made," Maudsley argued that mental exertion would severely deplete the physical reserves of young women. Like Clarke, Maudsley held that the vital energy of the human body was "a definite and not inexhaustible quantity"; because female education coincides with puberty, the vital energy needed for proper physical development would be taxed severely. Women already suffered periodic strains to this energy through menstruation, these men explained, and any additional strain through study would irreparably damage the body: "When Nature spends in one direction, she must economise in another direction." "It would be an ill thing," Maudsley concluded, "if it should so happen that we got the advantages of a quantity of female intellectual work at the price of a puny, enfeebled, and sickly race."[26]

The Japanese proponents of better education for women, most notably Fukuzawa Yukichi, by now a major intellectual authority, argued that it was shortsighted to refuse women an education. Taking pleasure in ridiculing Kaibara, he described "the so-called" *Greater Learning for Women* as "nothing but a philosophy to oppress the mind and, in the process, destroy the physical body too." Women, according to Fukuzawa's revolutionary argument, are born equal to men and no social distinction should be made between the sexes. Daughters, like sons, should be properly educated inside and outside the home. Education was not only for the sake of women as individuals, Fukuzawa stressed; it was for the good of posterity. "My idea for the improvement of our race," he wrote in *On Japanese Women (Nippon Fujin Ron)*, "is to enliven our women's minds and encourage their physical vigor to grow with them, thus to obtain better health and physique for our posterity." He, too, linked the education of females to their bodies—in them was the future of the Japanese "race." (Fukuzawa's argument, in fact, relies on an analogy with starvation.) Thus both opponents and proponents of women's education were using the same terms of argument: on one hand, the education of women would lead to race-suicide; on the other, lack of education would also lead to race-suicide. As the English eugenicist Karl Pearson put it: "We have first to settle the physical capacity of woman, what would be the effect of her emancipation on her function of race-reproduction, before we can talk about her 'rights.'"[27]

Anxious for change, Meiji Japan was even more anxious about its consequences. Such Western thinkers as Marx and Fourier had argued that the position of women in a society was an indicator of that society's civilization, an argument familiar in Japan. As the editor of one leading women's journal observed:

> Western scholars have said that when we examine the status of women within a country we can determine the level of civilization that country has attained. In present-day Japan the condition of women is such that Japan cannot be considered a civilized or cultured country. There is no reason to complain over what has been said. It is not to be extremely deplored that we are made light of by the world because of our mothers, sisters, and wives! . . . We should exert ourselves in the improvement of the condition of women; by combining Western women's rights with the traditional virtues of our women, we will produce models of perfection.

Progress, or at least the appearance of it, the Meiji leaders seemed to realize, could be initiated by raising women's status. Yet women were also expected to maintain Japanese tradition. The streets of Tokyo, for example, were full of men in Western dress—a sign of enlightenment that was actively encouraged—while women went about in kimono. One critic of foreign contamination condemned women but not men for wearing Western clothes. Similarly, when women began to follow men's example by abandoning elaborate hairstyles and cutting their hair, the government responded swiftly: in 1872 (one year after it decreed that all chonmage, the samurai's topknot, be cut off) it made short hair for women illegal; those whose health required shorter hair had to obtain a government license.[28] Men were to initiate the future while women were to preserve the past. By the 1880s, all that had really changed for women was the scope of their obligations: their chief duty now was to serve the nation.

Ume had returned at a time when the government, paralyzed by uncertainty, knew that something had to be done but was unwilling to do that something. So Ume, noting the conservative climate but failing to understand its far-reaching influence, waited throughout

1883 at the Azabu farm for the Ministry of Education to contact her. Her life was becoming the opposite of what she had imagined, and within two months of her return she was greatly discouraged: "Sometimes I wonder why we went to America," she wrote the Lanmans in January 1883. "I don't believe we can do any good, & the government seems to be indifferent as to our work, & we seem to be forgotten. What can we do anyway? To say improve society is to put a mountain before us which we could never surmount. . . . My being educated benefits no one, and only makes me feel the difference sadly." Lonely, isolated, and depressed, the pampered only child of an affluent urban household was now the miserable daughter of a large and straitened farming family, distracted by fleas and younger siblings.

Family life offered little solace. She helped look after the many Tsuda children and cared for her mother, who, after many pregnancies (she had twelve children by 1884) as well as the care of a large farming household and the student boarders of Sen's school, was a chronic invalid—Ume once estimated that Hatsuko spent at least half of each month resting in bed. Ume "did not like what she saw of marriage," a friend later observed. "Even in her own home. Her mother was worn out with children, and the women of the house were at it all the time, Mr. Tsuda bringing guests and having religious gatherings any old time." Ume found some comfort in her older siblings. She experienced release from formal restraints by playing with her oldest brother, Motochika, who spoke some English, and she formed a close bond with her older sister Koto. Koto's years at a mission school had made her competent, though not fluent, in English, and she understood Ume's frustrations, providing her with companionship. Koto had recently married, however, and her growing family responsibilities claimed most of her time. It was Sen who made Ume's life difficult. Although he proudly encouraged her American ways in public, he required her to act as a model Japanese daughter in the private world of the Tsuda family, a code of behavior of which she had little knowledge. Six months after Ume's return, Shigeko wrote Adeline Lanman that Ume was lonely and Sen was very strict. Sutematsu also remarked on Ume's unhappiness. In a letter to Alice Bacon, Sutematsu wrote that she felt sorry for Ume: Sen she considered an odd person, and his family was neither comfortable nor relaxed. No one, she noted, tried to understand Ume, and

Ume herself seemed to think that nobody in her family sympathized with her. Sutematsu concluded her letter with her worry that Sen would try to marry Ume off.[29]

And marriage was certainly on everybody's mind. Sutematsu had agreed to marry Ōyama Iwao, eighteen years her senior, recently widowed, with three children. A major architect of the new military system, he was both chief of staff and war minister during these years and so needed a wife who was familiar with foreign ways and capable of being a society hostess. Although Ume had many doubts about the marriage, she was happy to report in March 1883 that "it is however understood that she will be like a foreign wife, and have priveledges like foreign women, because Sutematsu could never be a true pure Japanese wife." Ume was particularly hopeful that Sutematsu would use her position to influence others to adopt Western forms of social intercourse. Sutematsu, she wrote, "will be able to have lovely entertainments, dances, dinner parties, bring ladies & gentlemen together, show the great men what a woman can be & can do & be *Madame Ōyama*." Yet, while hopeful, both women remained ambivalent about the marriage. Sutematsu, taking months to decide, "grew thin with worrying and pondering, & wavering, because it took much thought & foresight & resolution to do as she had because it is for a lifetime. It was simply whether she would choose this or be poor & be more independent & free alone," Ume wrote. As the wedding neared, Ume grew increasingly uncertain. "I feel as if we are going to lose Sutematsu," she confided to the Lanmans six months later. "She will have much care & much responsibility to pay for her rank & wealth, but a great future seems before her. . . . little doubts come over me."

While Sutematsu chose wealth and a prominent social position, Ume chose independence by remaining single. Marriage seemed too high a price to pay for social acceptance. The day-to-day drudgery of her mother's constricted life must have convinced her that she had to remain childless if she were to achieve any of her ambitions. Although she laughed off the possibility of marriage, the lighthearted tone of a letter to the Lanmans written in early 1883 barely conceals her real anxieties: "Just think how absurd it does seem. It is too dreadful, but as I feel now I would not marry unless I wanted to, no matter if I have to live like a hermit, & nothing would induce me to make a regular Japanese marriage where anything but love is regarded. I am sure that Father would not make me, as I don't know Japanese ways at all, & above all have not had anything said to me on the subject nor any offers. I am not going to worry in spite of Shige's lectures & Sutematsu's warnings as to my age." Marriage was still considered women's true vocation, and the social pressures on Ume to marry were great. No alternative was imaginable for most women. A single woman was more than an anomaly, she was an object of contempt. As it was considered unfilial not to have children, Ume would have to take a husband if she wanted to adapt to Japanese society. Marriage, moreover, would give her the respectability and authority that would enable her to carry out her plans. "And *they*," she complained in a letter to the Lanmans written in the summer of 1883, "the cruel they, says I can do most & best for my object, if I marry, but I shall not believe it nor shall I mind it. I shall never marry. Thank you for saying that you are willing, & that you too will bury the subject for good." It required considerable strength of will to determine to remain unmarried in a society that defined women solely in terms of the men (father, husband, son) to whom they were attached, and so when Adeline Lanman also became excited by the topic, Ume finally exploded in exasperation: "Please don't write marriage to me again, not once. I am so sick of the subject, sick of hearing about it, & discussing it. *I am not going to marry unless I want to.* I *will* not let circumstances or anybody force me into it." Ume disdained the social approval marriage offered, and the arguments of others only strengthened her resolve by helping her to restore her deeply shaken self-confidence: "I *must* live & work & do," she wrote that summer.

Ume recognized the near impossibility of her making a successful marriage in either Japanese or American terms. She knew that she could not fulfill the standards expected of a Japanese wife—silence, deference, and obedience—and she was unwilling to sacrifice her independence and unprepared to soften her forthright manner. Nor could she hope to follow the American process of courtship: in Japan it was virtually impossible for an unmarried woman to socialize with single men. Thus she believed Shigeko was lucky to have met Uryū in the relatively free social atmosphere of the United States. As for Sutematsu's example, "not for *worlds*," she wrote in October, would she make such a match; "I am never to be a great lady like

Sutematsu or marry for love like Shige, so I will be an humble teacher, & I like teaching so the way is marked out & I am willing."

With Sutematsu's marriage and Shigeko's growing family, Ume was even more alone than before. Sutematsu's marriage to Ōyama, she believed, put her beyond Ume's sphere. "Then Sutematsu will not teach of course for the government," she wrote. Ōyama's "wife teaching, would be absurd, & I am sorry to lose her help, when I teach for I must teach all alone." By the middle of 1883, realizing that the government would do nothing for her, she finally understood the political climate: "I do feel tempted sometimes not to try & brave out the opposition. . . . The alternative is so hard, so lonely, & so discouraging, but I suppose it is the right way." Believing that she was "placed as few are placed," Ume began to plan her own school, a boarding school "where I could influence most," and hoped to open it in autumn 1884. "It will subject me to much unpleasantness," she wrote, "the life would be hard, but then," she gamely added, "I am sure to like it."[30]

The boarding school was more a hope than a concrete plan—she had neither the money nor the connections needed to establish it. Ume was faced with an immediate choice: a court position or employment at a mission school. The first was unthinkable. She had heard rumors of her possible appointment as court interpreter to the empress and, although deeply flattered, easily decided against the post. Even if Ume were familiar with them, the formalities and traditions of court life would be stifling. Her Japanese, moreover, was still weak. The second alternative, though equally uncongenial, was at least practical. Teaching at a mission school was work for which she felt suited and would also give her experience and contacts. Early in 1883, Shigeko, who taught at the government-sponsored Tokyo Music School, had asked Ume to join her at the school, but Ume turned down the request because teaching music would not further her ambitions.

In May 1883, Ume accepted a temporary position at the Tsukiji Kaigan Jogakkō, a girls' school run by the Methodist mission, which Sen had helped to establish in 1874, sending a few of his daughters there. "The prospect," she wrote, "pleases me, and regular work it will be too, for missionaries are regular." There she taught geography, world history, and English. But the work was unsatisfactory.

What bothered her was the school's status: as one educated abroad at government expense, Ume felt it was beneath her dignity to teach at a mission school. The pay was low (twenty yen a month), and so were the backgrounds of most of the students, she believed. "Most of these girls," she wrote to Adeline Lanman that June, "are from very low, common people, and brought up miserably, & at first had probably many bad ways & habits, which had to be corrected." Theft, she noted, was "not very uncommon." Although she frequently assured Adeline that she was eager to spread the message of the Bible and to set an example of upright Christian behavior, she considered these students a waste of time; only the "respectable" classes were worth the effort. When offered the same job in the fall, she declined, still hoping for a government posting. "The missionaries," she wrote, "will be my last resort."

Even though Ume often scorned displays of wealth and social pretension—one of Ōyama Iwao's dinner parties, for example, was "very frenchy"—she was nevertheless greatly attracted to social power. Complaining of one party she went to, "I don't care for these little affairs," she confessed a desire to attend "a real big affair" where she could meet "great people & diplomats" who could help her in her career. When invited to a ball hosted by Inoue Kaoru, the foreign minister, she announced: "And I don't hide it that I do want to go to the government ball, for I shall meet a lot of the great people & I want to look nicely & may be it will help my school plans." The ball took place in the first week of November 1883 at the foreign minister's official residence. It was essentially a dress rehearsal for the opening three weeks later of the Rokumeikan, a magnificent pavilion and proud example of Meiji Japan's aspirations to establish what Inoue called "a new European-style Empire on the Eastern Sea."[31] Ume was impressed by the display of wealth and the assemblage of important people, both Japanese and foreign, and she was pleased to tell the Lanmans of her introduction to the American minister and members of his legation as well as the mayor of London. She also spoke to an acquaintance from the days of the Iwakura mission, Itō Hirobumi, who had recently returned from a visit to Europe, where he had studied the organization and working of constitutions in the major Western nations, and was now one of the most powerful members of the government.

Ume had at last met an important official who, for reasons of his own, took an interest in her career. A week later she was invited to Itō's house, where he told her he was "anxious to help women, education, & every way." He also informed her of a position he had made for her at a small elite school, Tōyō Jojuku, run by Shimoda Utako, a scholar of Chinese poetry and a great favorite of the empress. "Mr Itō," Ume told Adeline Lanman in November 1883, "wished to propose to add an English department to that school *to be given to me*"; and her students, she boasted, would all be from the upper classes and accomplished in "the most strict, formal, & difficult etiquette." Itō also persuaded Ume to join his household, arguing that as Shimoda's school was nearby, she would not have to make a lengthy daily commute from the Azabu farm. At first Ume turned down the offer, assuming that she would be no better than a servant at Itō's residence, but Itō then appealed to Sen, who saw it as a rare opportunity and told her to go. "Now just imagine what a prospect this patronage offers me," Ume wrote two weeks later. Believing Itō to be "kind beyond measure," she saw his actions as entirely motivated by benevolence. Yet beneath Itō's goodwill was a more serious purpose: he was shortly to become acting foreign minister and required her knowledge of Western life. Ume's education in Western ideals of ladylike behavior made her for a time a valuable addition to the Itō household, because Itō was required to entertain Western dignitaries. His wife, Itō Umeko, was unfamiliar with Western languages and customs and therefore could not preside over such functions as hostess. Thus, when she finished teaching at Shimoda's school in the mornings, Ume returned to the Itō residence and, after a formal luncheon with Itō Umeko and her oldest daughter, gave them lessons in English and "foreign ways." "He asks me to teach & do anything I like for them," she wrote, "talk to them, play with them, make myself at home." Ume also taught them the piano, having brought her own from Azabu at Itō's request, using Japanese music transcribed into Western musical notation by Shigeko. Her duties even extended to dress: shortly after her arrival at Itō's residence, she accompanied his wife and daughter on a shopping trip to Yokohama—the first of many—in order to outfit them, from head to toe, in Western clothing. "It is an awful bother to think of everything," she complained to Adeline Lanman that January. Ume was also required to help Itō Umeko act as hostess at official functions. At a New Year's dinner party for thirty diplomats, for example, she received the guests with Itō Umeko. "I was introduced as her friend and translator," she explained, "and though I felt awkward, & as if I didn't belong there, Mr & Mrs Itō were very kind." Ume felt that at last her goals were receiving the push they deserved.

At the center of the Meiji establishment, Ume received a taste, during the first half of 1884, of the social influence she so desired. She also made the acquaintance of a number of important men whom she was certain would help her career. "With Mr Yoshida, & Mr Ōyama, & Mr Itō & Mr Saigō, I have become acquainted with a good many of the high rank," she told the Lanmans. "Such powerful friends as Mr Itō are worth having I tell you in Japan where without influence one can never work up. . . . Mr Itō is certainly the most popular man of the day, so I have a *great* friend if I have him." Ume was also hired as English tutor for Mori Arinori's two sons, a part-time position, she noted, which was good for her "future reputation and use."[32] Now, she was certain, her future was clear.

Perhaps more important, Ume gained connections with the wives of the political elite. Because Japan remained concerned about appearing civilized in the eyes of the Western powers, the government, under Itō's leadership, was interested in promoting activities that it considered appropriate to an enlightened ladyhood. Thus, during the 1880s, a number of women's charities and self-improvement societies headed by women of the Meiji establishment were instituted. On 5 April 1884, Ume described the beginnings of the Women's Charity Society (Fujin Jizenkai) in a letter to Adeline Lanman:

> Only last week we planned this thing, and now it is hot & thick. Mr. Itō first started Sutematsu & I on it. You know the Japanese ladies do so little & are often so inactive and unenergetic that we have been wanting something that would stir them up. Mr Itō wants us to get all these ladies & make them join together in some work of charity and usefulness & the proposal has come as far as this. We are going to have a large fair & ask a great many ladies to make with their own hands as specimens of their own work, either sewing or painting or any kind of fancy work & these things will all be gathered & collected & sold, the proceed to go to help a hospital now just begun for the poor & sick. We are asking the ladies to help the women's department of this hospital now started. You don't know what an undertaking this

> is!! These Japanese ladies many of them, especially the high ones, never heard of charity, never worked to help, never probably gave a thought to it, & to work something with their own hands & give it and *sell* it!! is something unheard. To sell what they make is very lowering & to them it is very strange. . . . We therefore appreciate the difficulty of the undertaking and also the good effect also of such a thing. . . . we have started with best influence & names, Mrs Ōyama, Mrs Itō, Mrs Inoue of the Foreign Department & several such ladies are on the comittee of which I am one. . . . [The] ladies must arrange to sell the things *themselves* as they do in foreign countries! Now such a thing as that is unheard of. To think of a minister's wife selling things, but they have promised, & it is a good lesson of charity.

Given her consistent use of the pronoun "we," Ume clearly considered herself at the core of this women's society, and she was pleased to report in June the success of this Rokumeikan charity bazaar, the first of many:

> The great event of the months, the fair, is at last over, and one of the most brilliant successes ever imaginable. In the first place, about fifteen thousand tickets were published and distributed, however, with precaution so as not to let it get too generally spread. Even as it was, Mr Itō here was much afraid that it was too public and had a regular extra police force to keep order, & quiet. You can not begin to imagine the trouble taken to have it all nicely, & it was truly very bothersome, without any doubt. Two of the Princesses allowed their names to be sent in as Patronesses & one of them came on all the three days & spent a few hours there. All the newspapers are full of nothing but the bazaar, bazaar, & strange to say, there is not a single one of them but what has the greatest praise of it. . . . There were twelve tables & different ladies took care of each, & each had a different corp of workers. Each table had two or three men to help, to take money, give change, & make accounts. . . . The tea room, in which was given tea, lemonade, ice cream, & all things of that sort, was also under a corp of ladies & girls, & was a great success. The ladies all wore a knot of purple silkcord as a badge, & the gentlemen one of red. I suppose those that helped were more than a hundred in number, & all the great ladies, all the

> ministers' wives, & Mrs Yoshida, Mori, Saigō, Inoue & all came all three days & helped. . . . It had been decided that from ten to twelve, only the Legations, ministers & families, & high persons of a certain rank should be admitted, so all these came and had the first best pickings. . . . Until twelve, though business was lively, the crowd was very well kept out, while most of the ladies were very demure & quiet, only selling when people chose to buy. But you should have seen the change afterward. I never would have believed it of these quiet ladies, the most of whom think talking of money, of bargaining or anything of that kind, is a sort of disgrace & you know in Japan, these high ladies never attend to money matters or touch a cent of money themselves. Well, they got a good lesson, I suppose they caught it from the few of us who don't mind. Any how, after the first, the way they urged the people to buy & praised their own goods, & brought their own particular friends to their own particular table, & actually forced them to buy—if you could have seen the way the gentlemen were really robbed of all their money by the persuasion of the ladies you would not have believed that these were the shy, proper, dames of Tokyo. They entered so heartily into the spirit, feeling as they should, that for charity's sake they could do it.

Impressed with their strong spirit and independence, Ume was also pleased that these women could be assertively ladylike. No alcohol was available at the bazaar, according to Ume, "by the most decided vote of the ladies. And that was so nice." Such fastidious behavior was natural, she believed: ladies were ladies no matter what culture they came from. If women of the upper classes could so ably participate in what she considered proper womanly activities, she was certain that bourgeois respectability could take root in Japan, for these women could influence by example their families and social inferiors.

The Rokumeikan was the setting for other Western-style activities that offered Ume a place in the social world of the powerful. Used for government functions, most notoriously official balls—it was the focal point for critics of the government's "Western excesses"—the Rokumeikan was also used by a dancing club eager to master Western-style dancing and dining, a pastime that Ume felt would give unattached young men and women a chance to meet and learn how to socialize in a convivial setting: "I go quite often to the dancing club," she wrote in February 1885, "& you have no idea how popular dancing is. So many persons come and seem to enjoy it so much. It is such an informal affair, and every one of them seem to enjoy coming & participating. Every meeting nearly is crowded and they all seem to have a good time. Nearly all the members are of the highest & best kind of people & lots of counts & barons & lords are among them. I always enjoy myself when I go & think it is well to encourage such harmless sociability & amusement."

How much store Ume put in the civilizing effects of such activities can be judged from her reason for leaving the club a year later. Its members, she believed, failed to realize the significance of their club's edifying example by treating dancing as a frivolous amusement, an attitude typical of what she saw as the "gay world" of upper-class amusement, and one made suspect by her middle-class values of respectability: "I got disgusted because they carried the thing too far, & it became too fashionable, so I withdrew myself."[33]

While living with the Itō family, Ume sometimes passed the evenings playing cards with Itō Hirobumi, who enjoyed her forthright manner (others, a former student later recalled, considered the same behavior "bold" and Ume "the most unwomanly woman on earth").[34] The two often discussed conditions in the United States and Japan. Itō, in fact, occasionally used Ume as a source of information about the West: one evening in January 1884 he asked her about Christianity and they talked for two hours; this conversation led Ume to report, with some excitement, that he "is in favor of it, acknowledged that its morals & teachings surpassed that of any other religion, & that for Japan, Christianity would be a good thing." Itō was merely seeking information, however, for a few days later he had an official meeting with a group of missionaries and a bishop. Failing to understand his political motives, Ume remained impressed with Itō's many plans to introduce Western ways into various areas of Japanese life and praised one such scheme to the Lanmans two weeks after she joined his household: "Mr Itō & I have had some very serious talks on all sort of subjects. He seems very anxious to promote the interest of Japan in every way socially, morally, politically, intellectually. He is anxious to establish a school, & to have me learn Japanese. Sometimes when I tell him about many things, about books, or interesting things about women's work, he tells me I must tell Japanese ladies all these sort of things, about work, & taking care of sick, & the worth of knowledge, etc. He wants me to learn, & to bring me forwards so that I can, & he is very kind."

The Meiji government may not have wanted women in politics, but it did want its elite women to set the standard for *kifujin shakō* (ladylike social life), intended to buttress their husbands' official positions.[35] Thus another concern promoted by Itō was educating the daughters of the elite to be model young ladies. As the future wives of great men, they needed to be not only thoroughly grounded in the ornamental accomplishments thought necessary for women of their status but also, like Itō Umeko, coached in foreign languages and Western social behavior. Itō accordingly proposed that Shimoda Utako's school, essentially a finishing school for upper-class girls, be merged with the female branch of the Peers' School to form an independent institution, the Peeresses' School (Kazoku Joshi Gakkō). In early 1884 he discussed his plans with Shimoda and Inoue Kaoru, using Vassar calendars and course descriptions supplied by Sutematsu. As a teacher at Shimoda's Tōyō Jojuku and an associate of Itō, Ume saw an important future for herself in the new school: "Mr Itō is the head," she wrote in February, "& of course he will make all the plans. It was his idea & his own carrying out, & he will have the Empress take a personal supervision of the whole thing. Mrs Shimoda is I think to be the Principal, that is the understanding. The school is to be for the daughters of nobles, & will take in about a hundred & fifty. I have only heard these things lately, but I think I told you Mr Itō always was planning a school, & lately I hear he has been earnest in urging it on, & so the school will be begun I suppose before the end of the year. . . . If I can get a place and position in this school I should be very glad." Believing that meaningful change could come only from the top, Ume was particularly pleased that the school would be under the patronage of the empress and that its students would be from the Meiji elite. "Just think," she wrote, "only the highest girls, the best girls of the land can enter this institution. Think of the influence all these girls will have in the after fate of this nation." The prestigious teaching position she believed was her due was at last in sight. Nor was it any ordinary government post. The Peeresses' School was to be placed under the direct management of the Imperial Household Ministry and thus had the added éclat of being connected to the imperial court.

Ume's exposure to wealth and social power appeared to end abruptly in June 1884, when Itō dismissed her. She was no longer needed to teach his daughter, who was now fully acquainted with Western clothes and would soon be learning English at the Peeresses' School. Nor was she needed to help Itō Umeko entertain foreign dignitaries: after the return of the foreign minister, Inoue Kaoru, Itō had few Western guests. Ume's religion, moreover, presented a potential embarrassment to him. Itō was convinced that Christianity acted as a social adhesive in the West, providing the Western powers with a secure foundation for their political institutions. Japan, he believed, lacked a unifying national religion of its own. Itō's interest in Christianity alarmed his critics, and in May 1884 some newspapers, according to Ume, suspected him of urging the emperor to convert—an accusation he hotly denied. Thus Itō told Ume that it would "be politic in him . . . if he did not keep in his house a Christian girl."

The move back to the Azabu farm left Ume anxious and depressed. The Tsuda family was in straitened financial circumstances—unable to compete with the government's agricultural institutes, Sen had closed his school in early 1884 and thereafter had no regular work or income beyond the produce he sold—and yet another baby, the seventh daughter, was born just three weeks after Ume's return. The contrast to life in the Itō household, where Ume was given her own rooms and servants, and where a typical family meal consisted of soup, fish, two meats, vegetables, dessert, and fruit, was disheartening. As she confessed in a letter written that June: "It is a mingled feeling with which I leave the Itōs'. Kind they have been beyond measure. Luxurious the life, & yet I was a stranger, & the formalities & politeness & distantness, were often strange to free & easy going Ume. I feel that it was a very rich experience—an experience most helpful and useful, an insight into a new phase of life, a new lesson from which I shall reap reward & I shall never regret the peep into the rank so different from mine, so different from America. I feel too it is a thing all ended. I shall never go back again, I think. I do not know what will happen in the future." Though she assured Adeline Lanman that she was happy, Ume's protests suggest the opposite. "I am afraid you will think I am gloomy or dispirited," she wrote, "but you must not think so. I am very cheerful . . . though regretting to leave here of course, some."

While waiting for the Peeresses' School to open in 1885, Ume continued to teach at Shimoda Utako's school and earned income tutoring others in English. She also continued to help wealthy women purchase Western clothes. "It was quite amusing to go with them since they were perfectly ignorant, & I had to tell them everything," she wrote the Lanmans in April 1885 about one wife and her daughters. "It is strange that everyone wants to have foreign dress, & it is so fashionable. But some of the people look horrid in it." Her future still seemed uncertain when that same month she heard a rumor that the position of English teacher in the Peeresses' School was going to the daughter of an English consul. Convinced that the post was rightfully hers, Ume fumed in a letter to Adeline Lanman: "I think my reward ought to be a field to work in, a place to teach. It is my right, & my place." What was truly humiliating was the possibility that Ume would be hired to teach under the foreign woman. "I do not expect much of a place," she wrote, "though it does seem strange that the government does not use their own tools. Those who were sent by them, and educated for the purpose. I do not say I will not get any position, but I will have a subordinate one under this girl maybe." The rumor, however, proved groundless; shortly before the Peeresses' School opened in autumn 1885, Ume was appointed as English teacher with an annual salary of 420 yen. As a member of the imperial household, moreover, she was no mere teacher: "Mr Itō said that I was to be made *sonin* [an imperially approved civil servant] & that is very high. . . . And as there is no woman in the *chokunin* [an imperially appointed civil servant] rank, there is only one rank above me, in which women are. And not counting in the court ladies there are few who are *sonin* as I am." "This, of course," she proudly informed Adeline in September, "is quite a difference, & especially among Japanese."

Ume's optimism revived in autumn 1885, when she began to teach at the Peeresses' School. Her new position gave her the opportunity to leave Azabu permanently, and she moved to a rented house in central Tokyo with her younger sister Fukiko, a student at the Peeresses' School, and her father's half-sister, who taught needlework there. Living away from her parents and their crowded house allowed Ume greater independence and fewer constraints. Her steady income—"a great deal for a woman in Japan," she claimed that October, "many men keep house & support a family on half"—provided her some comfort, and at the Peeresses' School Ume was able to continue her acquaintance with a world of wealth and social prestige.

The school was physically imposing. Composed of substantial Western-style brick buildings, it was surrounded, according to Katō (Ishimoto) Shizue, by a high wall with "a tall ancient wooden gate with black painted iron fittings." In her autobiography Katō recalled that when she was a student at the Peeresses' School her classmates included four imperial princesses and many daughters of marquises, counts, viscounts, and barons, as well as the daughters of high government officials and prominent industrialists. Many girls arrived at the school accompanied by a small retinue: "Some girls drove to school in their coaches, but many came by rikisha with their gilt family crest painted on the back and drawn by rikishamen in black satin happi-coats embroidered with the same crest. Girls of the daimyo families arrived with maids in separate rikishas following their mistresses. When such a family had more than one daughter to send to school, each of the girls was followed by her own maid-in-waiting, sometimes even by a household steward, a man in Western frock coat, or in a kimono and hakama [overskirt]. Thus three girls in a family would have seven rikishas in their grand daimyo procession. Maids and rikishamen waited at the school until the classes were over." With such attention consistently paid to rank and status, much of the school's activities were taken up with formalities. When the school was invited to tour the new imperial palace, for example, merely getting the students off was a time-consuming effort: not only had each to be put into her own rickshaw, but each rickshaw with its passenger then had to be placed in the line of the hundreds of others according to the student's rank.[36]

Ceremonies naturally played a major part in the life of the school. Little was unregulated or uncontrolled. Opening and closing exercises, for example, as well as receptions for the empress on one of her frequent visits, were rigorously rehearsed by the entire institution. Ume described one such practice session for the school's official opening in November 1885:

> When the Empress arrives, all the scholars are to go beyond the gate to meet her, & also when she returns they go with her to the gate. I lead my own class and take them to the selected spot. We rehearsed this today, & went outdoors, the whole one hundred & fifty girls, with all the teachers. . . . Well, after we go back to the house, we go each to a class room, I to mine own, & wait the arrival of the Empress. . . . & her coming is made

> known by the opening of the door by the director, when I, by a motion of my hand, make the girls stand, respectfully, placing their hands & bodies in the polite position, which I must do too, standing before them all. Then when the Empress has come in they bow very low, & sit down & I must hear them read, & have their lesson. She will probably stay only a few moments, as she must go through nine classrooms in the hour. Accompanying her will be the Principal, the three directors, some of the Princesses, Mr Itō probably, & one or two attendants. . . . After that is all over, we all repair to the large building, & the Empress reads something to us, then the Principal does, then one of the teachers from the faculty side, & then one of the scholars, then perhaps, some of the teachers will go in privately, & bow before the Empress, so it will be three times I must go through all the forms, worse than the Emperor's birthday.

These imperial visits were so disruptive of the lessons that Ume, after her initial awe at the splendor and stately behavior of the empress and her attendants, soon found them tedious and trying. In a letter written the next May at school during a break, she remarked that the place was in confusion because chairs, screens, and other items for the use of the empress were arriving from the palace, indicating that another visit was in the offing: "I doubt if I will have anything to do, because I had my turn not long ago, & I am heartily glad I don't have to go through with it again."

The curriculum at the Peeresses' School was also stultifying in its rigid emphasis on formality. It was not aimed, according to Katō, who later became a prominent advocate of birth control and outspoken critic of the family system, "at cultivating or enlarging the mind but drove any imagination or curiosity into narrow boundaries of orthodox morality and formality." As in the public school system, the students at this school were trained to be "good wives and wise mothers." The boys at the Peers' School, Katō wrote, "were taught and trained to be 'great personalities'; girls were first and foremost taught to become obedient wives, good mothers and loyal guardians of the family system. This discrimination was not calculated to encourage girls to independent thinking." Their education was a sort of "negative education," she believed, its primary aim the indoctrination of the family system.[37]

The students were required to cover a range of subjects that allowed for little in-depth study: along with mathematics, physics, chemistry, geography, history (both Japanese and world), classical and modern Japanese literature (including the mastery of four to five thousand Chinese characters), and foreign languages, they had lessons in calligraphy, painting, drawing, music, and both Japanese and Western needlework and cooking.

Like all Japanese students, these girls were required to study ethics, and every morning before classes the entire school recited: "We girls in the Peeresses' School shall respect the imperial family, and try to be model subjects loyal to the Emperor and the Empress." In the ethics class they were taught, in the words of Katō, "that loyalty and filial piety are the chief and fundamental morals, that our conduct should be directed to expressing our sense of gratitude to the Emperor as obedient subjects, and to parents and ancestors as faithful daughters." The textbook for this class, *Fujo Kagami* (A mirror for womanhood), was written by an original member of the Meirokusha, Nishimura Shigeki, a Confucian scholar and lecturer to the emperor, who upheld the Confucian view of ethics as the basis of all education, with all other fields of study as supporting branches of moral training. Stressing the central importance of moral education to overcome what he considered the evils of Westernization, Nishimura believed that a proper education based on "national principles" should take the traditional education of Tokugawa times as its model: the Confucian classics, he argued, were "unrivalled in the world as texts for moral education." His textbook for the Peeresses' School was a collection of didactic tales about model women from East and West, such as Murasaki Shikibu and Joan of Arc, as well as such exemplary women as the mother of George Washington, and recounted such stories as that of one daughter's joyous self-sacrifice in order to save her mother from drowning and another who, after toiling long and hard in the wind and snow of a severe winter to support her aged parents, finally decides to answer the advertisement of a dentist and sell her front teeth. Because of the imperial favor *Fujo Kagami* received—the empress recommended it be used in all girls' schools—as well as Nishimura's various posts in both the Ministry of Education and the Imperial Household Ministry, this ethics text represents the official definition of ryōsai kembo.[38] Thus the state's view of the good wife and wise mother was little different from the Confucian ideal of self-denying obedience as praised in the *Onna Daigaku*—a far cry from Nakamura Masanao's vision of a competent and educated woman who takes charge of her children's education and her household's management.

At the Peeresses' School great emphasis was also placed on self-control and physical discipline. The class in ethics, according to Katō, was reinforced by a class in etiquette given in a special "etiquette practice-hall," which instilled in the students a disciplined sense of modesty and reverence. They were serious about this class, she recalled, "as if life consisted solely of formalities which, if carefully preserved, leave nothing more to be desired. Indeed, knowledge itself could be nothing but formality to us who were to take it from the voice of authority as the infallible guide for the movement of the mind. We were never to criticize or doubt it." Through instructing them in such complexities as proper ways of sitting and standing and the three forms of bowing to elders, equals, and inferiors, this class trained them to internalize the constraints of refinement.[39]

Another lesson that drilled into the girls a sense of obedience to command and strict physical control, and which received much comment from both students and visitors alike, was athletics. Full performances of Swedish exercises, Japanese and Western dances, and Red Cross drills were given twice a year by the entire school for the empress and members of the court. Hundreds of girls, all wearing long-sleeved purple kimonos, red cashmere hakama, and high-heeled shoes, and arranged before the temporary pavilions draped in purple, red, and gold brocade with the white imperial crests, must have made an impressive display of rigid self-control and military discipline as, in unison, they went through the motions of Swedish exercises or conducted a Red Cross drill in bandaging and carrying "wounded soldiers" on stretchers across the field. The Swedish system in particular, relying as it did on precisely coordinated movements performed in unison to the instructor's calls, concentrated on the students' obedience and instant response to the word of command.[40]

Against this background of formality and ceremony Ume attempted to acquaint her students with the more easygoing habits of nineteenth-century American girlhood. At Shimoda's Tōyō Jojuku, before it was incorporated into the Peeresses' School, she frequently took her students outside during the morning break and taught them games. Free outdoor play was a new but indecorous pastime

(Katō's mother, for example, feared that such lively activities would spoil her daughter's frail body and delicate looks), and many, after running about, had to go to their maids to have their hair fixed and noses powdered. Ume also introduced her students to tennis, a pursuit she considered more wholesome than dancing. Eager to have her students become adept at Western forms of socializing, she began her "Saturday evenings," a form of "at-home" only for her students to give them practice in English conversation and informal sociability. Nor was this extramural instruction limited to students' entertainment. In a letter marked "(Private)" she wrote to Adeline Lanman: "When I received the garters you sent me the other day in the box, those that come from the waist, I thought I would ask you if you wouldn't some time when you have chance send me one of those bands for ladies to use at certain times. I want one as a model, and should like to show the Japanese ladies, as their method is so uncomfortable, & I have none of the nice bands I used to have."[41] True to her intellectual background, which regarded a real education as the formation of character, a process of cultivation that permeated all areas of life, she was intent on bringing Western notions of ladyhood to every aspect of the lives of middle- and upper-class Japanese "ladies."

Ume, however, was making little headway in her efforts to teach her version of civilization and enlightenment to Japanese women. After her initial excitement about the high status of the Peeresses' School had cooled, she realized that the institution's activities were largely empty show. Her letters to the Lanmans extolling her students' ceremonious behavior quickly became letters of complaint. Resentful of their ascendancy—for after all, a high social position in both American and Meiji ideologies of meritocracy was supposed to be earned, not inherited—she often scorned the entire class. "Girls of the Nobility," she wrote in September 1885, "are stupid as a rule." Yet, drawn as she was to social power, her attitude remained ambiguous. One month later she revealed her ambivalence in the compliments and criticisms punctuating her description of the lessons she gave outside the Peeresses' School to the daughters of a former feudal lord:

> It is quite formal & ceremonious & I am led through long winding halls in & out of rooms by lots of attendants & then taken upstairs & there is a table & chairs. Here I wait, & presently the

> young princesses come up. They are always dressed beautifully & behave so shyly & quietly. . . . They are so shy I can hardly make them open their mouths & it is a great bother to teach them, for I have to be so polite, & I am so afraid I shall make some breach of etiquette & be scolded by the attendants, who are in the next room adjoining, & opening into it & who listen with all the ears they have to what I am saying . . . I wonder if these human dolls can learn much. I met their father, the big noble that he is, & he spoke very pleasantly & affably, for which I suppose I ought to be very proud, but I am not particularly.

Though a teacher of the daughters of the elite, Ume was not their guide. Far from acquiring the position of leadership that she had hopefully foreseen, she was as isolated as ever. "I am sometimes surprised at myself," she had noted while living in the Itō household, "and think with a start, how strange it is to be so alone & independent . . . and going as a stranger among strangers treated very kindly, but respectfully & distantly, like one distinct & separate." And indeed, her life while in Itō's employ represents much of her experience in Meiji Japan: at the center of the establishment, she was nevertheless at its margins.

Ume was not acquiring the influential role in society she had assumed would be the logical consequence of her Western education, and neither, to her disappointment, was Sutematsu. Although she was the wife of a great man, Sutematsu was hardly the Madame Ōyama of great social weight and influence that Ume had hoped. Instead of championing the Western ideal of the companionate marriage, which allowed for an expression of the woman's individuality and accorded her some respect as an autonomous being, Sutematsu was doing her utmost to conform to the traditional ideal of a Japanese wife. "I feel & so do many that Sutematsu's position is a great one for work," Ume wrote Adeline Lanman in the summer of 1885, "that she can do a great deal for Japan, but she does not feel so, she feels so bound in by customs & proprieties that she can not make any plunge for reform. She is trying to keep & get Mr Ōyama love & esteem as a Japanese woman would, not shocking him with foreign crazy ideas. Looking at it in that sense she is more helpless than you or I to do any reform or to help Christianity. She feels so & she feels she must be so—but I am sorry that she does take that view & not a more independent true one—the one natural to her."

Although she understood Sutematsu's dilemma, Ume was nevertheless disgusted with her timid behavior. "I do not have patience with such wifely tameness. . . . She is too submissive & seems to have lost her will. I am very sorry." Sutematsu "never seems to go out of her prison like home," Ume complained; what was worse, she "is getting very artificial in her dress & looks." Sutematsu, Ume was shocked to report, "paints her face." Clearly such behavior meant regression to Ume: Sutematsu was backsliding from the Western standards of individual worth into an unenlightened world in which women were nothing but caretakers. "She just stays in the house, & minds the children, and looks after things, & is a figurehead, while all her studying & accomplishments go for nothing." Yet Ume understood that Sutematsu was an easy target for criticism: "You see Japan is in such a whirl now," she told Adeline, "and the question of women's education etc, being so much agitated that any woman as Mrs Shimoda or Sutematsu, who is in any way prominent or well known is picked to pieces." In 1887 gossip appeared about Sutematsu in Japanese newspapers which was soon repeated in some American papers, and later that year it was rumored that Shimoda, principal of the Peeresses' School, was Itō's mistress. "You see the dreadful stories they get up against them," Ume wrote.[42]

By the late 1880s, the conservative reaction to the perceived excesses of Westernization was in full force. Women's causes and the individuals who promoted them were openly criticized. Tani Kanjō, president of the Peeresses' School, was forced to resign in 1887 because his ideas, according to Ume, were disliked. Two years earlier, in an official letter to the Imperial Household Ministry, the emperor had criticized Tani as too enthusiastic about female education. "Women's education is not the same as men's," he wrote, and thus Tani's position "would have been more appropriately filled by a person of calm, rather than active disposition." Conducting women's education "in a vigorous manner," the emperor complained, had numerous bad effects. "Therefore, a person of greater composure should have been selected to direct the education of girls." Tani was soon replaced by Nishimura Shigeki, an appointment that gave Ume cause for concern. "From all I hear," she wrote Adeline Lanman, "our next Principal will not be as progressive as our former one, and I do not know whether he will favor English."[43]

Although Nishimura acknowledged that Confucian morality was inadequate for Japan's modernization and admitted that it was particularly unjust to women, he nevertheless articulated his views on women's education according to Confucian ideals. It was wrong, he believed, to educate women too much or to encourage them to be too active. In a speech delivered to the Peeresses' School one year after his appointment, he stated: "Frivolous people are inclined to say that the old Eastern education of women is extremely subservient and bigoted and should be abolished quickly. This opinion is greatly mistaken. As is well known, the Eastern education of women emphasizes submissiveness and faithfulness. . . . In recent years, many foreigners who have stayed in this country a long time have admired the submissiveness and virtuousness of Japanese women." Many foreigners did indeed admire the traditional Japanese ideal of femininity and warned of the evils Japan would experience if it educated its women. In 1889, the same year as Nishimura's address, Erwin Baelz, a medical doctor at Tokyo Imperial University who sometimes attended the imperial family, outlined in a public lecture the ill effects Japan would suffer if Japanese women received a thorough education. Using statistics which purported to show that American college women either remained unmarried or, if they married, had few or no children, Baelz argued that women could not be good wives and mothers if they had an academic education. Members of his audience were some of Japan's most influential men, and the lecture was widely reported and discussed in the newspapers.[44] Coming from a Western medical man, this scholarly argument, relying on the new science of statistics, lent more authority to previous criticisms of women's education.

By the end of the decade Ume's future was less than clear. Although she was now a civil servant of intermediate rank (she was promoted in late 1886 to an annual salary of five hundred yen), the government remained equivocal as to her position. After her appointment to the Peeresses' School, Ume, like other members of the Imperial Household, was ordered to pay her respects at court on the emperor's birthday and New Year's Day. But, as there was no precedent for a woman government worker of her rank, court protocol could not accommodate her, and Ume was told privately to stay away. The situation clearly reflected her anomalous status in Meiji society.

Ume finally accepted that a position of importance would not be given her; to fulfill her ambitions she would have to take the initiative. This did not mean, however, that she would disregard the government and its resources. In a letter of May 1888 praising "a very ambitious class of women, who are really intelligent & well educated . . . & do a great deal of good," mostly graduates of the Tokyo Women's Normal School, Ume told the Lanmans for the first time of her desire to study again in the United States. While she identified with these energetic graduates of the Normal School, she also saw their ambitions as a possible threat to her career. Her position at the Peeresses' School was undoubtedly secure, but this rising generation of educated women challenged her self-ordained role as authority on enlightened womanhood. They goaded Ume to take decisive action in planning her future. "I think how nice it would be," she wrote, "if I could go for a little while for honest study, to fit me better for my work as teacher, so that not only I might be a teacher of English, but I might some time be at the head of my own Department." Such bald statements of ambition, however, had to be couched in patriotic language, and like many of her contemporaries, she wove her interests with those of the nation: "I intend to be a teacher all my life, as it is, but I should like to fit myself up to be a first rate teacher, & though I may have enough education to carry me along through life in its ordinary paths, I want more than that—I want to be well fitted for my work, & we need all our brains & ability in Japan I assure you."

Because of the increasing numbers of women graduating from the two normal schools for women, her education in American primary and high schools no longer sufficed. Ume now required a higher education from an American university. Even though she appealed to Japan's future as her motivation, her career was her immediate concern: in a letter to Mary Morris, a prominent Quaker from Pennsylvania who took an interest in Japan, Ume informed her that she was ready to resign her position at the Peeresses' School if she could not secure a paid leave of absence and instead would rely on Morris's offer to pay her expenses. She was also taking the first concrete steps toward establishing her own school. Alice Bacon, Sutematsu's close friend, had come to Japan in 1888 to teach for a year at the Peeresses' School; she and Ume shared a house, and the two began making plans for a school under Ume's direction.

Finally, after convincing her school to grant her a two-year leave of absence with pay so that she could study, in her words, "things important for Japan in regard to schools & education for girls," Ume, aged twenty-four, left for America in the summer of 1889. At the urging of Mary Morris, Bryn Mawr College had accepted her as a special student, waiving the usual preparatory study and entrance examinations and agreeing to give her free board and tuition.

Having made a far from triumphant return to Japan at the beginning of the decade, Ume left again at its end, determined to try once more for a position in Japanese society. The 1880s had been a decade in Ume's life characterized by her naïveté, a decade in which she was largely ignored by the official world of the government and the press, though she was well known among the Western-educated elite. Believing that her Westernization was sufficient to make her a leader among the emerging professional and upper-middle classes as an authority on cultivated ladyhood, she ingenuously assumed that her American education, acquaintance with men in high places, and the supposedly benign paternalism of the government would see her to an influential career. But, instead of being a secure member of the elite, Ume found herself at its margins. She was regarded, in the description of a friend, as a freak. Questions regarding her cultural identity (American or Japanese, Western or Eastern) and her proper allegiances (which country, which family) were richly symbolic of Japan's predicament.[45] With the growing backlash against the country's experimentation in Western ways of life and institutions, Ume represented what many anxious about Japan's identity feared. Far from achieving the status of an acknowledged pacesetter of the nation's future trends, she was instead an anomaly, an object of curiosity possessing some useful knowledge. Her departure for Bryn Mawr was thus both a step toward her future career and a needed retreat. While studying in the United States, where she felt more at ease than she did in Japan, Ume could plan new strategies to help her realize her ambitions and see her ideals put into practice.

Tsuda Sen and Tsuda Hatsuko, Umeko's parents.

The five girls dressed for their audience with the Meiji empress, shortly before their departure for the United States in 1871. Umeko, the youngest, is second from the right.

The five girls in the "ill-fitting, ready-made American garments" purchased for them in Chicago. Umeko is second from the right.

Charles Lanman, secretary at the Japanese legation in Washington and Umeko's guardian, and his wife, Adeline, Umeko's "American mother."

Umeko in Georgetown.

Umeko in the Lanmans' house, about one year before her return to Japan. This photograph suggests how estranged she became from her native culture: the kimono is improperly worn, the obi badly tied, the fan (probably Chinese) held awkwardly, and the hair ornaments out of place. Shortly after her return to Japan, Umeko asked Adeline Lanman to destroy this photograph.

Umeko at Bryn Mawr College, about 1892.

The Joshi Eigaku Juku before it was destroyed in the Great Kantō Earthquake of 1923.

Umeko in her last years—a rare smiling photograph.

Chapter Four

Woman's Paramount Sphere, 1889–1899

The 1890s were Ume's apprenticeship years, a decade that completed the education in woman's sphere she had begun twenty years earlier. Work in various social reform and charitable activities provided Ume with lessons in public speaking and fundraising and gave her useful organizational skills as well as valuable contacts with women's networks in both the United States and Japan. Study in the United States, visits to several schools overseas, and teaching at various schools in Japan gave her experience in the establishment and day-to-day operations of a school for women and familiarity with diverse teaching methods. And Ume learned from women leaders in Japan and abroad, women who became inspirational models for her.

The first such woman was M. Carey Thomas, dean of Bryn Mawr College. Arrogant, autocratic, and caustic in manner, she dominated the college: to a great extent she created the image of the American "college woman," ever promoting her vision of the ideal Bryn Mawr student. When in her address to the graduating class of 1899 she castigated President Charles W. Eliot of Harvard University for having sunspots on his brain (he had suggested that higher education was wasted on women), newspapers across the nation ran stories on the "Bryn Mawr woman." As the college was her school, so were the undergraduates her students. In her weekly chapel talks, and especially in private interviews with each incoming student, Carey Thomas made certain that all understood what it meant to be a member of Bryn Mawr. An inspiring if formidable example, she filled her graduates with the confidence that as women they, too, could do great things.[1]

Only seven years Ume's senior, M. Carey Thomas, like Ume, had no patience for the insipid life held to be the proper social world of young ladies. She, too, was irritated by feminine self-effacement. Working against those among the college's trustees who assumed that intellectual activity was damaging to true femininity, she adamantly opposed special courses for women and attempts to water down the curriculum: as an all-female school, Bryn Mawr had to maintain high academic standards if it were not to be dismissed as a mere finishing school. Through rigorous entrance examinations, she argued, Bryn Mawr would select only the ambitious, and their education ought to be as academically demanding, and as impractical, as that provided at Harvard. Carey Thomas's views of women's education were thus significantly different from Ume's. Domesticity and higher education were for her separate concerns: believing the world of the intellect to be wholly unrelated to sex, she held that an education to train women to be cultivated wives and enlightened mothers was beside the point. If a graduate were to marry, she would continue her work in a profession outside the home; she and her husband would be working companions. A traditional marriage, Carey Thomas believed, was the unhappy destiny of the second-rate. "Our failures only marry," she once said.[2]

Ume studied at Bryn Mawr during its exciting first years. Just five years old when she arrived in 1889, the college was self-consciously aware of the mandate it had to fulfill and sensitive to the readiness with which it would be criticized should it fail to live up to standards of academic excellence, not to mention ladylike decorum. These early students regarded themselves as the vanguard, ambitious young women eager to prove their abilities as individuals and, more importantly, as a sex. The atmosphere of the college was stimulating, disciplined, and intellectual: a student from England, for example, writing in an 1888 issue of the *Nineteenth Century*, an English monthly review, boasted of her classmates' learned lunch-table discussions of Grimm's Law. Using the opportunity to prove their ability to govern themselves responsibly in a spirit of sororal solidarity, the Bryn Mawr student body instituted a student government that included a house of commons and prime minister, thereby refuting the assumption that women were incapable of living and working together in harmony.[3]

This interest in politics naturally involved discussion of women's rights, and it was here that Ume was exposed to debates regarding women's suffrage. Ume's close friend Anna Hartshorne, who was also studying at Bryn Mawr in the early 1890s, noted that Susan B. Anthony had a great impact on many students. In addition to her usual schedule of public speaking and lobbying members of government, Anthony had devoted much of the previous decade to writing her share of the first three volumes of *History of Woman Suffrage* and, in 1888, had organized the first International Council of Women to celebrate the fortieth anniversary of the Seneca Falls women's rights meeting and its *Declaration of Rights and Sentiments*. Anthony was now working to unite the rival National and American Woman Suffrage associations as well as to give the women's rights movement a respectable image by forging an alliance with the Women's Christian Temperance Union (WCTU). These efforts of strategic importance were closely followed at Bryn Mawr, whose students would soon make their interest visible in such associations as the College Equal Suffrage League.

With these ambitious young women Ume at last found herself among her own kind. Many were well into their twenties, like Ume, and a large number had also been schoolteachers before entering the college. Eager for personal success, they shared an abiding sense of their duty to work for the advancement of women in general as well. At Bryn Mawr Ume had a full and rewarding social life. Popular with the other students—Anna Hartshorne wrote that "they were all crazy about her"—Ume made many friends, traveled with them, and stayed at their family homes during vacations. For once she was not a stranger.

Nor was Ume singled out as an oddity, although many at Bryn Mawr, both students and faculty, were curious about Japanese women, and she was often asked to give informal talks on the subject. She enjoyed addressing women's groups: her first such experience had been five years earlier, when she spoke to a group of Japanese women on the subject of Christianity at an Episcopal mission meeting outside Tokyo. Ume made a commanding figure, projecting to her audience calm and collected poise. Anna Hartshorne first saw her at a tea given by a Bryn Mawr faculty member at which Ume spoke of Japanese women and her past. Ume "made a wonderful impression" among the members of the college, she wrote, because of her powerful presence: "Like a princess, and for the same reason, that she was used to being looked at and no longer gave a hoot, so to say." Many American women were particularly drawn to Japanese women, seeing in the Meiji Restoration the promise of greater social justice for women, and were eager to contribute to what they considered their Japanese sisters' future happiness. The first schools for Japanese girls, after all, were established and staffed by American women, the first English-language descriptions of the life of Japanese women were written by American women, and the first Japanese women's organizations were begun or inspired by American women.[4]

Ume's informal talks about her countrywomen coincided with her work with Alice Bacon on *Japanese Girls and Women* (1891), now a classic study of the lives of Japanese women of all classes. Collaborating on this book helped Ume to clarify her ideas about Japanese women, their needs, and the contributions they could make to society. The structure of *Japanese Girls and Women* is fairly straightforward: the book traces the training and daily life of women of each class, invariably concluding that their lives are far from ideal. The typical Japanese girl, for example, leaves home "to become a wife at sixteen, a mother at eighteen, and an old woman at thirty."[5] But the book does manage to find hope: it discovers either a hidden good behind each bad situation or notes that the situation is changing. Despite its many criticisms of traditional and modern Japan, *Japanese Girls and Women* remains essentially optimistic.

Japan's progress, argues the central thesis, requires a radical change in the status of women, especially in the social and legal status of the woman within the family: "Until the position of the wife and mother in Japan is improved and made secure, little permanence can be expected in the progress of the nation toward what is best and highest in the Western civilization." Western civilization, its technology, arts, and religion, and the Western ideal of domesticity are held up as the elements of progress. Exposure to the home life of the West would transform Japanese men, the book suggests, leading them to open the narrow world of women by conferring respect on woman's sphere: "Better laws, broader education for the women, a change in public opinion on the subject, caused by the study, by the men educated abroad, of the homes of Europe and America,—these are the forces which alone can bring the women of Japan up to that place in the home which their intellectual and moral qualities fit them to fill."[6] The "blessed influences" of the Western home would thus extend to Japanese society, acting as a catalyst to initiate change from the top of the family hierarchy.

Just as Japan's progress is stunted, *Japanese Girls and Women* suggests, so, too, are its females: beautiful but pinched, nipped, and strangulated, rather like a bonsai. A Japanese woman's "greatest happiness is to be gained, not by cultivation of the intellect, but by the early acquisition of the self-control which is expected of all Japanese women." She is a "finished product at the age of sixteen or eighteen. . . . The higher part of her nature is little developed . . . just at that time when her mind broadens, and the desire for knowledge and self-improvement develops, the restraints and checks upon her become more severe." Unable to advance freely along healthy and natural avenues, she "becomes, in a few years, the weary, disheartened woman."[7]

Brushing aside the familiar argument that legislative reform was unnecessary because husbands rarely abused their power and wives were generally treated with affection, *Japanese Girls and Women* compares the position of the wife with that of the slave—an analogy popular with nineteenth-century American feminists and rooted in the abolitionist cause. It notes that no matter how well the slave is treated, his or her enslavement cannot be justified because "it was a condition that was wrong in theory, and so could not be righted in practice." So, too, "the position of the Japanese wife is wrong in theory, and can never be righted until legislation has given to her rights which it still denies." Although much of the book is vague in its repeated calls for legislative reform, never specifying what these rights are—probably to avoid the contentious debate about male and female equality—it does point to Japan's property laws as one area of change. If women could hold property in their own names, "much would be accomplished towards securing them in their positions as wives and mothers; and divorce, the great evil of Japanese home life to-day, would become simply a last resort to preserve the purity of the home, as it is in most civilized countries now."[8]

At the heart of the book lie its most strongly worded criticism of the family system and the clearest statement of its solution: "Legislation once effected, all the rest will come, and the wife, secure in her home and her children, will be at the point where her new education can be of use to her in the administration of her domestic affairs and the training of her children; and where she will finally become the friend and companion of her husband, instead of his mere waitress, seamstress, and housekeeper,—the plaything of his leisure moments, too often the victim of his caprices."[9]

The female education envisioned by *Japanese Girls and Women* has the Western domestic ideal as its foundation. That is, it would encourage what the authors assume to be the inherent, universal feminine characteristics and womanly virtues of Japanese women. Approving the public education system, which Tsuda and Bacon believed was creating "more independent, self-reliant, and stronger women," they urge a liberal education based on "the newer and broader culture, with its higher morality, its greater development of the best powers of the mind," tempered by "regular hours, healthful food, and gentle restraint." With their mind and character properly developed, Japanese women would become wives "of broad intellectual culture," "friends and confidants" of their husbands, "not simply housekeepers and head-servants"; their homes would thus become "centres of influence."[10]

Some such homes, according to *Japanese Girls and Women*, already existed. Headed by women of the former samurai class, they are described as "sending out healthy influences that are daily having their effect, and raising the position of women in Japan." The women of this class—Ume's class—claims *Japanese Girls and Women*, constitute the rightful leadership of Japanese women. The future of women, their possible roles and potential contributions to society, were being defined, the book repeatedly stresses, by these women under the enlightened guidance of the empress: "Wherever there is progress among the women, wherever they are looking about for new opportunities, entering new occupations, elevating the home, opening hospitals, industrial schools, asylums, there you will find the leading spirits always of the samurai class."

> The samurai women to-day are eagerly working into the positions of teachers, interpreters, trained nurses, and whatever other places there are which may be honorably occupied by women. The girls' schools, both government and private, find many of their pupils among the samurai class; and their deference and obedience to their teachers and superiors, their ambition and keen sense of honor in the school-room, show the influence of the samurai feeling over new Japan. To the samurai women belongs the task—and they have already begun to perform it—of establishing upon a broader and surer foundation the position of women in their own country. They, as the most intelligent, will be the first to perceive the remedy for present evils, and will, if I mistake not, move heaven and earth, at some time in the near future, to have that remedy applied to their own case. Most of them read the literature of the day, some of them in at least one language beside their own; a few have had the benefit of travel abroad, and have seen what the home and the family are in Christian lands. There is as much of the unconquerable spirit of the samurai to-day in the women as in the men; and it will not be very long before that spirit will begin to show itself in working for the establishment of their homes and families upon some stronger basis than the will of the husband and father.[11]

As the occasional slips into the future tense suggest, however, the great influence of the energetic and educated samurai women was more hoped for than real.

Japanese Girls and Women contrasts these active and modern women to the retrogressive and threatening presence of the geisha, "the great problem to the thinking women of Japan." Whereas the resourceful and forward-looking samurai women energetically cultivate themselves and uplift society, the decadent geisha and the disreputable influence their social prominence gives them impede the nation's progress toward Western civilization: as the women of the former samurai class resolutely serve virtue, on both a national and a familial scale, the geisha encourage vice, inciting men to indulge their baser instincts and leaving them "bewitched," "beguiled," and "enslaved." Unlike the educated samurai women, with their deep sense of honor, the geisha are uneducated in "the higher morality," their finer nature left undeveloped. "In their system of education manners stand higher than morals." They lack a "true education" based on Christian morality and Western ethics, and instead represent the glittering, sophisticated world of artifice: "Without true education or morals, but trained thoroughly in all the arts and accomplishments that please,—witty, quick at repartee, pretty, and always well dressed,—the geisha has proved a formidable rival for the demure, quiet maiden of good family, who can only give her husband an unsullied name, silent obedience, and faithful service all her life." Usurping the rightful place of the daughters of "good" families, many geisha "have been taken by men of good position as wives, and are now the heads of the most respectable homes." The geisha thus threaten what *Japanese Girls and Women* views as the proper class structure. "If the wives of the leaders in Japan are to come from among such a class of women, something must be done," the book warns, "and done quickly, for the sake of the future of Japan."[12]

Because *Japanese Girls and Women* was the first lengthy and informative description of its subject written in English, the book received considerable attention in the United States and Japan. But whereas the reviews in the American press were generally favorable, the reaction in Japan was hostile. Ume must have anticipated such criticism because her contribution to the work is heavily disguised; Alice Bacon's name alone appears on the title page. Ume, however, is named in the book's preface and is credited with more than the usual assistance. Alice also made certain that half of all royalties were sent to Ume, and she further acknowledged Ume's claim to coauthorship when she told her of her plans to write a will, giving Ume ownership of the copyright of "our book." "You had better keep this letter. I[n] case of my death without making a will," she instructed Ume in December 1890, "it would serve as evidence of your right to the copyright." But attempts to conceal Ume's contribution to shield her from criticism failed. In August 1891, shortly after copies of *Japanese Girls and Women* reached Japan, Sutematsu wrote an alarmed letter to Alice hinting darkly that the book was likely to cause Ume much trouble. Ume told Alice that she, too, had heard criticisms of herself. Sutematsu suggested deleting Ume's name from the preface, and Alice even offered to write a letter to the major Tokyo newspapers disclaiming Ume's responsibility for the book's content. They concluded, however, that it was too late to deny her connection, and nothing was done.

Ume nonetheless seems to have enjoyed the notice *Japanese Girls and Women* received, for the interest it generated encouraged her to transform her informal Bryn Mawr talks into a full-fledged campaign to seek support for Japanese female education from American women's organizations. In 1891, for example, in a speech with the snappy title "Education and Culture—What Japanese Women Want Now," she addressed the Massachusetts Society for the University Education of Women, an important group that raised scholarship funds for women students. The success of such public talks, as well as the concern for the future of Japanese women that she encountered at Bryn Mawr, enabled her to create a scholarship fund of eight thousand dollars; the interest would enable future graduates of mission schools and girls' middle schools to continue their education in the United States. After four years' study at an American institution (Bryn Mawr, the Women's Medical College of Pennsylvania, and the Drexel Institute were specified), the recipient would return to Japan to teach other females. Work on this scholarship fund honed Ume's considerable skills in public speaking and organization, while giving her valuable lessons in the art of fundraising. Most important, however, was the credibility this campaign gave her. With the scholarship fund, Ume was thereafter publicly connected in Japan and the United States to higher education for women and the values it represented.

Ume was well aware that many American women were willing to work for the education of Asian women. Seven months before she left Japan for Bryn Mawr, in January 1889, she had attended a public lecture in Tokyo by Pandita Ramabai. An Indian feminist, Ramabai was instrumental in campaigning for women's education and for the elevation of their role and status in Indian society, touring much of the United States in an effort to raise funds for her school for child widows. Her lectures and writings were successful—the American Ramabai Association was formed and guaranteed her Bombay institution support for at least ten years. Ume was greatly impressed by Ramabai. "I imagine her a very smart intellectual woman," she wrote Adeline Lanman that January, and she displaced the very unfeminine features of Ramabai's ambitious, public campaign onto her American companion, a woman doctor whom Ume characterized as "strong-minded"—that is, unladylike. Ume may have been recalling Ramabai's example when calling in her fundraising speeches for the education and elevation of the women of Japan—speeches, moreover, that flattered their American audiences while subtly reminding them of their obligations to their Asian sisters.

During her summer breaks and whenever her busy schedule permitted, Ume traveled (often alone) through the eastern United States giving what Anna Hartshorne described as "parlor talks" in the homes of women sympathetic to the cause of women's higher education. The core of these talks was her insistence that liberal education was the key to women's emancipation, an assumption also made throughout *Japanese Girls and Women*. Education, she argued, was central to improving women and, because of their influence within the home, their society in general. Asking her American audience to remember "a somewhat similar struggle, on a different plane, for the better education of women in this country," Ume addressed these women in the language of the domestic ideal: "While I have been in this country, the one thing which has struck me particularly, and filled me with admiration, is the position American women hold, the great influence that they exercise for good, the power given them by education and training, the congenial intercourse between men and women, and the sympathy existing in the homes, between brothers and sisters, husbands and wives." Appealing to the American ideals of charity, liberality, and faith in human potential, as well as to her audience's specific interest in the advancement of women, Ume virtually shamed these women into contributing by telling them that the scholarship "would be open to all Japanese women as an incentive to them—a free gift from American women—to show the interest which has been taken in them and the high value attached by American women to education." Such coercive tactics, however, were probably unnecessary: during the closing decades of the century American women's groups, such as the Massachusetts Society for the University Education of Women, that raised scholarships and loans for women students were on the rise.[13]

In her talks Ume emphasized again and again that Japan had advanced rapidly in the short space of twenty years and was now beginning to join the civilized nations of the world. But this progress, she argued, was superficial. In discarding the feudal past, men had gained advantages, but "no corresponding advantages have been given to the women." Japan's progress, she warned, also had its ill effects. Not only were women failing to make gains in the new Japan, but they were even losing former ground. Divorce, for example, was becoming more common. "The present time of change," Ume noted, "has seen the rise of many social and moral evils. . . . Men have broken down the old barriers; they no longer have the same restraint and greater freedom has been given them." Thus it was urgent that women be well educated. Using arguments already elaborated in *Japanese Girls and Women*, Ume enumerated the social advantages to be gained by offering women a higher education. In marriage, an educated woman would have a restraining influence on her husband, her cultivated companionship keeping him happily at home and her virtuous nature gently enticing him away from vice. And if her education trained a woman for paid employment, this would guarantee her some economic independence, granting her the freedom to choose when and whether to marry. The ability to earn a salary would also command respect from others. Should such women "prove their power and ability," she reasoned, "the Japanese men would soon cease to regard them as inferior."[14]

Throughout these talks Ume always returned to her central ideal: as intellectual companion to her husband and teacher of morality to her children, the educated woman served her society as an enlightened mother and cultivated wife. A modern progressing nation, she stressed, required modern progressive women:

> The old-time training and education was refining and effective in its way, but the present day is bringing many new wants to the home, and new duties to the women that call for a better preparation than was given in the old days. Japanese men themselves have begun to find out that, with the introduction of new ideas into Japan, the women must inevitably change too, with the new conditions. The present time demands broader education for women, new avenues of employment and of self-support, so that it may be possible for a woman to be independent. Wives must fit themselves to be companions of educated men, and mothers that they may wisely influence their sons, and there must be true sympathy of thought between them in the home.[15]

Educating women, Ume assumed, would result in a nuclear family based on the Western (more specifically, American) model: the respectful courtship of the bride-to-be who could freely accept or decline a marriage proposal, the companionate marriage that accorded the wife a position of influence within her proper sphere, and the happy and well-informed motherhood that gave the mother a position of authority within the family.

Ume again assumed that relevant social change could only come from above. It was the duty of women of the upper classes, she assumed, to set the example: "We should expect them to have the greatest influence." Yet these women were "the most backward" because of their secluded and restricted life: "Surrounded by servants who do everything for them, who think for them even, what have they in their lives to make them in sympathy with the men, so that they may win the respect, and gain the position women ought to hold by the side of their husbands? As it is, they are not fit to be the companions of educated men."[16] Although greater social change might just as readily have come from the thorough education of women whose social station did not decree seclusion—the women of the working and merchant classes, for example—this was unthinkable for Ume. She wanted to see the women of the upper classes in a position of leadership so secure as to be unthreatened by women beneath them either in class, such as working-class women, or in respectability, such as the geisha. She envisioned for these women an active social life in benevolent works and the organization of social reform activities, much like wealthy American women at the end of the century.

What was needed, Ume proposed, were Japanese women educated in the Western ideals of womanhood who could enlighten these upper-class women about the needs and requirements of a modern nation, thereby setting in motion a sort of chain reaction in which the women from the higher classes would fulfill their rightful role as influential pacesetters. The model Ume chose for these women educated to spread the gospel of gentility among the upper class was none other than herself: "A well-educated, cultivated, native woman, even though she is herself not of high rank, can as a teacher find her way to the homes of this exclusive class."[17]

Ume's depiction of a native woman, armed with the tools of enlightenment and gaining access to the private lives of the most inaccessible women in order to teach them the essentials of civilization, is very close to the image of the female missionary toiling in heathen lands. She must have had this role in mind when she named the "two great things" needed to "remedy the evil" of Japanese women's oppression—education and Christianity—sometimes blurring the distinctions between the two and thereby implying that they were virtually the same. This line of reasoning naturally appealed to another group Ume frequently addressed: women's church organizations. Certainly evangelist Christian churches, with their emphasis on personal choice, tended to support liberal education for women because it trained the mind to make decisions for itself. Japanese women's deficiency in this area, Ume believed, was the cause and the result of their lowly status. "Social customs have assigned a secondary place to woman, and she is considered unfit for responsible work," she noted, "because she has grown unfit to think for herself." Many church-affiliated organizations, moreover, promoted higher female education in the belief that women, as natural teachers, would spread the message of the Bible—an appeal also put to good use by such other advocates of women's education as Catharine Beecher, who argued that training women to be teachers (whether in the classroom or in the home) prepared them for their secular mission of reforming society. Teaching, in other words, had become accepted as the paramount female mission. By the mid-nineteenth century, American evangelicals were emphasizing the conversion of "heathen" mothers as the most direct means of Christianizing heathen nations, and it was a common notion that only females—whether foreign missionaries or native "Bible women"—could gain entrance to the secluded world of Asian women.[18]

Ume was preaching to the converted. The two themes stressed throughout her speeches, Christianity and education, were certain to strike a responsive chord in her audience, for these were the twin pillars of the nineteenth-century American women's movement and appealed to groups across the feminist spectrum, from conservative church groups to advocates of women's paid professional work. As the central elements of the domestic ideal, Christianity and education were fused in the profession of teacher, the focus of Ume's scholarship plan.

No wonder, then, that her campaign was successful. The Japanese Scholarship Committee, also called the Philadelphia Committee, was formed under the direction of Mary Morris, its chairman, and M. Carey Thomas. Its fifteen members, each of whom pledged to pay an annual subscription fee, came from the Quaker, Episcopal, and Presbyterian churches in the Philadelphia area. Yet although the committee members were prominent churchwomen, proselytization was not the goal of the scholarship. Despite Ume's use of the rhetoric of the mission field in her speeches—an appeal that led some of the committee to believe that an evangelical purpose was the fund's main concern—Christianity and church-related activities were entirely secondary to her plans, a point of view supported by Carey Thomas. Like Mary Morris, whose husband was a director of the Pennsylvania Railroad Company, most of the members were affluent women married to bankers or railway executives, and so the Philadelphia Committee began, in 1892, with over four thousand dollars in subscriptions and nearly fifteen hundred dollars already collected from lesser donors. More than halfway to the goal of eight thousand dollars and heartened by this success, the committee soon contemplated the sum of ten thousand dollars to provide the scholarship's recipient with an additional year at an American preparatory school before she entered college.[19]

In spite of her busy schedule of informal talks and public speeches, not to mention the time she devoted to *Japanese Girls and Women*, Ume did well in her studies at Bryn Mawr, living up to the college's high standards of academic achievement. Although it was generally assumed that she would emphasize languages in her course of study, she chose instead to concentrate on biology, a curious choice for one who claimed "to study things important for Japan in regard to schools & education for girls." Nor had she shown a special interest in the natural sciences during her Georgetown days. Ume was probably motivated by simple competition: in the early decades of the Meiji era, the majority of the (male) overseas students had studied in such fields as science, medicine, and engineering—subjects vital to Japan's modernization—and Ume, still smarting from the Ministry of Education's snubs, wished to prove that she, too, was capable of mastering what was regarded as a masculine subject. And biology, unlike medicine and engineering, could be studied at a women's college. She had the satisfaction of seeing herself vindicated with the publication in 1894 of an article in the *Quarterly Journal of Microscopical Science*, cowritten with Thomas Hunt Morgan, a professor of biology at Bryn Mawr.

Ume's three years at Bryn Mawr were full and rewarding. She had a rich social life among women like herself, and her college life, after the dreary years at the Peeresses' School, was stimulating. She was therefore reluctant to return to her lonely and monotonous existence in Japan and sought to extend her stay by asking M. Carey Thomas for work. It was quite within Carey Thomas's power to find a position for Ume, but she seems to have been indifferent to the request, even unwilling to make an effort. "Directly connected with the college," she wrote Ume on 25 March 1891, "there seems to be no post unfilled. All our secretaryships etc are already promised, but there would almost certainly be teaching of some sort. Still I feel that I ought not to assume any responsibility. I can only say that I trust the way will 'open', as Quakers say, for you to stay another year." When Ume, a year later, was offered a post as laboratory assistant and refused the position, Carey Thomas was furious.[20] The offer, however, had come too late: Ume had persuaded the Peeresses' School to extend her leave of absence for a year and now, her extension expired, was obliged to return to Japan.

Her years in the United States had provided precious experience that would later assist Ume in the establishment of her own school. Her informal talks at the college and her speeches throughout the American East were important lessons in public speaking and fund-raising. The enthusiasm shown her scholarship campaign, as well as the interest sparked by *Japanese Girls and Women*, confirmed Ume's belief that American women would be a major source of support for Japanese women's higher education. She was able to organize this enthusiasm, moreover, into concrete assistance, for she returned to Japan in 1892 with her scholarship goal of eight thousand almost entirely achieved.

These years in the United States also gave Ume an invaluable look at the operation of various schools. She spent a term at Oswego Teachers' College studying pedagogical methods, while at Bryn Mawr she was able to observe the workings of a newly founded women's college determined to prove that women were men's intellectual equals. She watched M. Carey Thomas, one of only three people ever to be granted the Ph.D. summa cum laude by the University of Zürich (she had been refused a degree at Leipzig and Göttingen because she was a woman), use every opportunity to drill into the students' minds the supreme value of a liberal education: the liberating effects of learning to think for oneself strengthened by the discipline of study. Although Ume never openly repeated M. Carey

Thomas's claims for women's equality with men, emphasizing instead that an educated woman would find her fulfillment as her husband's helpmate, she later adopted Carey Thomas's formidable image as an austere and sometimes autocratic educator.

Ume also observed a school that offered its students an education "appropriate" to their adult roles. In the summer of 1890 she visited Alice Bacon at the Hampton Normal and Agricultural Institute in Virginia, where Alice had been teaching intermittently for the previous ten years. Founded by Samuel Chapman Armstrong, whose missionary father (known as the Father of American Education in Hawaii) had promoted home economics instruction for girls and education in elementary agriculture for boys during his tenure as Hawaiian minister of public education, the Hampton Institute was established at the end of the Civil War with the support of the American Missionary Association to teach emancipated slaves, and later native Americans, in "industrial education." Its founders were interested, in the words of Armstrong's biographer, "in training black men and women to be teachers and leaders of their people." The school's faculty included Booker T. Washington, an early graduate, who promoted Hampton's well-intentioned but blinkered philosophy, one that failed to extend to its students the white (male) standards of a liberal education. Hampton's students were, Armstrong believed, intellectually and morally deficient. "The north generally thinks that the great thing is to free the negro from his owners," he wrote. "The real thing is to save him from himself." A manual training that included moral education and the three Rs was deemed sufficient.[21]

In 1890 Alice Bacon was also working to establish Dixie Hospital, an institution dedicated to training black nurses. Although an improvement over the "industrial education" of the Hampton Institute, the education offered at Dixie was nevertheless limited to vocational training tied to the domestic ideal of women's service to others. Ume approved of the "civilizing" mission of these two schools, and Hampton and Dixie probably confirmed her assumption that woman's sphere was universally the same, neither culturally nor socially constructed, and that an appropriate education for young women would therefore emphasize the values of late nineteenth-century white American middle-class society.

When Ume returned to Tokyo late in the summer of 1892, she immediately set to work promoting her scholarship. A committee of eight—four women and four men—was formed to act as the Japan arm of the Philadelphia Committee. Chaired by Ume, the committee had to be composed of individuals "anxious for the spread of Christianity and the elevation of women in Japan," according to its constitution; all eight members were connected with either government or private schools, but none was associated with a mission school. The other committee members were: Uryū (Nagai) Shigeko, Ume's friend and fellow student from the Iwakura mission; Takeda Kin, who had attended Wellesley College; Dr. Okami Kei, who had studied at the Women's Medical College of Pennsylvania; Iwamoto Zenji, the principal of Meiji Jogakkō (Meiji Girls' School); Shimada Saburō, who taught at Meiji Jogakkō; Dr. Motoda Yūjirō, professor of psychology at Tokyo Imperial University; and Takamine Hideo, who had studied at Oswego Teachers' College.[22]

From its administrative office in the compound of Meiji Jogakkō the scholarship committee sent official notices in early 1893 to the major girls' schools in Japan, and advertisements appeared in such journals as *Jogaku Zasshi* (Women's education journal), edited by Iwamoto Zenji. Candidates, the scholarship's description specified, were to be between the ages of seventeen and thirty, single, and would have to take competitive examinations set by the committee in Japanese history, Chinese, English, and mathematics. Each applicant's knowledge of English, the advertisement noted, "must be such that the student can at once enter and pursue studies in English in an American school." The scholarship, however, provided an extra year beyond the usual four years of study for precollegiate preparation. In a cover letter, Ume spoke of the necessity for women's higher education, noting the benefits to be derived from employment before marriage, and emphasized that the scholarship was not a prize: the achievement of "mere knowledge" was not the aim of the scholarship. She envisioned a patriotic young woman who was prepared with "a zeal and readiness to give to others on her return what she had acquired, and to use this knowledge to elevate the position of Japanese women." Again, Ume was the model. The scholarship's ideal candidate was a cultivated, educated woman who could "be a leader and helper among the women of Japan."[23]

Although the Philadelphia Committee insisted that the scholarship be open to all Japanese women, Ume limited its pool of applicants by requiring that its recipient pay her passage to the United States as well as meet the considerable expense of purchasing Western clothing and other incidentals. Several applicants for the scholarship were forced to withdraw when they could not meet these expenses.

Even though just eight applied for the first scholarship in 1893, it received great publicity. The scholarship spoke to a desire common to many middle-class girls who, having reached the end of the limited female educational track in Japan, longed for a higher education. For many young women a university education, which could be gained only in the West, promised freedom and a degree of control over their future. The heroine of seventeen-year-old Kimura Akebono's best-selling novel, *Fujo no Kagami* (A mirror for womanhood), embodies the dreams of many Japanese women for an overseas education. Certainly the phenomenal popularity of *Fujo no Kagami* indicates that it tapped a profound desire: serialized in the *Yomiuri Shimbun* in 1889, it was a source of inspiration for many women who relied on newspapers and magazines for information about the outside world as well as for educational material and entertainment. The exuberant optimism that fuels the preposterous plot suggests that Kimura saw higher education as a form of liberation: Yoshikawa Hideko, the heroine, attends Newnham College, the "first college for women [that] has been lately founded in Cambridge University," Kimura notes, "as if for the very purpose of receiving this extraordinary daughter of Japan who, blessed with beauty, talent and an intellect of the highest order, is destined to become a mirror for the womanhood of her generation."[24] At Newnham, Hideko excels all others, proving to be the most brilliant student in the college's short history. After her graduation—accomplished within months of her arrival and with the highest of academic honors—she travels to New York, where she sets out to alleviate the poverty and misery of the city's slums. Having introduced silk and its production to the United States through the benevolent offices of a group of American "noblewomen," Hideko then returns triumphantly to Japan, where she establishes a textile factory that employs impoverished women, providing them with such progressive amenities on the factory grounds as a nursery for their children.

Kimura offered Hideko's university education and social work in the West as experiences that gave scope to her heroine's native intelligence—only outside Japan, she implied, could Hideko claim freedom of action and thereby fulfill her innate excellence. That this freedom was not intended as an immature expression of self-indulgence, moreover, is indicated by Hideko's social conscience, for she uses her education to better the lives of others and, at the story's close, to serve her country. Thus Kimura touched on a related concern of the 1890s: social reform.

In the early decades of the Meiji era the call had been for a sense of nation; now it was for a sense of society. With the promulgation of the constitution in 1889 and the opening of the national Diet in 1890, attention turned to the social problems brought about by the turbulent change and the furious pace of Japan's rush for the attributes of modernity. *Shakai mondai* (social problems) became the focus of intellectual discussion. Indeed, shakai was considered a new word recently introduced to Meiji Japan, becoming the topic common to various writings and speeches of different political stripes in fin-de-siècle Japan: social problems, social reform, social stability, social education, social policy, social novels, and, most ominously, socialism and social revolution.[25]

National unity had been forged with elementary school education and military conscription, and an "inner spiritual revival" was needed to confirm that unity. In 1890, shortly before the first session of the Diet convened, the Imperial Rescript on Education was issued. A logical outcome of the nationalistic trends within the Ministry of Education, the rescript was a counterweight to the political rights offered in the new constitution. Designed to strengthen loyalty and obedience to the state, it celebrated the family-state and its correlative, the patriarchal family system, emphasizing filial piety in classroom and family life as the source of national virtue: "Our Imperial Ancestors have founded our Empire on a basis broad and everlasting. . . . Our subjects ever united in loyalty and filial piety have from generation to generation illustrated the beauty thereof. This is the glory of the fundamental character of Our Empire, and herein also lies the source of Our Education," it read in part. Sent out to all schools within months of its issue, the Imperial Rescript on Education joined the imperial portrait as a sacred object reverently maintained by each school (a practice instituted in 1889); thus it became more a religious text than a secular document as it was read with solemn sanctity at each ceremonial assembly by a white-gloved principal before an audience of schoolchildren bowed in reverence. It was reinforced that same year by the Elementary School Regulations, which named ethics instruction as the first "objective of education," and was followed in 1891 by the Explanation of School Matters, which identified "the spirit of reverence for the Emperor and patriotism" as the "first objective" of education.[26]

With the Imperial Rescript on Education and its praise of deference to authority came increasingly voluble attacks on women's education, for a quality education gave women an identity outside the family, suggesting the possibility of their abandoning traditional roles. The president of Tokyo Imperial University, Katō Hiroyuki, for instance, declared at a meeting of the Japan Women's Education Association that attempts to extend higher education to women were misguided and a waste of time. Public middle schools for women became the focus of intense controversy, and critical speeches in both the Diet and prefectural assemblies suggested that funds for such institutions—already few in number—be cut. Mission schools, often the only source of higher education for girls, were again the object of criticism in an atmosphere that was increasingly hostile to Christianity. And such schools as the progressive Meiji Jogakkō, whose Christian founder, Iwamoto Zenji, advocated women's rights, were criticized for supposedly encouraging sexual promiscuity in their students.[27]

Ume taught at Meiji Jogakkō during these years—Iwamoto Zenji had been a student of Tsuda Sen and a disciple of Nakamura Masanao—and its tradition of a liberal education based on Christian ethics had a profound and lasting influence on her, for Ume would later duplicate much of the school's curriculum in her own school. Many of her values and beliefs were also shared by other members of Meiji Jogakkō. Iwamoto opposed the traditional family system, promoting a family ideal based on the central partnership of husband and wife. Like Ume, he believed in encouraging social contact between young people before marriage, so that marriages could be based on ties of love and companionship. This emphasis on individual worth was embodied in the school's innovative approach to teaching. Instead of learning by rote, the students were challenged to think for themselves; cultivation from within, instead of imitation of Confucian models, was the central goal. The school's faculty members were mostly young and intellectually creative. Many took their inspiration not only from contemporary German philosophy and the Christian teachings esteemed by Iwamoto but also from the early romantic literature of Kitamura Tōkoku, an important social reformer and the main influence behind the school's noteworthy literary journal, *Bungakkai* (Literary world), and Shimazaki Tōson, a teacher there.[28] These innovators helped foster the central value of Meiji Jogakkō: the dignity and merit of each human being. The teaching methods at the Peeresses' School and the Tokyo Women's Normal School, where Ume also taught a few hours a week, must have been as different from Meiji Jogakkō as night is from day.

This emphasis on self-discovery was central for the advocates of higher female education, who argued that offering a quality education to women was the solution to social problems, not a problem itself. Against the Confucian moralists, who advocated ethics instruction, or *shūshin*, were those like Ume who urged moral education as essential to Japan's progress and future civilization. Employing the latest theories of pedagogy from the West, educators had debated the difference between instruction and education of character beginning in the 1880s and continuing well into the 1890s. The attention paid to women's role as moral educators of their children soon expanded to an awareness of women's possible role in the moral well-being of Japanese society. Women should be properly prepared for their social obligations, these advocates urged, not denied them. The feminist Shimizu Toyoko, for example, argued in the pages of *Jogaku Zasshi* that women ought to be prepared for economic survival. Like Kishida Toshiko before her, she suggested that it was foolish to try to shelter women from the realities of society. Marriage could offer no such protection; in fact, it was the "real" world. Women could serve themselves and society as a whole, Shimizu argued, if they were adequately educated to meet their social tasks.[29]

Ume voiced similar views about the connection between social welfare and women's education in an article entitled "The Future of Japanese Women," published in the *Far East* in early 1897 and aimed at an educated Japanese and foreign audience. Repeating warnings already sounded in *Japanese Girls and Women* and her scholarship speeches, Ume noted that many of the traditional safeguards that had protected women in the past were being discarded in the present. Women were now also in danger of losing any gains first made possible by the Meiji Restoration. Japan was thus perilously close to reversing the great strides it had only recently achieved and soon would be able neither to compete with the West nor, by implication, to consider itself superior in the East. Comparing the educational opportunities offered to women in England and the United States to those available in Japan, she suggested that the limited schooling given to Japanese girls would soon be a source of national disgrace: "While Japan may have advanced, it has not begun to advance as America has done, and the danger is that each year of progress in this new era of enlightenment for the world, will only see our women, who are the boast of the East, more and more behind the women of the West."[30]

To establish Japanese society on a firmer foundation and therefore assure its future progress, Ume argued, women needed a liberal education so that they, too, might be schooled in the essentials of civilization. If women were not properly educated to become capable mothers and fit companions of men, she warned, they would impede the progress of enlightenment. The "moral training and the building up of the character of our girls should be the highest aim of the educator," she wrote. For this they required "a knowledge of the facts that are the heritage of the human race, and a training of the reasoning faculties that they may clearly distinguish the good from the bad, reason from prejudice, and duty from misplaced emotion." "This does not mean," she was careful to add, "that a woman is to be taught exactly as men are taught, that any training which fits her for her own special life work should be neglected, but it does mean broader foundations, and a liberal education far beyond what she is getting at present."[31]

Arguing that such an education would prepare Japanese women for their true vocation of marriage and motherhood by giving them the means to confront the realities of the harsh and unreliable world, Ume stressed that they thus might reproduce the home life considered to be one source of Western strength:

> Can it be said that our women are capable of meeting the problems of the day; that they have the power to restrain the men as the American women do in keeping up the standards of morality and purity; that they can make the home the restful heaven it should be away from the world's temptations? Can they give that influence for good, that broad sympathy and help that a man has a right to demand from his wife, a help so much higher than the mere supplying of his physical needs? Are our women

> so trained that they are capable of judging of the temptations and trials of a man's life, and knowing his mental and spiritual needs, of helping to support and comfort him? Without culture, education, and experience, women can only share the lowest side of a man's life and must indeed fall short of the ideal wife and mother. The loss in this is not only for the women themselves, but for their husbands and for future generations.[32]

In addition to a liberal education, "The Future of Japanese Women" concluded, women should receive training to furnish them with the means of supporting themselves. Alluding to the families reduced to poverty by the death of their principal breadwinners in the war with China of 1894–1895, Ume suggested that such families could have avoided destitution if the women had had the means of honorably earning an income. She noted that in most cases, however, it was not necessary for women to earn their living, but they could nevertheless benefit from training in such womanly occupations as "teaching, writing, nursing, cooking, or sewing." Even if this training might never be called on, it was more valuable than "the richest dowry": by implication, women could thus avoid the dishonorable professions of the prostitute and geisha. The defense offered by such training made it far nobler than the "many frivolities" customarily thought appropriate for female education.[33]

The appeal of "The Future of Japanese Women" was that it asked for so little. As Shimizu had done in her *Jogaku Zasshi* article of 1890 and, earlier, Kishida Toshiko in her Ōtsu speech, Ume contrasted the narrow life expected of most women to the realities of the outside world and demanded better female education. But there the similarity ends. Unlike Kishida and other feminists, Ume shunned political arguments for women's rights. She contributed to *Jogaku Zasshi* articles on such topics as Helen Keller, women nurses, and the history of female education in the West as well as source materials, often passing on to Iwamoto Zenji the American newspapers and magazines that Adeline Lanman sent her, and she may have been aware of Shimizu Toyoko's article. But she certainly was not consciously echoing Kishida Toshiko's ideas about the equality of men and women. Deeply conservative, Ume was unsympathetic to the values and methods of the popular rights movement and its members (a distaste shared by the *Jogaku Zasshi*, which was hostile to the proletarian membership of the movement). With her respect for hierarchical authority, she was impervious to egalitarian arguments for women's rights and placed the onus on women to prove their worth. If women were given the opportunity to show themselves "capable of greater things, there will come the day when they can take a higher place in society, as they certainly will in the home, and in the esteem of their husbands." The legal system would then be reformed to offer fair divorce and marriage laws and "individual rights . . . for a woman as for a man."[34] All that Japanese women required, Ume reasoned, was a liberal education equivalent to—though by no means the same as—the higher education their brothers received. Ume's article was thus not a call for women to act; rather, the plea was directed at men to provide an adequate education for their daughters. Women were simply to await this change, and after they had proved themselves fit for intellectual work, social and legal reforms would fall into place. By presenting men as solely responsible for reform, Ume circumvented, though not reconciled, her ambivalent ideas about female power and her equally ambiguous attitude toward male authority.

Ume was voicing in her writings and speeches ideas that constituted the mainstream of late nineteenth-century feminism. In Japan as in America and Europe, motherhood was the great unifying theme of what was then called "the woman movement"; the related issues of the sanctity of the home and the wife's position within it were the central concerns of the social-reform movement. Such women as Hatoyama Haruko, a noted Meiji educator and associate of Ume, spoke for many women of the middle and professional classes when she argued for the power of women in their homes.[35]

More direct measures to strengthen the position of women within the family and, by extension, Japanese society were taken by such reform groups as the Kyōfukai, the Japan Women's Temperance Association (also called the Tokyo Women's Reform Society), under the leadership of Yajima Kajiko. Yajima had been moved by the impressive speeches of Mary Clemmer Leavitt, a representative of the Women's Christian Temperance Union who toured Japan in 1886. Leavitt's words spoke to the anguish Yajima had experienced during her marriage to a drunken and abusive husband and her bitterness at the criticism she had received for divorcing him. The Kyōfukai began as a temperance society modeled on the WCTU but was less concerned with drinking than with institutionalized male privilege, society's sexual double standard, which encouraged in men for what it punished women. "The purpose of this society," its bylaws stated, "is to develop the dignity of women by reforming corrupt social practices, cultivating morality, and prohibiting drinking and smoking."[36] Prostitution and concubinage, the unspecified "corrupt social practices," were the main concerns of the Kyōfukai, with "the dignity of women" its fuel. As in the West, efforts to establish the standards of temperance and social purity easily shifted to struggles for women's social freedom, higher education, and legal rights.

The Kyōfukai rapidly turned its attention to politics, especially government policy on prostitution, monogamy, marriage laws, and the family system. Although Article 5 of the Police Security Regulations prohibited women from participating in politics—women who formed a political association, joined a political group, or even attended a political meeting could be fined or imprisoned—the Kyōfukai influenced local politics through skillful use of the lecture circuit and the press and addressed petitions to the national Diet, all the while camouflaging its politics in the language of social reform. As with women's reform groups in Anglo-American Victorian society, the philanthropy of this reform society inhabited an undefined space between the family and the state by taking women's issues from the private sphere into the public domain.[37]

The Kyōfukai's campaign to eradicate prostitution and the concubine system is commended in *Japanese Girls and Women*, and Ume praised the association and its leader in another publication aimed at an English-speaking audience. Yet she never joined the organization. The significant political implications of much of the Kyōfukai's actions may have put her off, for she firmly believed that women should avoid politics. Ume was surprised, for example, when Alice Bacon showed an interest in Japan's adoption of a new constitution, and her own description of the event, written on 5 February 1889, sounds more like a newspaper editorial than her ideas: "It is a most unprecedented thing, the voluntary giving up of the power of a monarch to the people—a reformation without feud or bloodshed, & a most wonderful reformation in the government of Japan. . . . From now onward will be a most exciting time for Japan, and of course a time of danger too, as too much liberty might intoxicate the public mind, and rash things might be done." Coupled with her ingrained indifference to politics was Ume's equally deep-seated caution. Although the Kyōfukai was not a political organization, it was openly critical of the government, a stance that could have made Ume's position as an employee of the Imperial Household Ministry vulnerable.

Ume, moreover, was pessimistic about the possibility of organizing large groups of women to perform meaningful social work. Discounting the obvious example of the Kyōfukai and its well-publicized actions, she responded to the proposal to establish a Japanese YWCA in another publication published in the *Far East* in 1897, "Letter to an American Friend": "I do not see how it is possible at this time to do any extensive organized work. The time at present is to try and raise workers. It is an educational period, rather than a time of direct work. Our women are yet in the very beginnings. . . . They have not yet begun to take up any work." The reason that little significant reform work was being carried out, Ume argued, was the lack of a large number of Western-educated Christian women (like herself) among the middle classes, who would provide leadership:

> Of course, I must ask you to consider the few educated women in Japan, and also the fact that women have no property in their own right. There are no institutions of learning higher than a high school course of three or four years above the primary school, and these schools are very limited in numbers. The Missionary schools send out graduates, but these are very few among the mass of women, and they are scattered far and wide. I do not see at present how any great work can be undertaken by them. Whatever is done must be small and such as they can carry on, and then as time goes by it can be gradually increased. There are several associations already started among Christian women, as the King's Daughters, the W.C.T.U., and others, but although they do good, yet much of what they wish to do is hampered by want of means and also of leaders in organizing such work. . . . Thus our Christian women have not a very great influence to back them in whatever work they take up.

Ignoring the value of the work performed by such women as Yajima and her followers, very likely because of their active interest in government policy—a "strongminded" attitude that disqualified the Kyōfukai from the disinterested altruism commonly believed to characterize true womanhood—Ume nevertheless repeated the central concerns of the association when she named prostitution as the most pressing social issue of the day: "We want new laws, new public opinion, and new moral influences, to go out from all sides on this question."[38]

Ume's charity work, moreover, paralleled the social reform efforts of such groups as the Kyōfukai. Philanthropic work was one way for women to gain authority in the public world of social policy, and Ume was not to be left behind in this visible movement. She shared characteristics common to many advocates of social reform, like Hatoyama and Yajima: the reform movement's leaders were typically educators, either Christian or influenced by a Christian teacher, who had some experience abroad or at least a Western-style education that gave them an outside view of the position of women in Japanese society. The Kyōfukai, seeing factory conditions and women's general lack of economic power as causes contributing to prostitution, began a number of shelters for young women, starting with the Tokyo Jiaikan in 1893. Ume voiced a similar connection when she suggested in her "Letter" the establishment of houses for working girls in "one or two of the Tokyo districts" (and also a "nice Christian Students' Home" for students coming to Tokyo). After 1895, the society became increasingly involved in relief efforts for victims of earthquakes, floods, and other disasters, and Ume undertook similar work when she organized aid for the families left destitute by the war with China, and later the war with Russia, charitable work that also mirrored the endeavors of the Aikoku Fujinkai (Japan Women's Patriotic Association), a prominent government-supported women's organization established in 1901.[39]

It was to "rescue work"—the reclamation of prostitutes—an area highly publicized in the 1890s by the Kyōfukai and various church groups, that Ume devoted most of her social reform energies. "It is the crying need of our country now," she wrote. "This is a work I am hoping my countrywomen will take up. I shall, indeed, do all I can to encourage and urge the work of rescue." Deeply disturbed by geisha because many had transgressed class lines by occupying positions of social power that she believed ought to belong to respectable women, Ume was equally class-bound in her attitude toward prostitutes. Her view was typical of middle-class women in the West: a social pity that signified class position and social status, for only a lady could rescue a prostitute and elevate her to respectability.[40] The image of the prostitute offered in *Japanese Girls and Women* and "Letter to an American Friend," moreover, is largely sentimental. Unlike the sophisticated geisha, she is presented as either an innocent country lass led astray by the iniquities of city life or a heroic daughter who sacrifices herself for the benefit of her family.

Behind Ume's philanthropic concerns were painful personal motivations. Many years earlier, Sen had fathered a son by one of the household maids, a common enough occurrence that nevertheless rocked the family. The outrage Ume felt at this example of male privilege and abuse of power fired her rescue work, and the shame of her father's lapse later led her to begin a novel in which she tried to work out her complicated feelings of dejection and anger.

Her unfinished novel, *Ine, A Story of Modern Japan*, is a romantic potboiler based on the life of a prostitute named Isa whom Ume had helped to reclaim. A good example of Ume's resourcefulness (she began the novel in an effort to earn money, aware of the popularity of Japanese subjects in the United States and elsewhere), *Ine* begins as an examination of the social havoc brought about by Japan's modernization and the clash between contemporary and traditional values, an opposition apparent in the novel's opening description of modern technology ripping across the pastoral landscape of "old" Japan:

> The long summer day was at last drawing to a close as the crowded train on the Tokaido line, which connects the two great capitals of Japan, was rushing past the charming scenes around the Hakone mountains. Now and then, with the evening sun already behind it, Mount Fuji in all its majestic glory would appear, its perfect outlines, with only a few traces of the snow left on it, surrounded by the crimson and purple clouds of a glorious sunset. The nearer mountains stood out in luxuriant verdure. Picturesque pine trees, rolling hills and waving bamboo groves, a restless mountain stream that followed the railroad in its course, and miles and miles of vivid green fields of rice that waved in the evening breeze, made a constantly changing series of charming pictures that the artistic eye might long to linger upon, but by the many weary passengers, hot and dusty, and crowded together during the long hours of travel, all these things were unheeded and lost.

With the introduction of her heroine, Ine, and the description of her plight, however, Ume abandons this focus to narrate Ine's victimization by an irresponsible and selfish father.

Ine—a name similar to Ume—is a "great beauty, of the best Japanese type," and though poorly dressed bears "an innate refinement written on her face" that distinguishes her from the coarse country girls about her. Entirely alone, she is on the train bound for Tokyo, where she hopes to make her fortune to pay for her brother's education—a plot device typical of the time and one which suggests that Ume endorsed the prevailing assumption that a boy's education took precedence over his sister's future, even requiring her self-sacrifice. Like the six-year-old Ume arriving with the Iwakura mission in a strange and overwhelming America, Ine loses her courage: "The loneliness that had haunted the child all day became overpowering. No one had spoken to her for hours, and the unaccustomed scenes around her made her head whirl, and bewildered and frightened her.... At last, she turned her head to the window in her corner, where no one could see her, and covering her face with the long sleeve of her dress, she cried bitterly." A motherly woman—one in a series of such women—buys Ine a cake and tea, and after she leaves the train, Ine longs for the lost comfort of her dead mother, a yearning that parallels Ume's desire to overcome her isolation from her mother, Hatsuko.

In describing Ine's mother and father, Ume voices her troubled feelings about her parents. For Ine's mother she expresses great pity, portraying her as a worn-out but dignified and refined samurai woman from a reduced Edo family who had made an unfortunate marriage.[41] Ine's father—by implication, Sen—is described as an incompetent and selfish failure, a feckless man whose early signs of promise proved empty and who soon brings financial ruin on his family:

> It was true that the mother had never become reconciled at heart to the narrow ways of the little village and to her hard life of toil. In his younger days, the father had been prosperous, having succeeded to some wealth, and the marriage between the daughter of a poor *samurai* whose fortunes had been ruined by the Revolution of 1868, and a well-to-do *heimin* [commoner] had not seemed inappropriate to the families, when it was arranged. But the wife had inherited centuries of refinement and

> culture, and though she accepted her lot, and adapted herself to her new relations and her changed position, with a Japanese woman's meekness, never uttering a word of murmuring to any one, her husband's coarse speech and lack of delicacy, his pettiness and ill-temper, and the ways of the household into which she had entered never ceased to jar upon her sensitive nature. There was not much time, however, to brood over such troubles, for the days of prosperity were soon over for the family,—the husband, a careless man with no business capacity, gradually lost the greater part of his inherited property, and a life of hard toil opened up for the delicately-bred wife.

Ume erases Sen's samurai status by presenting Ine's father as a parvenu commoner, suggesting the great distance that Ume, proud of her heritage, wished to place between herself and her father. She may have written *Ine* after Sen's death in 1908 (although the manuscript is undated, the story is set in the war with Russia of 1904–1905), and his death may have released her to express, albeit in disguised form, her long-suppressed hostility toward him.

Ume sanitizes the occupation of the real-life prostitute Isa by having Ine find work as a maid in a teahouse, but this occupation brings her close enough to the demimonde of the geisha to place Ine in peril. The landlady of the establishment where Ine finds work has designs on her virtue. Herself a former geisha, though "clever as she was pretty, and with plenty of opportunities," she had not "risen as some of her less famous sisters had done, but was content to wield her power in the lower ranks of life over her husband and his establishment, having long before given up her profession when her beauty faded." Placing Ine among geisha, Ume contrasts the shallow glitter of "the gay talk [of] these sirens, whose aim was to bewilder the soberest guest by their brilliant dresses, their merry songs and their bewitching dances," to the sober dignity of Ine's samurai heritage:

> Little by little faded the glamour which covered the beauty of the gay world into which Ine had entered with such joy. She saw more and more the follies and the deceits and the emptiness of it. Much of the life was coarse and low. The women, apparently so gracious, sweet and innocent were immensely clever, but without true refinement of thought or feeling. It was

> a vain, hollow world she was in, with much misery, envy, and suffering beneath the cloak of gay words and pleasant speeches.

Ine's "inherited refinement and delicacy of mind" attract the noble hero of the novel, Lieutenant Murata. But with his death Ume was unable to finish the story. Because she consistently portrays Ine as a passive victim who relies on others to save her, she could not conceive a plot in which Ine helps herself. Ume's identification with Ine's victimization also made it difficult for her to maintain the authorial distance needed to analyze the social costs of Japan's modernization. *Ine* thus fails to fulfill its initial promise to be an investigation into the social conditions that contribute to prostitution; its reliance on melodramatic villains even implies that prostitution is due more to individual wickedness than to social inequity.

Remorse over his earlier sins led Sen in later years to champion reform efforts aimed at alcohol and prostitution. By the 1890s he was a prominent spokesman for antidrinking and antismoking campaigns and, as proud testimonial to his success in persuading others to forego tobacco, Sen presented a bell cast from over a thousand relinquished pipes to the 1893 World's Columbian Exposition at Chicago, even lecturing the president of Northwestern University on the evils of smoking. Sen's greatest efforts, however, were in the temperance movement. He, too, was in the audience when Mary Leavitt argued that alcohol was not an individual problem but a social one that contributed to immorality, crime, and the break-up of the family. Shamed by his past infidelities—a disgrace doubled for him by the fact that he had been drunk when he got the maid pregnant—Sen took to the temperance platform, embodying the evangelical role of the repentant sinner who is called upon to show others the evil of their ways. He addressed the Kyōfukai in 1887, and his speech, "The Ill Effects of Sake," was later published. Encouraged by the success of this pamphlet, Sen began a monthly abstinence journal with the patriotic title *Hi no Maru* (The rising sun). Though it enjoyed the support of other prominent Christians and *Rikugo Zasshi* associates like Uchimura Kanzō and Uemura Masahisa, however, the publication failed. Sen's efforts for the temperance cause also failed to gain him a position of secure authority, and his role remained secondary: repentant sinner rather than charismatic leader. He was relegated to the background when, after helping to establish the National Temperance League, he was passed over for the position of leader and was instead made one of the society's many vice presidents in 1898.[42]

Not surprisingly, Sen's manner had become that of "a revivalist preacher," according to Anna Hartshorne, "whether the cause was Christianity, anti-tobacco, or bee keeping." Always unconventional, he had become an eccentric, coming up with various projects but unable to focus his attention on any one idea. "He knew a tremendous lot," Anna Hartshorne recalled, "really knew—scraps of science perhaps, but he pigeonholed them all and fitted the bits into his schemes for introducing new products—and gadgets." So impetuous was Sen in each of his many enthusiasms that she wondered how "he could ever have been repressed into the Samurai mould." It was as if Sen's irrepressible energies and ambitions, thwarted in every enterprise, finally turned inward and reemerged as a harmless and ineffectual dottiness.[43]

Leadership in the Meiji enlightenment had proven elusive for Sen, and now, at the end of his life, he had become "a genial explosive old gentleman," in the words of Anna Hartshorne. The causes he had chosen to promote, like the fruits and vegetables he grew, remained outside Japanese tastes, for though he became prominent within his own circle, Christianity and such endeavors as the antismoking and antidrinking campaigns remained marginal to modern Japanese society in spite of brief moments of popularity. Similarly, his school and experimental farm had not been the bright success he had confidently predicted. After an encouraging start in the early years of the Meiji era, the Nōgakkō became a disappointment as Sen's own peculiar blend of Western knowledge—Christianity and agriculture—began to lose its luster. And the Azabu farm could neither compete with government facilities nor rely on a stable local market. The basic diet of the ordinary Japanese remained rice, miso soup, and pickles.[44] Sen's edibles were curiosities as exotic in Meiji Japan as they were in Tokugawa times.

Nor had his family fully regained its lost status. Outside the small world of the Japanese Christians and foreign missionaries, the Tsuda family had little prominence—with the notable exception of Ume. And even that world was becoming smaller and more insecure. Although there was great interest in Christianity in the 1870s and early 1880s—some missionaries even assumed that Japan would be evangelized by the turn of the century—the anti-Christian mood now building put its adherents on the defensive. Sen's sons who lived to maturity had also not fulfilled their father's high hopes. The oldest, Motochika, educated at Niijima Jō's Dōshisha in Kyoto and sent to the United States to study railroads (Sen had planned a government position for Motochika in the growing Ministry of Railroads), was unsuccessful in his various jobs; he died in 1901 of a brain tumor. The second, Jirō, inherited the farm in 1897 after studying agriculture at Amherst and was now struggling to turn a profit. Jun, the third son, would soon become a minor government official and serve as a clerk in the military courts in Manchuria. It was richly ironic that Ume, the child whose birth had so infuriated Sen, had inherited her father's enterprising ambition and became the only successful child in the Tsuda family.

By the turn of the century, the social reform movement's call for better education for women, and its celebration of the cultivated wife and educated mother as the moral center of her home, were countered by a government policy that allowed women superficial authority as wives and mothers but resulted in greater state control of what it deemed to be women's proper roles. The concern of the social reformers for the sanctity of motherhood and the purity of the home was mirrored in the state's view of the family as a bulwark against social chaos and in the increased emphasis that it now placed on the surveillance of motherhood and such specific groups as students. "In the future the source of the government's difficulties will not be foreign," the statesman Yamagata Aritomo observed in 1901, "but domestic affairs."[45]

If women were to be the natural mainstays of state-sponsored morality within the family, then these good wives and wise mothers had to be carefully produced and monitored. The Sino-Japanese War of 1894–1895 underscored women's importance as the nurturers of patriotic children—the future soldiers and workers in the empire as well as the next generation's guardians at home—and once again female education received renewed attention. "Since the family is the root of the nation," explained an official from the Ministry of Education, "it is the vocation of women who become housewives to be good wives and wise mothers, and girls' higher schools are necessary to provide appropriate education enabling girls from middle- and upper-middle-class families to carry out this vocation." While the specification of families from the middle and upper-middle classes belies the universally natural attributes claimed for the domestic sphere, it was the elements of this sphere that constituted the "appropriate education" for girls. As Alice Bacon commented in the revised edition of *Japanese Girls and Women* (1902): "The schools are to teach simply such subjects as are necessary for females; anything more would be superfluous, possibly dangerous."[46]

With the increased emphasis on government control of female education came the Girls' Higher School Law of 1899, which required each prefecture to establish at least one middle school for girls. This diminished the importance of the private (mostly mission) schools for girls, which had been the only major source of female higher education; ten years earlier, there had been at least forty-five such institutions, more than three times the number of public girls' schools. An ordinance of 1899 also aimed at restricting mission schools, possibly the only schools that provided an alternative to the government's definition of appropriate female education, by prohibiting religious education and ceremonies in schools. These schools were compelled to either cease religious instruction, their raison d'être, or close.[47]

Domestic ideology—*ryōsai kemboshugi*—had now become a tool of the state. During the late 1890s there was growing pressure in the Diet to standardize school textbooks and after a textbook scandal in 1902, the compilation of elementary school textbooks was placed under the authority of the Ministry of Education. The government text for elementary-school ethics instruction used nationwide included a lesson on "the duties of a man and the duties of a woman," in which the teacher explained the separate spheres of a husband and wife:

> After you are grown up, man must become master of a house and pursue his calling, woman becomes a wife and takes charge of the house, so husband and wife must help each other and make a home: the occupations of the two are thus naturally different. The moral precepts must of course be observed by both men and women, but men should be specially active, women specially gentle; neither must neglect good manners. So also it is important that both men and women should cultivate knowl-

> edge, but each such as will enable them to fulfill the duties of their own proper sphere. Man is stronger than woman, but it is a very bad thing if a man, relying on his strength, should not pay proper regard to woman; it is a great mistake that some people make who suppose that woman is inferior to man; they are both lords of creation, and there is no reason whatever to look down upon woman. Only the duties of a man and a woman are not the same, and each must not forget his or her own proper sphere.[48]

Central regulation of ethics education had been specifically demanded in the Diet so that the state might foster "the spirit of loyalty, filiality, and patriotism and advance the nation's civilization," in the words of one such conservative resolution. This view was summarized for a Western audience by Kikuchi Dairoku, a former minister of education, in 1907: "We regard education as an affair of the State, to be regulated, controlled, and supervised by the State, and not to be left to individual will or private enterprise." Parallel to the efforts made by the social reform movement to bring such family issues as concubinage into the public domain was the government's entry into the supposed private realm of the family—both used the domestic ideology as justification. Individuals, according to Kikuchi, were obligated to the state, and thus their only worth could be achieved by meeting these obligations: men as diligent workers, women as their caretakers. The ideology of separate spheres was not only naturalized, it was now politicized. "Man goes outside to work to earn his living, to fulfill his duty to the State; it is the wife's part to help him, for the common interest of the house, and as a share of her duty to the State."[49] Any attempt to offer an alternative view of Japanese women's roles would be disloyal to the state.

The family ethic preached in the schools and emphasized in the ethics textbooks was buttressed in 1898 by the promulgation of the Civil Code. Based on the feudal samurai concept of the *ie* (house or family), it positioned all familial relationships within a rigid hierarchy that paralleled the structure of the family-state, a hierarchy that was applied to all public institutions as well, most notably the army. The authority of the family patriarch was made absolute, like the absolute authority of the emperor-patriarch; male family members were superior to female family members; seniors were superior to juniors;

and the oldest son was superior to younger sons. In the extended family, "branch houses" were subordinate to the "main house." In this new Civil Code only men were legally recognized as persons; a married woman (placed in the same classification as the "deformed and the mentally incompetent") could neither enter into a legal contract nor bring legal action without her husband's consent. The husband had the right to dispose of his wife's property as he saw fit and the right to any of its profits (unmarried women and female heads of household could control their own property, but they were a small and mostly temporary minority). Adultery was a crime only for married women; only the wife's adultery was legal grounds for divorce. The husband was not obligated to support the wife after a divorce, and any children were considered to be solely the father's.[50]

Ume Kenjirō, one of the drafters of the Meiji Civil Code, defended these legal restrictions placed on the married woman as necessary "to guarantee the husband's authority." The subordination of women, he wrote in 1908 in his commentary on the Civil Code, was not "because the woman as woman is legally incompetent. . . . The unmarried woman and the widow in their legal capacity are no different from a male; however, the wife as wife is legally incompetent." The subordinate status of the woman as wife bolstered the authority of the *ie* system and, by extension, the authority of the family-state. Asserting its power by controlling women and excluding them from political participation, the Meiji government used the Civil Code as the final consolidation of its legitimacy.[51]

The Civil Code undercut the authority within the home that the ideal of good wife and wise mother seemed to offer women. The "home" was economically and legally the husband's house; it was his property and, now that the *ie* system had been codified, his domain. With industrialization and urbanization, moreover, the woman's small sphere of significant activities in the house was shrinking. Goods and foodstuffs traditionally produced by the women of a family were now being produced commercially and in large urban centers could be readily purchased at reasonable prices. This development decreased the status of women in the home: as an industrialized society leaves behind its agrarian roots, it increasingly values only that work which is paid. Furthermore, with compulsory elementary education, children came under state control at an early age; instead of being a dispenser of "wisdom," as ryōsai kemboshugi suggested, mothers lost much of their traditional role as teacher of household skills to the public school system, which instructed their daughters in "domestic science." The home was becoming a place of little real power.

In this repressive environment, in which women were given the appearance of meaningful participation in the workings of Japanese society but denied political rights, Ume's discouragement deepened. She was especially lonely and depressed in 1894. Her father, her older sister Koto, and Koto's husband had left for the United States the previous year, leaving Koto's two daughters with Ume, and in March 1894 her brother Motochika left for Hokkaido. In May her twenty-year-old sister Fukiko, who lived with Ume, suffered heart and kidney trouble and died in August after a lengthy illness. "This spring was of all times the hardest & saddest for me," Ume wrote years later in some autobiographical notes. "The trial was very hard to bear. No one can quite take her place with me."

Four weeks after Fukiko's death Ume confided to some Bryn Mawr friends that "now I feel quite at a loss, and do not seem as if I could pick up the threads of life again," concluding her letter: "Nothing has changed in the aspects of affairs out here, educationally or otherwise. We still remain, as before, at a dead stand. Sometimes I think I shall get on board of a ship and steal away from it all, and not care or try any more, but that, I suppose, you would think very weak and cowardly." She still had little influence, her students even less. The Peeresses' School, according to Anna Hartshorne, remained a feudal, stultifying, rigid institution where proper behavior was more important than learning. Ume was "more than ever the caged thing" after her return from Bryn Mawr, and her work was "elementary lang[uage] teaching to society girls who would not be allowed higher even if [they] wished." These students were educated parrot-fashion, repeating what was told to them rather than thinking for themselves. Trained always to please, they blithely answered "yes" to any question asked of them. Wanting to "lash these girls into personal consciousness," a former student remarked, the exasperated Ume succeeded only in frightening them.[52]

As when she first returned from the United States in 1882, the authorities were again indifferent to Ume's educational achievements. The government did, however, show an interest in her facility in the English language and her knowledge of American ways: she was used as an attractive spokeswoman for the official view of Japanese women and their proper education.

Ume was asked in 1893 to contribute to a publication, *Japanese Women*, by the Japanese Woman's Commission for the World's Columbian Exposition at Chicago. The book offers the familiar history of Japanese women and a description of their contemporary life, work, and accomplishments. Following a brief introduction, the opening observation of *Japanese Women* sets the tone: "A precept has been inculcated in this country from time immemorial, and, let us hope, is destined to continue for all ages to come, that men should concern themselves with matters outside their homes, and women with domestic affairs; that, in short, men should lead and women follow."[53] Although Ume's contribution to *Japanese Women* is not identified, she probably wrote the final chapter, on contemporary philanthropic works and female education, an indifferent description of various charities and schools. "My long labored over manuscript for the World's Congress is at last done," she wrote Adeline Lanman that September. "The subject was such a wide one—and people who promised to get information for me did not, and so it went. It now lies before me forty pages of good foolscap paper, and a whole month of hard work. I think I ought to have some reward for it, but don't see when it is to come, except in the honor of having done it for Japan."

Five years later Ume was asked by Ōkuma Shigenobu, then prime minister and foreign minister, and Tōyama Shōichi, the new education minister, to represent Japan at the 1898 Convention of the General Federation of Women's Clubs in Denver, Colorado. The importance placed on her appearance at this meeting is revealed in the summons Ume and her companion, Ogashima (Watanabe) Fudeko (another teacher at the Peeresses' School), received to report to the empress on their return. Yet, because of the great haste with which Ume's attendance at the conference had been arranged—within a week of the government's request, she was aboard ship headed for North America—she had little time to prepare a thoughtful address to an influential audience (the GFWC, founded in 1890 as a confederation of two hundred clubs representing 20,000 women, by 1900 had 150,000 members). She therefore chose the comparative safety of platitudes and adopted the role of a wide-eyed visitor from a remote and archaic country:

> We of the Far East find much to wonder at and admire every day of our stay since we have landed, an admiration on my part as new and vivid as though this were my first visit here. The great extent of your country, which has taken us many long hours of rapid travel to get to this city, which is not even half way over the vast continent, and comfort and luxury and wonderful facilities for traveling, the wealth and beauty of your cities all impress us. But passing over the admiration which must come to any traveller in this land, there is a richer store of pleasure than in seeing the material wonders of your country. It is the intercourse we are having with the advanced women of America. We know already something through our friends, the magazines and books, of the wonderful strides made in woman's work and woman's education in the last few decades, and now we have come over to see, ourselves, something of this grand work, to know what the foremost women of the world are doing for the advance of womenkind in every way. It is impossible for me to thank you sufficiently for the opportunity extended to us at this time. The many kind greetings we have received, the warm welcome and friendly hospitality extended us, the facilities that are being afforded us for study of your methods of work, and the insight which we have obtained in the short time we have been here of your organization, your energy and progress—all this we shall remember and bear back to our country.

To her credit, Ume was not pleased with the Denver speech. "Do you care for it?" she asked Adeline Lanman when she received her copy. "I do not want it printed and please do not show it around."[54] Given the official nature of her assignment, she could have said little else, but the speech nevertheless represents a missed opportunity for Ume: by its innocuous nature it failed to catch the attention of some powerful American women's networks.

Part of Ume's assignment was a tour of female schools, from the elementary to college levels, in England. She left the United States at the end of 1898 and spent five months in England—mostly London, Cambridge, and Oxford—where she received another valuable opportunity to observe schools for women which, after a lengthy struggle to prove the value of female higher education, were now consolidating their reputation. Though officially on government business, Ume had a more immediate interest in observing these institutions, for she had finally decided to start her own school. Her position at the Peeresses' School, while prestigious and well paid (by now eight hundred yen a year), could not satisfy her ambitions. Ume had advanced there as far as she could. In the summer of 1898, looking to the Philadelphia Committee for support, Ume discussed with Mary Morris her plans to start her own school to prepare young women for the government examination for the teaching certificate and wrote Morris in December that she wanted to "try the experiment for five years." Alice Bacon had written that she was ready to come to Tokyo to help with the school.

While Ume visited such women's institutions as Bedford and Queen's colleges in London, Girton and Newnham in Cambridge, and Somerville College and Lady Margaret Hall in Oxford, meeting with such leaders in women's higher education as Christine Mary Burrows (later principal of St. Hilda's College, Oxford) and Elizabeth Phillipps Hughes, principal of the Cambridge Training College (Hughes Hall), she was most interested in Cheltenham Ladies' College and its teacher-training college, St. Hilda's, Oxford. Under the skillful leadership of its principal, Dorothea Beale (friend and supporter of Pandita Ramabai), whose conservative educational philosophy accorded with Ume's, Cheltenham had become a financially secure institution with a large student population. It was an establishment of magnificent neo-Gothic buildings with lofty rooms dominated by stained glass windows, sculptures of allegorical subjects in every nook and cranny, and Dorothea Beale herself sitting at a large desk on a dais at the end of the Great Hall, from which she kept a close watch on her students and teachers. The college's success, not to mention the palpable authority of Dorothea Beale, clearly spoke to Ume's aspirations. "I had another talk with Miss Beale," she wrote on 16 December 1898 in a journal kept during her stay in England.

> She is a very interesting person. One of the pioneers of girls' education in England & has been an educationalist for over twenty-five years. She has been the founder and sole organizer of this whole school which has now over 900 pupils and it is this school which has affected so much the Girls' High Schools of England. There are over 90 instructors and they seem a very able staff of women. . . . Yesterday morning I visited Cambray

> House, which is an overflow school of the Ladies' College. Miss Beale first began her school there, and it has grown up from a little beginning into this great institution. It is encouraging to see how education has progressed in England, for we are at a stage in Japan no worse than when Miss Beale began her life-long work.[55]

Ume was also impressed with the class of students Cheltenham attracted. The college, in fact, imposed a class barrier so that, in Dorothea Beale's words, "none are admitted but the daughters of independent gentlemen or professional men." "It must be a very wealthy college," Ume approved in her journal. "In fact I hear that only well-to-do high class girls come here—daughters of gentlemen—not tradespeople."[56]

In England, Ume encountered the same interest in Japanese women that she had met in the United States. An informal talk she gave at St. Hilda's drew an audience of nearly seventy. Ume was especially gratified when Florence Nightingale—as popular in Japan as she was in England—granted her request for an interview. "I would rather have seen her than royalty itself," she confessed. Ume presented her with photographs of the Red Cross Hospital work in Japan as well as a copy of her life written in Japanese, and answered Florence Nightingale's questions about Japanese women. "I spoke of the future prospects for our women," she wrote in her journal on 29 March 1898, "and how their work was gradually broadening out. She said, 'It was quite the same in England. Forty years ago, women had such narrow lives. Nothing but marriage was expected of them by their parents. I am sure it was so with my mother.'"

Florence Nightingale was an important model for Ume—never one to miss an opportunity for self-improvement, Ume had read Nightingale's *Notes on Nursing* while caring for her sister, Fukiko, in 1885 when she was dangerously ill with typhoid fever. Both women had avoided the conventional life of marriage and children to fulfill their ambitions within the wider scope allowed by the womanly professions of nursing and teaching. While spurning the domestic world, they nevertheless relied on the domestic ideal as the pretext for their careers. Presenting her ambitions as a feminine calling, Florence Nightingale was able to leave the constraints of the domestic sphere and even the confines of England itself.[57] Ume, too, turned the contradictions inherent in the domestic ideology to her own advantage, moving beyond the restrictions of Japanese society to achieve her goals.

This theme of service to society united the various women who inspired Ume: M. Carey Thomas, Pandita Ramabai, Yajima Kajiko, Hatoyama Haruko, Dorothea Beale, and Florence Nightingale. All had taken part in the public struggle for better education for women, and all justified their highly visible participation in this campaign with appeals to social welfare. Service to society was what these women approved, and service to society was what they demanded of their followers. As Dorothea Beale, who conceived of her mission chiefly in religious terms, urged a group of students preparing to leave college: "May you ever understand better the meaning of that 'service which is perfect freedom' and make the words true for your own life—'No man taketh it from me, but I lay it down of myself.'" Such exhortations were reinforced by a special service in which the students dedicated themselves to work for humanity.[58]

Ume returned to Japan in the summer of 1899 filled with the moral certitude that her motives to begin her own school were entirely disinterested, expressing her desires, like Florence Nightingale and Dorothea Beale, in a language of vocation and self-sacrifice. Disturbed by her very unwomanly ambitions, she had sought the sanction of the highest spiritual authority available to her: after meeting the archbishop of York at Christmas 1898 and telling him of her aspirations, she had received his blessing. "I told him that I really wished to do something, and to grow in grace and that I had had many advantages," she confided to her journal two days before her thirty-fourth birthday, "but I must do something to pass them on to others, and how the weight of responsibility hung on me, although I was so unworthy of the blessings that God had given me in comparison with so many of my countrywomen, that often I felt I would be glad of not having seen and known and heard so much. Ah! that is what often comes to me—why one so unworthy should have been chosen for the life which I am having. The blessing of the Archbishop I shall take back with me as a strengthener, and how can I doubt that the prayers of such a good and holy man will not be heard of God!" Bolstered in her conviction that she was guided in her work, an unsought-for mission undertaken in the name of her God and her nation, and for the sake of her countrywomen, Ume could justify her aggressive ambitions.

The 1890s were richly rewarding years for Ume, despite her feelings of frustration. She witnessed the workings of various female schools and had gained direct experience in female education from schools as diverse as the Peeresses' School and Meiji Jogakkō; her public-speaking and fundraising efforts sharpened her organization skills and polished her persuasive style, and the enthusiasm American and English women showed for the future of Japanese women, coupled with the prominence of the social-reform movement in Japan convinced her of the substantial pool of support on which her school could rely. Ume's participation in this variety of philanthropic works, as well as her direct connection with several female schools, also gained her a considerable reputation as an authority on women's education. Yet her awareness of the suspicion and frequent outright hostility shown to mission schools, as well as the conservative atmosphere of the Peeresses' School, also taught Ume caution: female education of substance had very shallow roots in Japan. There was no solid native tradition to support such an undertaking. Daughters were often withdrawn from school during times of adversity, and girls' schools were the first to be closed when the political or economic climate made such institutions seem luxuries. Ume realized that she would have to look outside Japan for financial support of her planned school, while at the same time working cautiously within the country. "I know in Japan every one will be on the look out and ready to criticize all I do," she wrote Adeline Lanman from England in November 1898, "so I have to be doubly careful about the matter. . . . I hope that all may go right for the sake of my future work."

Chapter Five

To Know the Contents of Life for Ourselves, 1900–1929

By the early decades of the twentieth century Tokyo had acquired the features of modern mass society. The appearance of suburban railways was followed by the subway system, and buses and electric trolleys crossed the city carrying tens of thousands of passengers each day, making the rickshaw obsolete. By 1920 there were several hundred motorcycles and ten thousand automobiles in Tokyo, and the crowded streets were redesigned to give less room to pedestrians and more to vehicles. Business offices and department stores proliferated, and tourist buses showed visitors from the countryside the wonders of the big city and the achievements of a civilized nation. Pleasure and consumption were the visible forms of a more individualistic ethos. Radio, movie palaces, and music halls, featuring light opera and chorus-line revues, provided new forms of entertainment, and tea-rooms, *baa* (bars), and *kafuee* (cafés) attracted "modern boys" and "modern girls," the so-called *mobo* and *moga*. Some began to seek new ways of life in artistic and bohemian circles, while others embraced radical politics. After the 1904–1905 war with Russia, the term *modanizumu* (modernism) appeared, replacing the conventional adjective *Western*.[1]

Modernism, however, often reflected uncertainty and disaffection. A series of labor strikes in 1907 turned violent, and Tokyo was the scene of mob violence in 1905, 1906, and 1913. The economy had experienced a boom and bust period during World War I, and rampant inflation caused rice riots across the country in 1918. The rioting reached Tokyo in August, lasting for nearly a week, and expressed not only anger over high prices but also social discontent. A prolonged period of strikes the next year brought new attention to workers' rights and the socialist cause. Industrialization, urbanization, national education, mass transportation and communication, and now mass protest, had produced, in the eyes of the authorities, *bunmeibyō* (civilization disease).

What most disturbed authorities was the growing discontent among students. The publicity given to the suicide in 1903 of a student at an elite boys' school in Tokyo drew attention to the "anguished youth" of the late Meiji era. Newspapers across the nation ran stories on the sixteen-year-old boy's sensational death: to many it seemed to signify a disenchantment with the Meiji promise of rising in the world through education. The seemingly limitless opportunities for educated men of the previous generation were now in sharp decline. Many could only look forward to a career as a petty official or rural schoolteacher, causing them to repudiate the values of the older generation. Some were criticized as "educated idlers," others as "decadent youth" dabbling in "erotic-grotesque nonsense" and "dangerous thought." Ideologues warned that anguished youth, uncertain of their future, might turn to socialism.[2]

By World War I students were developing a political consciousness—a survey of public school essays reveals that the most popular topic in 1915 was cherry blossoms; in 1920 it was workers' strikes—and the mobo and moga were joined by the "Marx boy" and "Engels girl." Nor were these students the social deviants the authorities assumed them to be: a Ministry of Education investigation into the personalities and family background of arrested leftist students indicated that 65.9 percent of those interviewed were classified as "good," showing themselves to be "modest, decent, sober, and diligent." Alarmed by the spread of socialism and fearing the contagion of unhealthy thought among middle-class students, government leaders and conservative educators alike concentrated their efforts on suppressing student activism.[3]

These political activists came from a generation who believed that the gradualist policies of the Meiji leaders were inadequate to meet the social and economic problems of the day. Many rejected the notion that the purpose of personal fulfillment was national advancement. A new wave of Japanese feminism, established in the Taishō era (1912–1926), spurned the standards of true womanhood advocated by Ume and other Meiji feminists by popularizing the ideal of the cosmopolitan New Woman. The title of a journal published by a group of socialist women, *Suiito Homu* (Sweet home), for instance, offered a tongue-in-cheek reference to the ideal of good wife and wise mother. Like the New Women in England and America, these women rejected the constraints of the domestic ideal, but their thought was less a refutation of the nineteenth-century women's movement than a continuation of it. In spite of their flamboyant behavior and radical politics, the Taishō feminists, many of whom were educated at major female institutions in Tokyo, publicized ideas that were the logical outcome of Meiji feminism.

Ume had been arguing for women's right to a higher education, the need to make economic independence available to women, and the authority of the wife and mother in the home—all fundamentals of the nineteenth-century women's movement. But like many of her generation in Japan and the West, she could not approve of the next development in the movement: women's political involvement and their demand for the vote. As the next generation of feminists came to intellectual maturity in the Taishō period, Ume became increasingly isolated from their aspirations, offended by their values, and distressed by their actions.

The year 1900 seemed an appropriate time for Ume to break with the past and start anew. She regarded the beginning of the twentieth century as an opportunity for rebirth: two years into the century, she formally changed her name to Umeko, an act symbolic of a new identity for a thirty-seven-year-old woman embarking on her own enterprise. The year 1900 also seemed a propitious time for Umeko to begin her Joshi Eigaku Juku (Women's English School). With the increase in the number of girls' middle schools brought about by the Girls' Higher School Law of 1899, the number of vocational schools for women grew markedly in the first decade of the century. Umeko's colleague and principal of the Peeresses' School, Shimoda Utako, had founded her own school, Jissen Jogakuen, in 1899. Another woman, Yoshioka Yayoi, established Tokyo Women's Medical

School in 1900. Naruse Jinzō was planning to open Nihon Joshi Daigakkō (Japan Women's College), and the preparations were causing much anticipatory excitement. Umeko could afford to wait no longer.

Umeko's resignation from the Peeresses' School created considerable ill will, but it also brought her a sense of freedom, and the opposition she encountered simply elicited her fighting spirit. "It has been a more difficult thing to leave the school than anyone in democratic America could realize," she wrote M. Carey Thomas on 9 August 1900, "but I have been able to do so, I think, honorably." In a letter written later that same month to two Bryn Mawr friends, she was more informative about the problems she experienced but also more disingenuous about her motives in leaving the school:

> I can not go into all the details of the backings and fillings in regard to my connection with the Peeresses' School (which was so hard to break). No one would believe me when I asked to resign and I had some fights to go thro' and some yet before me. But I am now *free* and have burned, so to speak, all my ships behind me. You have no idea what it is to be connected with the Court and a Court School & to be regarded as a member (however humble) of the Imperial Household Dep't. However, I had to do it once for all. There were more reasons than merely the starting of the school that made me want to leave, but do you know I broke off a 15 years' connection with the highest rank school in Japan, and gave up my official rank & title. Worthless to me, but valued so among our people. Most of my acquaintances were surprised, and many called to ask what was the matter, when it was published in the Official Gazette, but I was glad to say that I wanted to get away from all the Conservatism and Conventions of my old life, and now I am only a commoner, free to do what I like, and free also from my salary, which, however small, still in Japanese eyes was ample! You in democratic America can not realize all this fuss, and I in my heart am glad to take my stand for what is right and true, and not for the rank & conventions and name.

The Joshi Eigaku Juku, Umeko explained in this letter, was to offer a three-year course to graduates of the girls' middle schools, which would prepare them for the government examinations for the teacher's license in English for the public schools. "We call it a School of English, but some day," she hoped, "it will be more than that, and will offer other courses of study."[4]

The teacher's certificate was merely a means to an end. Umeko wished to raise the status of women, and the quickest way to achieve this, she understood, was to enable them to be self-sufficient. With the abolition of the feudal system, social status was increasingly defined in terms of education, occupation, and salary—material wealth was becoming the prime indicator of individual worth. Business schools were on the increase (the Tokyo Higher Business School, for example, which had difficulty recruiting students before the Sino-Japanese War, had 2.8 applicants for each seat in 1897 and 4.7 in 1904), and a number of new magazines devoted to succeeding in the business world appeared. *Jitsugyō no Nihon* (Business Japan), first published in 1897, ran articles on "the secrets of success" and offered minibiographies of such wealthy men as Andrew Carnegie and Cornelius Vanderbilt. *Seikō* (Success), another such journal begun a few years later, popularized the rags-to-riches story and reached a circulation of fifteen thousand by 1905.[5] As money was becoming the measure of worth, Umeko fully realized that women's independence was connected to their ability to be independent wage-earners.

Even if a student did not move on to a teaching position, possession of the means to earn a living, Umeko believed, would command respect. Paid work gave women financial power and the more intangible force of social status. As she said in 1915 in an address to the Japanese YWCA:

> Economic independence is the one thing that can save a woman from an unsuitable or distasteful marriage urged on her by relatives. . . . To be able to earn even a mere pittance often makes every difference to a woman, & educators should think of this in the training they give a girl. A practical course often means to her more than accomplishments or theoretic knowledge of no use. Even with the best kind of an education for culture, I believe every Japanese woman sh[oul]d have some training which is of commercial value, be skilled in some speciality which is useful & practical & for which there is a market.

Aware of its radical implications, however, Umeko did not follow this line of reasoning to its logical conclusion: economic independence gave women the freedom to abandon traditional roles, "spoiling" them for family duties. Constantly compelled to affirm the orthodox role for women, she told a group of graduating students in the same year that "the home must always remain woman's paramount sphere."[6]

The Joshi Eigaku Juku started in a small rented house with four teachers and fifteen students recruited from notices sent to girls' mission and middle schools. Its opening ceremony began with a solemn reading of the Imperial Rescript on Education followed by a hymn in Japanese, psalms read in English, and a prayer in Japanese. Umeko then explained to the small assembly the significance of their enterprise and the responsibility each student had to the future of Japanese women:

> There is one thing I must warn you as students to be careful about. This school is the first of its kind in making a specialty of its higher courses of study. We may be criticized on many points. Perhaps some of these may not be of much importance, but even then, if such criticism impedes the progress of the higher education for women, it would be a matter of great regret to all of us. And criticism will mostly come, not so much on our courses of study or methods of work, but on points which simply require a little care and thoughtfulness on your part—the little things which constitute the making of a true lady—the language you use, your manner in intercourse with others—your attention to the details of our etiquette. So I ask you not in any way to make yourselves conspicuous or to seem forward, but be always gentle, submissive and courteous as have always been our women in the past. This need not in any way interfere with the standard of your studies, for you may as true women endeavor to get the same grasp and hold of knowledge and attain the same standard of study as those of the other sex.[7]

This warning to each student to act as a "true lady" and especially to behave in the submissive manner of Japanese tradition arose from Umeko's awareness of the distrust, disparagement, and general disapproval shown to women's higher education. Her students, she knew, would have to maneuver among the suspicion and hostility set in their way.

Higher education in Japan was still very much a male preserve; indeed, it was proudly misogynist in its claims to privilege. The elite boys' schools that prepared their students for entry into the imperial universities displayed great concern for manliness and the rituals of privileged masculinity. Freshman students at these schools were exhorted to "Demonstrate your manliness!" and were initiated into such fraternal rites as "dormitory rain": communal urination out the dormitory windows. Secluded as a united family of men, these higher schools scorned the world beyond their gates as vulgar and feminine, despising even the physical presence of women. In 1891, when a woman was discovered at a special assembly at the First Higher School in Tokyo, for instance, the ceremony was immediately halted, the main lecture hall closed, and bags of salt poured over the seats to repurify the place. In 1916, the actress Mori Ritsuko attended the same school's Anniversary Day celebrations, one of the few times when the gates were open to the public, because her brother was a freshman there. Outraged at this pollution by the presence of a "vulgar actress" on the school's sacred soil, the classmates of Mori's brother bullied him; two months later, the boy committed suicide. The higher schools and the quality education they provided were truly exclusive.[8]

Very much aware of this contempt for women, Umeko reasoned that respect for women's higher education might come from imitating much of the curriculum taught at the male higher schools. And it was the elite nature of these schools especially that Umeko strove to emulate. Just as M. Carey Thomas was determined to prove that her students could successfully pursue the Harvard curriculum if given the opportunity, Ume was set on showing that the Joshi Eigaku Juku students could match their male counterparts if given the proper training.

The higher schools for boys emphasized a liberal education; no matter what each student planned as his future, he was required to study a humanities-centered curriculum: pure science, the Japanese and Chinese classics, and, especially, English and German language and literature. Easy familiarity with a European language and its literature was the mark of distinction for the university-bound elite.[9] Umeko's students underwent a similar course of Japanese and Chinese literature, history, social ethics, and physical education (and later domestic science), with a special focus on English language and literature. In the preparatory year students read such works as the immensely popular *Little Lord Fauntleroy*, Palgrave's *Golden Treasury*, and translations of Hans Christian Andersen. They then moved on to such greats as *Silas Marner, A Tale of Two Cities, The Last Days of Pompeii, John Halifax, Gentleman, Cranford, Baron Münchhausen*, and the novels of Sir Walter Scott, as well as the poetry of Tennyson, the Brownings, and Milton.

Like many early female educators, Umeko was forced to compile her own textbooks. She chose stories from diverse sources for her readers, but the essential plot of these various selections, one student was quick to note, resembled Umeko's childhood experience in the United States: the hero or heroine was usually a lonely child who is suffering some form of disability (loss of parents, poverty, or physical handicap) but is always cheerful, optimistic, and willing to help others—a goodness usually rewarded by the kindness of adult strangers.[10] The didactic lesson of most of these works also embodied the ethos of self-help. Dinah Mulock's *John Halifax, Gentleman* (1857) is typical of Umeko's selections: the story of a hard-working orphan who, by endeavor, education, and the reward of his superiors, rises in the world, the novel emphasizes that nobility of character is greater than nobility of birth—a point made without challenge to the class structure.

Umeko attempted to expose her students to what she described in her first report to the school's alumnae as "the good and noble thoughts of great English writers," certain that such exposure would transform them into better human beings. She also believed that the foreign ideas embedded in English literature would liberate her students from the constraints of Japanese tradition: "English literature leads us also to the best ethical thought and teachings, which [have] already done much to mould new Japan," she wrote in the *Bryn Mawr Alumnae Quarterly*. Such new ideas, Umeko argued, were essential for Japanese women if they were to prosper in a modern society, with its threatening destruction of the restraints of traditional sexual and class barriers:

> Our women are coming forth from secluded lives, and taking up new responsibilities, and the spirit of progress has come to stay. The feudal lord and the old ties have gone, and our women are pushing aside the restraints of the narrow old ethical code. They need those higher qualities which fit in with modern civilization and modern life. We educators feel that if the Spartan

> simplicity of the past and the old habits of self-control are lost, and the day of materialism and freedom and self-assertion come in without higher education, giving mental training and mental balance, together with moral teachings and Christian ideals to lend their force, then the new civilization is a menace to our people, and the change a retrograde one. We need the best education in these critical times for our women.

Umeko's self-ordained role in this educational growth was that of cultural filter. Familiar with both Japanese and American cultures, she believed she could act as a transmitter of wholesome Western thought while keeping out noxious influences. "I trust that they may thus escape some of the dangers which lie in wait for the progressive and radical women of our day," she reasoned, "dangers which do not exist for conservative ones. How important it is to have them think for themselves, and realize the perils about them in these times of reconstructive work taking place among the wreck of our old social system!"[11]

Using the teaching methods she had absorbed at Bryn Mawr and especially at Meiji Jogakkō, Umeko and the other instructors challenged the students to think for themselves. This shocked some of the pupils and sparked others. One graduate recalled her surprise when she saw that she and her classmates would not be allowed to follow the customary pattern of writing down the teacher's words and memorizing them for examinations: "We were required to prepare thoroughly beforehand and give our opinions in class. We could argue with the teacher and did not have to agree with her if we were not convinced. It was a revelation for me to know that a girl might have her own idea about anything and argue with her honorable teacher."[12] To have their opinions encouraged and solicited in the classroom was exhilarating for many students, for the teaching method showed respect for their ideas while encouraging them to speak up in public.

This emphasis on individual thought was at the center of Umeko's educational philosophy. She wanted to inculcate in her students the habits of self-reliance and self-respect—characteristics that had helped her throughout her own uncertain career and that would help her students in the Darwinian struggle for survival in the corrupt world of modern life. These young women, Umeko believed, had to be prepared psychologically as well as intellectually. "Japanese girls are timid, lack confidence and independence," she told her YWCA audience in 1915. "They dislike taking responsibility beyond all things, especially for fear they may be blamed for what they do. They have never been taught to think and act for themselves. Emotion, and not reason is often their guide, so they are impulsive and over-sensitive. They are only too glad to have their opinions thought out for them, to have every detail in life planned for them by a capable person, to follow a leader, to worship a hero." Schools should thus "consider the practical uses of their courses of study," she continued, "& try to provide a girl with weapons to defend herself in the actual fight for existence." In an explanation of the philosophy and methods of her school written in 1905, Umeko stressed the need to overcome her students' habits of dependence:

> Every effort has been made towards the encouragement of study on the part of the students and of independent work and independent thought. The time is fast coming when such qualities will be needed in our women, as they are called for in men, and education which only encourages reliance on teachers and dependence on others is the education which comes to an end as soon as the gates of the school are passed. The memorizing of ready made opinions of others is not a sufficient help to meet the intricate and changing problems of life before us, while experiences in the school of life will only give added power when the reasoning faculties are fully developed. Constant effort has been made to appeal to the reason, and to teach the pupils to form for themselves reasonable opinions on various subjects. At the beginning the results show less than when memorizing is made the chief factor in the work, but the ultimate gain is beyond calculation, and in any case the development of the mind and the formation of a true judgment are results much more far reaching than mere gain in language study.[13]

Umeko understood that if her students could learn to value their thinking, they could learn to value themselves.

Though seemingly unexceptional, such ideas differed fundamentally from the views of other leaders in Japanese women's education. Miwata Masako, who helped Naruse establish Japan Women's College before founding her own school, advocated the "way of the wife" and the "way of the mother" as the heavenly calling of women, a service to society and the nation that was the sole reason for schooling girls. Any attempts to move beyond woman's sphere she considered a deviation from nature. "And so," she wrote, "the one and only purpose of women's education is the nurturing of good wives and wise mothers." In a clever conflation of the ryōsai kembo slogan with the "Western technology, Eastern morality" idea, Miwata invented a new slogan, *tokusai kembi*: women were to fulfill the Confucian ideal of womanhood while mastering the practical skills known to Western women.[14]

Atomi Kakei, the founder of another famous female school that specialized in such womanly arts as painting, flower arranging, and the tea ceremony, also promoted the official version of ryōsai kembo. Women who sacrificed themselves for the family, she believed, "would be celebrated as good wives and wise mothers. This is the real life for women." Atomi, however, extended this traditional virtue to include service to the state: a proper education, she maintained, consisted of inculcating in the students "the concept of the holiness of the national policy." Shimoda Utako advocated similar views emphasizing duty to the state. "The state gives education to the people," she wrote, "to accomplish the national ideals." It was necessary to educate each girl to become a "perfect woman," she reasoned, one who was "perfect for the nation" because her education had instilled in her the desired qualities of patriotism, "national morality," "intelligence and techniques suitable for national character" (what Shimoda elsewhere described as women's "true work": sewing, cooking, and the like), and had also developed in her a "splendid physique."[15]

Although Umeko stressed service and self-sacrifice in her understanding of what constituted a good wife and wise mother, she did not accord preeminence to the claims of the state. At the core of her educational philosophy was a firm belief in the value of the individual. Though she held that every woman had obligations to society, these duties were undertaken for the social good, not for national policy. As she had objected twenty years earlier in her description of the officials' wives who had been educated so that they might appear at government functions, "this is not right."

Umeko thus had a low opinion of female schools that, believing it improper or even impossible to encourage thought in their pupils, emphasized feminine skills at the expense of intellectual effort. Her article of 1897, "The Future of Japanese Women," had dismissed such establishments as "so-called schools." Anna Hartshorne, who had come to Tokyo in 1902 to assist Umeko in her school, was openly contemptuous of the Atomi Girls' School, wondering of its students: "The young faces were—vacant? Gently smiling masks? Were thoughts and emotions ironed out for company occasions, or—not present?" In contrast, the standards of the Joshi Eigaku Juku were high. Umeko repeated M. Carey Thomas's strict requirements and refused to soften the school's stiff entrance standards, knowing that the prestige of her school would be damaged by lowering the entry level to admit students insufficiently prepared. Each applicant wrote an entrance examination that, according to Anna Hartshorne, "required quite as much as men's Kōtō Gakkō [higher schools], plus enough spoken English to allow the First Year student to acquire thoughts and ideas through actual language lessons." "Naturally letting down bars and making things easy and then stamping 'Female Standard' was not [her] pace. Hence the Prep," she wrote. If a student could not complete the preparatory year, she was "gently advised to try music or flower arrangement" at some other school.

Graduating classes were small. Many students failed, others quit, and some left for marriage. A few were even withdrawn by alarmed family members: Anna recalled that the brother of one student took her away at the end of her second year because, he told Umeko, "If she graduates she won't do as I tell her." The school nevertheless flourished, drawing a steadily increasing number of applicants each year, so that within three years of its opening the Joshi Eigaku Juku had an enrollment of over one hundred.

An austerity that reflected the school's strict standards characterized school life. The first rented house that held the Juku was cramped, leaky, and bitterly cold in the winter, necessitating a move to a larger house, tumbledown and said to be haunted, but cheap. When the rapid growth of the school required yet another move, the new site was soon overflowing. The dormitories were small—two girls to a nine-foot-square room—and lacked heat or electricity, forcing students to study together in the dining room under electric lights and, during the winter, by a coal stove, before going to bed (at nine o'clock, when the dining room closed) in a dark and freezing room. The members of the school, however, were proud of this ascetic life, seeing it as a mark of honest poverty that distinguished their school from others ("Naruse and this flamboyant Joshi Daigakkō," sniffed Anna Hartshorne), as if their spartan life was proof that the school was not a finishing school for pampered daughters.

The facilities at the Joshi Eigaku Juku were also poor. When the school opened, a blackboard, Alice Bacon's typewriter, Umeko's books, and her battered piano, brought from the Peeresses' School, where it had migrated after she had left the Itō residence, were the only equipment. Books trickled in from the United States and England: Bryn Mawr donated over a hundred books and an *Encyclopedia Brittanica*, Mary Burrows of St. Hilda's sent collections of English verse, and others gave Bibles and hymn books—the students even using the hymnals as textbooks. In 1910, Umeko received a gift of over three hundred reference books from the Philadelphia Committee, and this time most of them were new.

A paucity of books and lack of proper facilities, however, did not greatly bother Umeko. In offering a higher education she wanted to see her students cultivated, but she was not interested in seeing them become overly cerebral; acquiring a phonograph, for example, was just as important as building a library. "In order to cultivate the taste and give home entertainment," she wrote the Philadelphia Committee, "I have often thought a good phonograph would be a good addition. Has any one of our friends an old one, not in use, who could spare it to us?" When some students did assume intellectual pretensions and turned to feminist and socialist discussion, the school resorted to such high-handed tactics as threatening to withhold a student's graduation unless her involvement in political issues ceased. Kamichika Ichiko, for instance, was forced to withdraw from a feminist group. The thrust of Umeko's teaching methods was character-building—the formation of what she called "the complete woman"—not scholarship. "True education does not depend upon the school buildings, apparatus, and other accessories," she told her first group of students. "It has seemed to me quite possible, therefore, to carry on the true work of education, even with greatly restricted means, if the teachers and pupils have with them the true spirit of work."[16]

Cultivation of the complete woman could be achieved, Umeko believed, by providing students with the beneficial influences of American middle-class home life. Taking a parental interest in "my girls," as she regularly referred to them, she cast her school as a harmonious family. In her early fund-raising efforts in the United States, Umeko emphasized the homely environment of the Joshi Eigako Juku by underscoring the private household connotations of the word *juku* when she translated the school's name as the Girls' Home School of English. Cultivated home life also characterized certain extracurricular activities. Along with the home entertainment provided by the phonograph was the lesson "in the ways of a foreign home," as Anna Hartshorne put it, that students received when their turn came to have tea with Umeko at her house on the school grounds. Eager to have her students become acquainted with the general forms of socializing that constituted the genteel behavior of the polished hostess, Umeko tried to inculcate in them the standards of table talk and manners that characterized the Western model of womanhood. She tried, according to Anna Hartshorne, to have "things just a little better than the average household." Philanthropic work was another facet of the domestic ideal she encouraged in her students. During the war with Russia students staged benefit concerts, made clothing for families left destitute, and knitted for soldiers engaged in battle. They also held an annual bazaar to raise funds for the school. "The girls enjoy these things," Umeko wrote Adeline Lanman in November 1901, "and it is good for them."

Operating on a shoestring budget forced Umeko to rely on the contacts she had made in the 1890s. The Philadelphia Committee was now renamed the Committee for Miss Tsuda's School for Girls, which regularly raised funds in the United States while it continued with the scholarship scheme. Alice Bacon, who had returned to Tokyo in 1900 to help establish the school, received no wages for her two years of teaching and gave Umeko most of her earnings from the Tokyo Women's Normal School, where she also taught. Associates of the American committee and Bryn Mawr friends, most notably Anna Hartshorne, who replaced Alice Bacon in 1902, were asked to come to Japan to teach in the school for very low or no wages. Anna, too, gave the school most of her earnings from the Tokyo Women's Normal School and Peers' School. Of the school's full-time staff there were generally two Japanese women, two foreign women (Anna Hartshorne was a permanent member and the second woman usually came to Japan for two, sometimes three, years), and four Japanese men. Many of the men, however, did not take their work seriously, forcing Umeko to supervise them closely and to substitute for them during one of their many absences. In late December 1910 she poured out her frustrations in a letter to her sister Yona: "If only the school would run of itself, but Mr. Sakurai is worse than ever about helping out in the office, and since Mr. Shimizu has gone, no teacher ever helps as much, and then Miss Kawai is away, and the teachers must be kept up, and many of them are irregular and stay away. None of the regular Japanese teachers are as faithful as the foreigners in their work, and it is always an effort to keep them regular and doing their work and if one does not try very hard to keep them up and to take their places when they are absent, then the girls fail and get slack, and so there is unusual amount of worry about teaching. My work would not be half as hard if the teachers were more faithful. . . . If only there were one Japanese man as faithful and kind as [the foreign women] are!"

The school also relied on a large number of part-time and temporary teachers. Even though Umeko disliked missionaries, she was not reluctant to ask American, English, and Canadian missionary women to donate time to the school. (One woman began a singing class, wrote Anna Hartshorne, "as a gift to a Christian institution.") Men from Tokyo Imperial University, the Peers' School, the Higher Normal School, and Tokyo Foreign Language School gave weekly classes, and Umeko even persuaded such famous educators as Iwamoto Zenji and Nitobe Inazō to deliver weekly lectures, thereby enhancing the school's prestige. She could also count on a sense of obligation to her or the school: most of the scholarship students taught at the Joshi Eigaku Juku after their return from the United States, and Tokyo alumnae also took late afternoon classes for no pay, often after a day of teaching elsewhere. It required considerable strength of character and determination palliated by a magnetic sense of dedication to keep this assortment of people to their promised duties.

Umeko's tenacity soon paid off. At the beginning of the academic year in 1904 the school received official recognition as a *senmon gakkō* (vocational school). Although well below university status, it was the highest rank a women's private school could achieve. "Our school has been recognized by the Educational Department as being of the standard above that of high schools [kōtō jogakkō, girls' middle schools]," Umeko wrote Adeline Lanman in April. "It is of course a card for the school to have this recognized standing." Official recognition, however, also meant greater government control: "They require certain changes and regulations which we must fulfill if we wish to keep the recognition," she explained, including more emphasis on domestic science and ethics instruction approved by the Ministry of Education.

Further official approval came in 1905 when the graduates of the Juku were no longer required to take the government examinations for the teacher's license. "It is the first private school for girls granted this privilege," she wrote Adeline in September. What Umeko did not tell her, however, was that the nation needed teachers, and needed them quickly. Elementary school enrollment was rising rapidly, but the number of qualified teachers was falling. The work, traditionally regarded as a "heavenly calling," had lost its prestige—what had previously been an honorable profession dominated by those of samurai birth was now peopled by the children of farmers—so that the occupation was now held in contempt. ("School teachers!" scoffed the writer Kunikida Doppo in 1902, "I despise them. Sitting around like fat toads blinking their eyes after having just missed a mosquito.") By 1900 the salary of a teacher was little different from the wages of an artisan or laborer, with an average monthly pay of thirteen yen. The government was forced to hire poorly trained personnel such as the so-called stopgap teachers (*koshikake kyōshi*), who worked as instructors for a very limited time before finding a position in another sector, as well as the *demo kyōin* and *taran sensei* (would-be teachers), who taught because they could find no other employment. Consequently, by 1908, only 26 percent of the nation's licensed instructors had passed through a teacher-training program. This shortage of qualified male teachers plus the low wages that could be paid to females made the graduates of Umeko's three-year course very attractive indeed; the number of women school teachers doubled between 1905 and 1915.[17]

With this demand for female teachers the Joshi Eigaku Juku grew steadily. Its only serious rivals in the capital were the Women's Normal School, Japan Women's College, and, after 1918, Tokyo Women's College. As the school became better known among advocates of women's higher education in the United States, American tourists carrying letters of introduction arrived at the school in ever increasing numbers. Most expected a guided tour of Tokyo but instead were shown about the school and those places on the grounds where Umeko hoped to build additional rooms. This subtle pressure for donations often worked: Phoebe Hearst, mother of William Randolph Hearst and a generous supporter of female education, was among a party of American women visiting the school and left a donation; another visitor from Chicago wrote a check for five hundred dollars on the spot; and one woman, whom Umeko could not remember, persuaded her parents after her return to Boston to donate six thousand dollars and to establish a scholarship to support one student.

Not all of the increasing number of students attended Umeko's school because they wished to become teachers of English. Many were sent to acquire a general higher education that would raise their value in the marriage market. Most were daughters of the generation labeled the "young men of Meiji" by Tokutomi Sohō, men born in the late 1860s and 1870s, with roots in lower samurai, landlord, or wealthy farming families, who had moved upward through education and achievement. These men were of the new upper middle and professional classes—career officials in the central bureaucracy or members of such government institutions as the imperial universities and the military.[18] (The school, appropriately, was located in a neighborhood of government offices, official residences, and foreign legations.) Aware of the economic and social mobility to be gained from a higher education, these men were willing to invest in a better-than-average schooling for their daughters, not because they expected these girls to advance to brilliant careers of their own, but so that they might acquire a well-educated husband and thereby achieve a higher status through marriage. Eager to consolidate their status, they approved of a cultivating education for their daughters that was both appropriate for their daughters' sex and distinctive of their families' rank. Umeko's connection to the Peeresses' School, moreover, added cachet to her school, drawing these daughters of upper-middle-class families anxious to distinguish themselves from the middling ranks of the middle class. "They come of good families," Umeko said of her students in a letter to Adeline Lanman in April 1906, "and I feel very proud of them."

The school also attracted applicants eager for knowledge beyond that offered in the government schools and dissatisfied with the traditional Confucian model of womanhood emphasized in most upper schools, both private and public. The Joshi Eigaku Juku drew students from all over Japan. By bringing them together in the intimate world of the small school and crowded dormitories, it offered a mix of various backgrounds, dialects, and local customs that broke down provincial concerns and suggested a world of possibilities beyond the traditional boundaries imposed on these daughters. It provided a meeting ground for intelligent, ambitious, and dissatisfied young women who had come seeking growth and experience and found that there were others like themselves. Mishima (Seo) Sumie, was a typical student. The daughter of a professor father and a mother who came from a wealthy Okayama manufacturing family, Mishima saw a higher education as "the key to my liberation and all my future happiness."[19] A number of the Juku's students thus arrived at the school with an incipient rebelliousness.

The most famous of Umeko's students are those who joined a group of young women who called themselves the Seitōsha, or Bluestocking Society, after the literary circle formed by a group of intellectual Englishwomen more than a hundred years earlier. Taking the educational philosophy of Umeko and her peers to heart, these students challenged the authority of their families, their society, and—to Umeko's great displeasure—their teachers.

The founder of the group, Hiratsuka Raichō, had briefly studied English at the Joshi Eigaku Juku in 1906 after graduating from Japan Women's College. While a student at Naruse's school, she soon became disheartened by the school's emphasis on womanly virtues and Naruse's conservative views on female education (a dislike later reciprocated by the school when it erased her name from its records because of her notoriety). After her graduation in 1906, she began an informal postgraduate course of study, attending various schools and joining literary and reading circles.[20] In 1911, with money earmarked for her wedding expenses, Raichō brought out the first issue of the group's literary journal, *Seitō* (Bluestocking), which offered the following manifesto:

> Our group has as its objective the birth of a feminine literature. We are animated by an ardent sincerity and our ambition is to express and produce feminine genius; we will succeed through

a concentration of spirit. That genius, which is of mysterious essence, is an important part of universal genius, which has no sex!

When Japan was born, woman was the sun, the true human being. Now she is the moon! She lives in the light of another star. She is the moon, with a pale face like that of a sickly person.

This is the first cry of the Bluestockings! . . . We are the mind and the hand of the woman of new Japan. We expose ourselves to men's laughter, but know that which is hidden under that mockery. Let us reveal our hidden sun, our unrecognized genius! Let it come from behind the clouds! That is the cry of our faith, of our personality, of our instinct, which is the master of all the instincts. At that moment we will see the shining throne of our divinity.[21]

This self-conscious posturing shifted in the early years of the Taishō era to an awareness of the need for serious discussion of the problems facing women; but for the first two years of its existence, as the journal's circulation rose to three thousand and the group attracted members from other women's schools and literary circles—its membership reached between two and three hundred—the Seitōsha were wholly interested in the "modern" concerns of self-discovery, self-expression, and, most shocking, women's sexual experience. "We are eager to know the contents of life for ourselves," Raichō declared. That *Seitō* should begin as a purely literary journal was only logical, given that literature was one of the few areas available to women: Meiji society, with its emphasis on the utilitarian aspects of life required for efficient modernization, had relegated literature to the margins. Women had relatively free access to this form of self-expression—though their artistic reputation was often connected to their ties to literary men and their circles—and through it, inevitably, they overcame the isolation that characterized their lives. *Seitō* enabled a number of Japan's foremost women writers to publish their work in a conspicuous journal.[22]

Because of their emphasis on self-fulfillment, the Seitōsha appeared to Umeko and others as selfish, willful, even dangerous. Yet in many ways the members were a logical outcome of nineteenth-century feminism. Having received the decent higher education championed by Umeko and others of her generation, they desired to go beyond the traditional nurturing roles of wife, mother, and teacher by widening the boundaries of the feminine sphere. They scorned the main goals of the nineteenth-century women's movement, which had accepted the existing social order by trying to create a meaningful space for women within their society. Severing past connections to respectability and sexual purity, these twentieth-century women spurned traditional notions of femininity and woman's sphere. The Japanese press first called them New Women, a characterization popularized by contemporary American and English college-educated and career-minded women, and a cosmopolitan name the Seitōsha happily accepted. Self-expression, not self-sacrifice, was the New Woman's goal. As a founder of Heterodoxy, a contemporary New York feminist group with similar goals, put it: "We intend simply to be ourselves, not just our little female selves."[23]

By 1913 the literary exploration of self gave way to overtly political writing. *Seitō* began publishing translations and original articles devoted to such topics as marriages contracted on the basis of mutuality, women's paid work, vocational and higher education that would lead to women's financial independence, prostitution, and the exploitation of women under the capitalist system. The scope of these problems—issues that went beyond the Meiji generation's concern for the good of the nation—also indicated that the Seitōsha considered themselves part of a global women's movement. In the April 1913 issue Raichō published her famous article "Yo no Fujintachi ni" (To the women of the world). Arguing that women should be given the opportunity to discover and develop an identity outside the family through adequate higher education, a line of thought rooted in the arguments made by Umeko and others for women's education, Raichō developed these ideas into a criticism of the family system and an awareness that the traditional ideal of submissive womanhood was based not on women's nature but on the necessity of women's subordination to the family in Japanese society:

> We are now doubtful of women's conventional way of life from the roots up. We can no longer stand to continue that sort of life. "Should women marry?" This question itself is the one which we ought to have already asked ourselves. We can believe no longer that women should sacrifice themselves throughout their lives on account of the need to preserve the species, or

> that reproducing offspring is woman's only work, or that marriage is the sole possible way by which women can maintain their lives, or that to be a wife and mother is all women's vocation. I suppose that, outside of marriage, women's way of life should have limitless possibilities arrived at individually, as should women's choice of vocations, outside of being a good wife and wise mother, be without limit. It would go without saying that each woman should have her own choice. We, therefore, require as high a cultural education as possible. We require high spiritual education for the meaningful lives of women as persons independent of men's lives. . . .
>
> No longer can modern women who have achieved more or less individual self-awareness be sure that so-called womanly virtues, for instance obedience, gentleness, chastity, perseverance, self-sacrifice and so on, which have long been compelled by men or society are welcome. We have thought them over, tracing back to their origins why these things have been required of women, and questioned why society has come to permit them as womanly virtues and why they have ultimately come to be believed as our essential nature. . . .
>
> Though we don't intend to cry out against marriage itself, we will never submit to the current idea of marriage and the present marriage system. Isn't marriage in the present society the relationship of obedience to power throughout women's lives? Aren't wives treated as if they were not yet of age or they were cripples? Don't they have proprietorship over their property nor any legal rights to their sons or daughters? Isn't adultery committed by wives punished, while that committed by husbands never punished? . . . We would never marry nor be wives to yield to such an unreasonable system. Once we have been awakened, we cannot possibly fall asleep. We are now living. We are awake. Our lives will not become a reality without exhaling something which is burning within us.

The Home Ministry, to the dismay of some in the group, declared this essay offensive to public morality and harmful of virtues, and even considered banning the entire issue. Two members of the Seitōsha, Nakano Hatsue and Yasumochi Yoshiko, were summoned to central police headquarters and warned that future issues of *Seitō* would be carefully studied for any items that could be deemed damaging to traditional morality and disruptive of social order.[24]

An analysis of the family system and its ties to the exploitative nature of capitalism was elaborated by another student at the Joshi Eigaku Juku, Yamakawa Kikue. Intellectual, scholarly, and committed to the socialist cause, Yamakawa after her graduation translated a number of key works that discussed "the woman problem" from a Marxist and socialist point of view, including August Bebel's *Die Frau und der Sozialismus*, the American socialist Philip Rappaport's *Looking Forward: A Treatise on the Status of Woman and the Origin and Growth of the Family and the State*, and writings of the Russian feminist and revolutionary Alexandra Kollantai. In the pages of *Seitō* she debated the issue of prostitution with the magazine's second editor, Itō Noe (an anarchist who published a partial translation of Emma Goldman's *Tragedy of Woman's Emancipation* in *Seitō*), both women concluding that philanthropic efforts were not enough: only a radical restructuring of society would eradicate prostitution. Women's groups had to commit themselves to bring about social revolution, Yamakawa argued in print and from the lecture platform, if they were to achieve real change in women's status.[25]

These radical views forced some members of Seitōsha to leave the society, thereby allowing the political stance of *Seitō* to drift further left. Authorities warned that indiscriminate reading was fostering "unhealthy thoughts" that poisoned the minds of Japanese youth, while conservative politicians, educators, and social commentators sounded the alarm about "frivolous and dangerous social thought" and "rampant individualism" among the young. In 1906 the Ministry of Education issued a morals directive stating that students were "neglecting completely their duty to society" because of decadence, licentious self-indulgence, and socialism. "Dangerous thoughts are infiltrating the world of education," it declared, "threatening to shake the very foundation of our school system." The sources of this unwholesome influence were "the recent publications that have increasingly tempted young men and women with dangerous opinions, world-weary attitudes, and depictions of the baser sides of life." Therefore, "those entrusted with the responsibility to educate must pay careful heed to stamping out extremist biases and damming the flow of social poison." Teachers were instructed to scrutinize their pupils' books and to promote what the ministry deemed wholesome reading—officials in Japan Women's College, for example, regularly checked students' mail for subversive literature—while the family-state ideology received even greater emphasis in new ethics textbooks.[26]

The dangerous thoughts generated by feminism were seen to be especially linked to the influence of the government's bogeys: Marxism, socialism, and anarchism. Before the Russian Revolution, which intensified official concern about student activism, authorities used the Red Flag Incident of 1908, in which a Tokyo demonstration of leftists waving red banners and chanting "anarchy" resulted in a street fight with the police, and the execution nearly three years later of twelve leftists charged with plotting to assassinate the emperor (the Great Treason Incident) as a means to wipe out the "contagious epidemic" of socialism. "The first essential in the eradication of socialism," wrote Yamagata Aritomo, president of the Privy Council, "is the diffusion of full and complete national education and the cultivation of moderate thought." Thus in April 1913, the month in which Raichō's "To the women of the world" appeared, the Ministry of Education demanded the regulation of publications critical of the official view of good wife and wise mother. The Home Ministry followed with instructions to its officials to consider the "extreme doctrines pertaining to the 'new woman'" as "dangerous thought" and issued a list of banned women's journals.[27]

Umeko, too, was alarmed by the radical politics advocated by the Seitōsha. She is said to have regarded the group as "agents of the devil," and Yamakawa recalled in her memoirs a prayer offered by another teacher when a Seitōsha member, Kamichika Ichiko, returned from a meeting: "Oh God, please save these poor girls from Satan." Although the society undoubtedly offended Umeko's conservative sensibility, it also gave her a more immediate cause for concern: higher education for women still had its vocal and well-placed critics, and the activities of radical students only seemed to prove the opposition's worst fears about educated daughters getting out of hand. Umeko warned her graduates in 1908: "A new generation of selfish women bent on self-improvement regardless of the rights of others would be taken to show that women are unworthy of the freedom and the new privileges of this generation."[28]

Umeko was especially worried that the Seitōsha would blacken the good reputation of the school she had spent years to establish.

Raichō had already achieved considerable notoriety for her part in a failed double suicide with the writer Morita Sōhei, and the Seitōsha soon attracted the hostile attention of the press. Sensational stories appeared in the Tokyo dailies: Raichō, according to one, had seduced a young boy and kept him for her amusement. Others hinted that some were man-hating lesbians or frustrated spinsters. "Such thinking bespeaks a deep despair and resentment toward the male sex," wrote one commentator, "feelings born out of failure to win husbands and settle down as young brides. As women of Imperial Japan, we would hope that you will not forget your patriotic love for your country even while weeding the fields or mending clothes at home." The newspaper *Kokumin Shimbun* ran a series of articles entitled "The So-Called 'New Woman'" after a group of Bluestockings visited the Yoshiwara, the licensed pleasure quarter, in the summer of 1912. "New Women Amuse Themselves at the Yoshiwara!" screamed one headline. So outraged was public opinion at this alleged depravity that crowds gathered at Raichō's house several nights in a row and threw stones. The press used every opportunity to vilify the Seitōsha as degenerate and dissipated and often ridiculed specific women leaders in cartoons that trivialized their ideas and criticisms.[29]

When in November 1916 Kamichika Ichiko stabbed the anarchist Ōsugi Sakae, who had rejected her for Itō Noe, the newspapers had a field day. Umeko, however, remained cool. "It has been a sad time at the Juku," she wrote a former student that month. "I am sure you too have been very sad about Miss Kamichika. There is nothing now we can do but pray for her, so it is too sad to write or talk about." Afraid that the incident would give her school a bad name, she asked this graduate to write something for the school magazine "so that people outside may know our good graduates and how they are and how they feel. If we [sic] can write anything good about the Juku now is the right time to do so. Even if it is a letter to me I shall be glad to print it and it will be a great comfort to many. I hope you will write something. You might take for your subject the dormitory life—or else what you gained at the Juku, or what Juku gives its pupils. Perhaps if you can speak a good word for us, it will be very good."[30] Thus it could be demonstrated, she hoped, that the school had a wholesome influence on its students and that *Seitō* and the Seitōsha were mere flashes in the pan.

Umeko nevertheless judged the Seitōsha's ideas a sufficiently serious threat to her authority to warrant a response. In April 1915, six months after *Seitō* ran translations of writings by Emma Goldman and Olive Schreiner, Umeko's short essay, "Japanese Women of the Present Day," appeared in the *Bryn Mawr Alumnae Quarterly*. Opening with a reference to a translation of Schreiner's *Woman and Labor*, the translated text of a speech by M. Carey Thomas on women's suffrage, and an oblique allusion to *Seitō* (apparently unworthy of a more specific regard), she presented these writings as recently published items that indicate that "the most radical thought of the West comes in and influences a certain portion of our people." Umeko went on to claim, however, that this interest in feminist thought—which she perceived as entirely foreign in origin—was insignificant: "There are no great women's movements, apparently nothing seems to change in the world of women, and there is little to report of new work for the past year." Women's activism, she suggested, was disruptive and even destructive, and thus not native to Japanese women: the "English suffragettes," for example, cause trouble, something unthinkable of "our mild, reserved, conservative little ladies."[31]

Significant change, however, was coming, Umeko argued. An inexorable progress, seemingly beyond human agency, was occurring in the everyday lives of women. The theaters were full of women, "many of them a party among themselves without men escorts," and women were now going to restaurants alone and ordering a meal "as if it were a matter of course. One can recall the time barely five years ago when it was unheard of for women to go to these same places alone." Such changes, she stressed, "come about unconsciously, without a question." The source of this progress she located, once again, in the women of the imperial family, the living embodiment of supreme authority. The planned enthronement ceremony of the new Taishō emperor in November, she noted in concluding her essay, would include the new empress, an unprecedented act that appeared to acknowledge woman's importance in her role as wife. "In regard to this matter, there has been no discussion, agitation or objection. The common sense of the nation and the ideas of the new era guide in such things, without a struggle on women's part."[32] With these closing words, the implications of Umeko's reasoning were obvious: women were to wait for meaningful change to be granted them from above, not agitate for it; freedom would come from obeying authority, not struggling against it.

In the early months of that year, nearly one year after Germany invaded Belgium near the beginning of World War I, Umeko demonstrated women's altruistic behavior, which ideally transcended politics, in the campaign she helped organize to raise funds for Belgian relief. Advertising in the Japanese- and English-language newspapers, she raised fifty thousand yen, a substantial undertaking for which she was honored by the Belgian government at war's end. This public campaign, grounded in female benevolence, allowed women to show their concern for military aggression while remaining outside politics.

Umeko's belief that women's activism and political involvement were inexpedient led her to explain that Japanese women were "not yet ready for suffrage" to Carrie Chapman Catt, the American president of the International Woman Suffrage Alliance, when Catt visited Japan in 1912 as part of a well-publicized official tour to investigate the condition of women in Asia.[33] Political rights, Umeko assumed, would be extended to Japanese women once they proved themselves worthy of the privilege. For the vote was indeed a privilege in her eyes, and she opposed women's suffrage in part because she could not accept the principle of universal equality that underlay arguments for universal suffrage. Not all women were equal, she believed, and certainly not all were equally qualified to vote. Like many antisuffragists in the West, Umeko wanted equity for women but not equality. It seemed to her premature and counterproductive for women to demand the vote.

These ideas also found expression in a speech Umeko gave in 1915 to the Japanese YWCA at the missionary resort town Karuizawa. Asked to speak on "The Woman Movement in Japan," Umeko used the opportunity to denounce the Seitōsha, giving the group pride of place at the end of her lengthy address: "They are not a healthy product. Their principles are not clearly defined or logical. Their knowledge & ability (beyond the power of a little clever writing) is limited, but their doctrines are lawless, & their teachings immoral. They advocate free love."

Like other conservative educators and officials of the Ministry of Education, she warned against the indiscriminate reading of "extreme literature which is fast pouring into our country, tainting the minds of not only the men, but of our innocent women"—the plays of Ibsen (*Seitō* had published an open letter to Nora, heroine of *A Doll's House*, in 1912), the novels of Tolstoy, and the works of the naturalist school—all described by Umeko as "the scum of European literature." According to Umeko, young women students, in a "reaction against the old fashioned stoic doctrines of Bushidō, or Kaibara's teachings for women," were eagerly devouring "the latest works of Ellen Key" (the Swedish feminist greatly admired by Hiratsuka Raichō, who published her partial translations of Key's works in *Seitō*).

Umeko ended this address with a conclusion similar to that of "Japanese Women of the Present Day." Significant change in the status of women would not be achieved through the radical ideas of such groups as the Seitōsha. True progress, she argued, was instead being achieved in unnoticed ways in the home: "The real work is now being done in quiet ways, which are after all our Oriental ways. For if Woman's Suffrage ever does come . . . it will probably come without procession or banners, without rallies & militants, for such is not the spirit of our Japanese women." The process may seem slow, "but each day brings progress." The women of Japan, Umeko ended, "above all, work in quiet places, in quiet ways, but nonetheless they attain their ends."

Umeko's attitude to the Seitōsha, however, was considerably more ambivalent than she cared to show. Even though she consistently presented deference to authority as the proper behavior of young women, she nevertheless grudgingly admired the Seitōsha's unorthodox spirit. She had always been impatient with the docile character instilled in most Japanese girls, as shown in her frustrations with the students of the Peeresses' School, and she openly criticized the traditional ideal in a speech of 1913: "Japanese women under the old ethical codes have led, many of them, pure, noble, unselfish lives of devotion; but their virtues were passive, they lack breath, fire, life."[34] Umeko was thus able to identify with their spirit of unrest. And so, despite her displeasure with the Seitōsha, she was sympathetic to their feelings of discontent. She, too, had once been ambitious and rebellious, dissatisfied with her life and disapproving of Japanese society, and likewise convinced of women's power to be a transforming force in their world. As she reminded her readers in her essay of 1915, "Japanese Women of the Present Day," she, too, was "known as progressive." Umeko understood, moreover, that the taste for radical literature she so deplored was rooted in a general disaffection brought about by the decline in opportunities for educated youth and in an increase in the political awareness of students.

The repressive nature of Japanese society, she saw, only exacerbated their rebellious spirit: "The most serious indication of the times is a spirit of unrest and rebellion against restraints and authority which has grown up in certain quarters," she observed in her speech before the YWCA.

> It is not definite or organized enough to be called a movement. There are one or two groups of women under a leader, but they have no very defined platform as a rule. The spirit of discontent against existing conditions is the main point. It is not always shown openly. It spreads in hidden places & so is the more dangerous. We find it among men students as well as women and [it] points out the danger of the age for it is the rebellion against undue restraint. In its worst form it is not a reasonable sane rebellion against unjust oppression, but against all authority & law. Among women, it is seen in an extreme degree in a band of women who called [sic] themselves *Seito* "Blue Stockings" & also "new women."

The Seitōsha were in many ways Umeko's intellectual heirs. They had taken to heart her emphasis on material and spiritual independence. Independent thinking, a firm belief in women's ability to work for the well-being of society, and a determined commitment to bettering women's lot were ideals they shared with their teacher. Like Umeko, they were fired by an evangelist impulse for social reform. Similarly, the Western feminists most popular with the early twentieth-century Japanese feminists were those women whose central concern was motherhood, the great unifying theme of the nineteenth-century women's movement. Ellen Key celebrated women's eroticism and presented motherhood as the greatest expression of female sexuality, while Margaret Sanger, who found a champion in her friend and fellow birth-control advocate Katō (Ishimoto) Shizue, incorporated Key's ideas into her own vision of the supreme value of motherhood. Raichō's definition of the New Woman, despite its self-regard and heroic pretensions, embodies values very similar to those Umeko had developed:

> The new woman; I am a new woman.
>
> I seek, I strive each day to be that truly new woman I want to be. . . .

The new woman is not satisfied with the life of the kind of woman who is made ignorant, made a slave, made a piece of meat by male selfishness.

The new woman seeks to destroy the old morality and laws created for male advantage. . . .

The new woman does not merely destroy the old morality and laws constructed out of male selfishness, but day by day attempts to create a new kingdom, where a new religion, a new morality, and new laws are carried out, based on the spiritual values and surpassing brilliance of the sun.

Truly, the creation of this new kingdom is the mission of women. . . .

The new woman is not simply covetous of power for its own sake. She seeks power to complete her mission, to be able to endure the exertion and agony of learning about and cultivating issues not unknown to her. . . .

The new woman today seeks neither beauty nor virtue. She is simply crying out for strength, the strength to create this still unknown kingdom, the strength to fulfill her own hallowed mission.[35]

Of all the students of the Joshi Eigaku Juku, members of the Seitōsha, whose radical ideas and sometimes outrageous actions Umeko feared would reverse the few advances already achieved by women, continued in their careers to make the greatest gains for Japanese women. Many were prolific producers of speeches, writings, and translations that championed women's issues. With Ichikawa Fusae and Oku Mumeo, Hiratsuka Raichō founded the New Women's Association (Shin Fujin Kyōkai) in 1920 and campaigned for women's suffrage and revision of Article 5 of the Police Security Regulations of 1890, which prohibited women's participation in politics. In 1932 she became involved with the Women's Birth Control League of Japan, whose president was Katō Shizue. Yamakawa Kikue established the Red Wave Society (Sekirankai), the first socialist women's organization, with Itō Noe and Kondō Magara in 1921. She later became the first director of the Women's and Minors' Bureau in the reorganized Ministry of Labor in 1947. Kamichika Ichiko also campaigned for women's suffrage. After World War II, she was elected to the national Diet, where, in the face of criticism and ridicule, she presented an antiprostitution bill in 1955 and saw it enacted the next year.[36]

Umeko's struggles with certain of her students and other anxieties connected with running her school contributed to a permanent breakdown in her health. For many years she had suffered from asthma and respiratory problems, and the stress from worry and overwork culminated in heart disease. The insecure finances of the school, despite its steady expansion, forced Umeko to continue teaching at other schools and to tutor students privately. A shortage of teachers at the Joshi Eigaku Juku plus her desire to remain connected to the classroom meant that Umeko taught many hours while also seeing to the full-time duties of the school's administration. Along with the many textbooks and readers she regularly compiled for students of English, she also made time to help edit two magazines devoted to the study of English, in the hopes, as she put it in June 1903, "that there may be millions in it, and that our school may be built up with the funds of it." This heavy workload and the voluminous correspondence she maintained—Umeko once estimated that she received 150 letters in the space of six weeks—left her no respite. Even when she was sent to the United States specifically for a leisurely vacation away from the worries of her school, she soon resumed the busy fund-raising schedule of previous visits, lecturing in major cities in the East while squeezing in visits to friends.

Money was always her greatest worry. Unlike the two other major private women's schools in the capital, Tokyo Women's College and Japan Women's College, Umeko's school had no institutional support. Tokyo Women's College, founded in 1918 as one of seven Union Christian Colleges in Asia in an interdenominational effort of six Protestant churches, could rely on church funding and mission support. Similarly, Japan Women's College could look to a powerful network of support within Japan: Naruse Jinzō used his connections to solicit substantial sums from such prominent friends as Itō Hirobumi (prime minister when the school was established in 1901), Saionji Kinmochi, and Ōkuma Shigenobu, as well as the Mitsui and Sumitomo enterprises. Though private, Japan Women's College nevertheless received official support. Umeko was hampered primarily by the fact that her school was a female establishment. Private schools and colleges for men seldom experienced the financial worries and fund-raising humiliations Umeko endured. Many statesmen who warmly encouraged her aspirations—Itō Hirobumi, for example—failed to make their enthusiasm reality with their money, while the imperial court, which also claimed a great interest in women's education, was also unforthcoming with needed funds. Umeko may have received audiences with the empress and the occasional imperial gift, but her school never received the generous imperial grants given to the leading private men's universities: Keiō received fifty thousand yen in 1900, Waseda thirty thousand yen in 1908.[37]

The Joshi Eigaku Juku continued to look to the United States for most of its support, and the Philadelphia Committee regularly sent what money it could, but it was increasingly difficult to interest other Americans in Japanese women's education. Many now viewed Japan's modernization with fear, seeing it as part of the so-called yellow peril. Umeko experienced this prejudice during her visit to the United States in 1907, when she and her sister Yona were refused service in a California hotel diningroom until a friend from Bryn Mawr, who happened to be present, vouched for them.[38] Not until the Great Kantō Earthquake of 1923, when individuals and organizations donated money and goods to rebuild a devastated Tokyo, did American interest in the school revive. The Joshi Eigaku Juku, which, like so many other wooden buildings in the capital, burnt to nothing, received substantial sums of money and needed supplies from friends and strangers alike, and the school was able to rebuild on its present site.

Umeko also received a blow from the Philadelphia Committee when she tried to make some money from the scholarship program by offering, in 1902, to prepare future recipients of the scholarship for a year at her school for a fee of five hundred dollars. The committee turned down the suggestion, preferring to have scholarship students attend a preparatory school in the United States. A few years later Umeko tried to co-opt the scholarship for her students with the request that the Japanese committee, which she chaired, be given the authority to "always choose a student for the scholarship from Miss Tsuda's school or at least . . . from among the friends of the committee in Japan." The Philadelphia women again refused, pointing out that such preferment went against the original spirit of the scholarship, which was created to give every girl in Japan an equal opportunity of competing for it. Stung by what she took to be a lack of confidence in her powers, Umeko resigned as chair of the Japan committee.[39]

Family worries contributed to Umeko's poor health. Charles Lanman's death in 1895 had left Adeline lonely and despondent, and she wrote Umeko many long and grieving letters. Distressed, Umeko answered with frequent assurances that Adeline was not alone and that she would return as often as possible to the United States. "And altho' I can not be at your side," she wrote Adeline on her return to Japan in July 1899, "still do not think of me as gone from you or lost, as long as we can write to each other, and think of each other, and feel for one another as much as I do." During her final visit to the United States, in 1913, she found Adeline Lanman in an alarming state. The Georgetown house, once her great pride, had become rundown, and Adeline herself, old and feeble, was now becoming senile. Convinced that she was penniless, Adeline was living in penury until Umeko broke open the locked door to her former bedroom and discovered bankbooks recording money deposited in Adeline's name. Before returning to Tokyo, Umeko saw that the house was repaired and Adeline was properly outfitted in new clothes. Quite naturally, Umeko was overwhelmed with anxiety at the situation. With Charles Lanman long dead and the rest of the Dodge family gone, she was the only person left in Adeline's life. "Oh, Mrs. Lanman," Umeko wrote her from Tokyo in June 1908, "how I long to see you and help you!" Umeko also felt constrained to assure Adeline in many letters that her American childhood had indeed been happy. "It is pleasant," she wrote her in 1910, "to recall old times, and I *do love* the old home and Georgetown. . . . I send you a kiss and a hug. How I wish I could see you sometime."

In Japan, Umeko found little consolation with her few friends and family. Her sister Yona provided companionship when Koto's family and financial worries—Koto's husband had been bankrupted in 1903—kept her at home. But, like Koto before her, Yona's marriage in 1909 took her from Umeko. Umeko's social circle, moreover, was small. Beyond Sutematsu and Shigeko, whom she seldom saw, she had few friends. Umeko was devoted to Anna Hartshorne, but their close relationship was threatened for her by Anna's friendship with Mary Nitobe, the American wife of Nitobe Inazō. The two often traveled together, leaving Umeko to spend many of her vacations alone, bitter, and jealous of Mary. In December 1910 she wrote a rancorous letter to Yona describing the Nitobes' new house: "I have not seen the building, but I hear it is very large and very fine—indeed almost a *goten* [palace]. It will cost a great deal to keep up, but she likes that sort of thing, and she has the money for it, and as she likes to spend in that way, no one can say a word. I do not like such display. It does not help Dr. Nitobe—I think it hinders him and his reputation, but still it is no doubt a pleasant luxury to live every day better than our peers and our daijin [cabinet ministers]. How poor we all in Japan must appear to Mrs. Nitobe." In the last years of Umeko's life Anna was her only friend, but Anna's busy schedule left Umeko largely alone. A diary Umeko kept during these years reads like a logbook in which she obsessively noted the times of Anna's comings and goings.

The cerebral hemorrhage that partially paralyzed Umeko's older sister Koto in 1910 also distressed Umeko greatly. The two sisters had been especially close—Koto had looked after Umeko when she first returned to Japan and had always understood her difficult life—and so Umeko blamed Koto's stroke on the constant demands of her husband and children. "She has grown like a child," she wrote Yona angrily.

> She does not worry, she never scolds, and can not ever get angry. Her mind does not seem able to make such efforts as these, but she is like a child, laughs, is pleased, and enjoys simple things. They bring her always *omiage* [small gifts] as to children and although she says she is weary of being ill, yet she is not altogether unhappy or sad. If only in all these years, she could have rested fully one month each year, as she rests now all the year, month after month, she would even now be a nice woman and strong, not to speak of the money used in such an illness. But no one spared her. It was Kaasan [Mother] this and Kaasan that. Each made his demands, and she herself got into the habit of nervous overwork. I think Mr. Ueno is getting his penalty fully now—poor man, it is very, very hard now, and he can appreciate as he never did what he has lost in my sister's health.[40]

Koto died in 1911 at age forty-nine. It seemed to Umeko that all those she loved were dead: her mother had died in 1909, one year after her father had died, and in 1914, just three months after Umeko returned to Japan from her final visit to the United States, Adeline

Lanman died. Alice Bacon died in 1918, and a year later Ōyama Sutematsu followed.

In 1917, when Umeko was fifty-two years old, she was admitted to a Tokyo hospital so ill that she was certain she was dying. "It is hard to think of life, of work, of friends," she wrote from her bed in St. Luke's. "Somehow everything has changed for me in these few weeks. I feel like one who has been doomed." The diagnosis was diabetes, a debilitating condition that led to two cerebral hemorrhages—one severe—two years later. Umeko was forced to lead the sheltered life of an invalid for the remaining ten years of her life, unable to use her right arm fully and thus capable of writing only with great difficulty and pain. The loss of her spirit soon followed the loss of her health. Umeko "put the whole of her force of will to not getting another stroke," Anna Hartshorne recalled, "to being on the watch every second, and training herself not to think or feel anything at all lest emotion bring it on. Maybe I'm wrong, maybe the apathy was part of the disease—and at least she did achieve a sort of content. She told me once 'It seems strange after the life I've had that I can be happy this way doing nothing, but I *am* happy.'" By 1920, according to Anna, Umeko "was entirely out of it." Housebound, she had little contact with the outside world, and isolated from her students, she appeared stern and unapproachable. She often referred to her students as her "family," but Mishima Sumie remembered seeing her only a few times and "was rather afraid of her, as most of the girls were."[41]

Umeko was now intellectually isolated from her students and out of touch with their sympathies. The Seitōsha, for example, were not the insignificant aberration she had portrayed them as. By 1920, according to Mishima, a spirit of rebellion had overtaken the Joshi Eigaku Juku as it had other Tokyo schools: by 1925 "social science study groups" of the left-wing student movement were established at Japan Women's College and Tokyo Women's College. It was "perhaps a great transition period in the history of Miss Tsuda's School," Mishima recalled, most marked by "a tendency on the part of the students to neglect the study of English books and run to wild speculations."

> In fact, we did not have enough command of English to read the language freely, and Miss Tsuda's intention was to have us

> study English and American classics by consulting dictionaries and get at the Christian spirit shown in them. But we were too confused in that speculative age to concentrate our minds entirely on the reading of Milton, the Brownings, Tennyson, Emerson, etc. Moreover, the upheaval of liberal and democratic thought of the time made the girls blindly rebellious against conventions and existing rules. When the teachers tried to lead the girls to a critical study of the social problems and political movements of the time, the girls got hot—there were some girls who were afraid of touching these subjects—and declared that all authority was tyranny, all capitalists were enemies of the labor class; that all human beings must be equal and there should be no such things as parents and teachers demanding respect and obedience from children and pupils.[42]

Although she was aware of the repressive nature of Japanese society, Umeko regarded it as beyond criticism, or certainly beyond women's criticism. She continued to stress social reform and philanthropic good works as the proper concerns of women, accepting the class and gender divisions that characterized these efforts. In her last discussion of modern Japanese women, "The Woman Movement in Japan," Umeko still pointed to the geisha, "this class of low albeit attractive women," as "the most important and difficult" problem facing women, more important even than licensed prostitution. By the end of the Taishō era in 1926 Umeko's feminism, developed during the last decades of the nineteenth century, failed to address contemporary issues: Umeko advocated "influence" rather than action, believing that women should wait for privileges rather than struggle for rights.[43]

Umeko's isolation in the last decade of her life has a parallel in Natsume Sōseki's observation in *Kokoro* that the spirit of the Meiji era had died with the Meiji emperor, leaving those born and raised in that age to live on as anachronisms. Born shortly before the end of the Tokugawa era, she had lived through two imperial reigns that witnessed some of the greatest social and political upheaval in Japanese history, the progressions and frustrations in her life often reflecting the twists and turns of Meiji and Taishō Japan. In the summer of 1929, in the fourth year of the Shōwa era, Umeko, aged sixty-four, died. The "real work now being done in quiet ways," the work that kept itself to the standards of the domestic ideal that she had celebrated as belonging to the true nature of Japanese women, was appropriated in the 1930s into state-sponsored women's organizations when the expanding empire in Asia, and later the war effort, required that all women over age twenty be mobilized to work for the nation.

After Umeko's death the school was renamed Tsuda Juku to honor her memory as an austere educator dedicated to the advancement of her countrywomen and the enlightenment of her nation—a reputation she maintains today—and with the other major women's schools in Japan, Tsuda Juku was granted university status after World War II. It continued to maintain a good reputation, training generations of well-qualified teachers and a number of scholars, sending selected graduates abroad for postgraduate study. In the postwar era some graduates ran in local and national elections, many successfully. Tsuda Umeko's stress on ladylike behavior and firm belief that women should remain outside politics, however, left a mixed legacy. When a former college president tried for a seat in the Diet, her self-effacing manner severely hindered her campaign: few voted for her because they did not recognize her name on the ballot.[44] The Japanese government, again concerned about its image overseas, appointed some graduates to official and semiofficial posts at international forums, where they were articulate spokesmen for the nation, often holding positions of high visibility but little power.

Ironically, Tsuda Umeko's school became a victim of its own success. Like other women's colleges in Japan, Tsuda Juku was forced again to struggle after coeducation and equal opportunity in education reforms were initiated during the American Occupation. Ambitious young women often chose to enter the former imperial and prestigious private men's universities in ever increasing numbers once these schools began to accept women students. Women were also entering the workforce in greater numbers, opting for jobs in a variety of fields other than traditional womanly vocations, although many occupations and upper-level positions remained closed to most women. Teaching lost much of the attraction it had held for the ambitious or intellectually curious. The gradual elevation of women's status within Japanese society—the goal of Tsuda Umeko and other advocates of women's education—meant that the position of institutions of higher learning for women remained precarious, albeit now for different reasons.

Chapter Six

Conclusion: In Quiet Places, in Quiet Ways

From her departure for America with the Iwakura mission in 1871, Umeko's life became a quest for security, status, and authority, reflecting the efforts of the newly formed nation of Japan to achieve equality with the West and power in the East. Sent to the United States by her father in an attempt to regain some of her family's lost rank and privilege, and by the government to help rectify the poor image of Japan's treatment of women, Umeko was groomed at government expense for what she assumed would be a position of leadership within the Meiji establishment, a role that she believed would be similar to the influential posts attained by the male students dispatched abroad to study for their nation. Yet the very factor that first made such a prospect possible—her sex—made that same future seemingly impossible: sent abroad to absorb, as a female, what could benefit Japanese women, she was denied any official distinction on her return to Japan because she was female. Umeko was forced to create a role for herself by polishing her image as an authority on the education, both formal and informal, needed by modern middle-class Japanese women.

She assumed this authoritative voice by appealing to notions of true womanhood, a domestic ideal that dovetailed with ryōsai kemboshugi, the ideal of good wife and wise mother first articulated by early Meiji intellectuals and later adopted by the government. As defined by Nakamura Masanao and others, the concept began as an important advance for women by granting some power to the mother and raising the status of the wife. The official definition of ryōsai kembo, however, grew increasingly restrictive as the government presented it as the only proper role for women. By granting women some security and limited authority within the family, moreover, the government-sanctioned ryōsai kembo version of domesticity united Meiji interests with those of the family. It thus became increasingly difficult for women to criticize the family system and, by extension, the family-state, as well as the moral code that confined them to restricted roles.

Umeko was forced to maneuver within the narrow confines of the official ideal of womanhood. Though willing to argue woman's worth, she cautiously avoided following this line of reasoning to its logical conclusion: woman's autonomy. Women should be made capable of independence and self-sufficiency, she believed, but only in relation to the domestic sphere, the source of their importance. By thus avoiding controversy and respecting the general orthodox ideas about women's role, Umeko was able to offer a quality higher education to the daughters of the middle and upper middle classes.

In trying to maintain a balance between the aspirations of some of her students and the expectations of their society, Umeko encouraged in them a sense of achievement and worth but was careful not to discourage the claims of the traditional female sphere. Teaching therefore seemed an acceptable occupation for her graduates: it gave them paid employment while staying within the bounds of womanly behavior. But teaching, ironically, enabled some to move beyond the feminine role of nurture and service celebrated in the domestic ideal. The first profession to which women were allowed access in great numbers, teaching attracted ambitious young women who used it to advance beyond the domestic realm: many later leaders of the women's movement began as teachers, while others went on to establish their own schools.

Umeko's own life showed that the conventional role of wife and mother was not the only future available; certainly the education she offered suggested other possibilities for women. Once encouraged to serious study and independent thought, some of her students turned to books outside those sanctioned by the authorities and participated in discussions of contemporary social and political issues. From Umeko's school came a number of independent and enterprising women who, like Umeko, were filled with a moral certitude in their cause. She may have deplored the methods of many twentieth-century feminists, but they were the logical outcome of the ideas she had promoted.

For twentieth-century feminism had its roots in nineteenth-century notions of domesticity. Women's progress, Umeko and others of her generation believed, did not conflict with the domestic sphere. By proclaiming the central importance of the home and the family, and by characterizing women's work in the home as a vocation, these spokeswomen attempted to raise women's status. The proponents of the domestic ideal hoped to enhance women's self-respect and thereby gain for them a measure of independence; hence they argued for better education for women and a greater scope for their contributions to society.

What seemed to be widening opportunities, however, proved to be constricting bonds. Although Umeko worked to increase women's educational opportunities and prove their capabilities in the professional world, she nevertheless bound women to a single sphere of action even as she aimed to broaden their futures. Nor did she intend these expanded opportunities for all women. Rather than challenge the existing social order, she sought to enlarge middle-class women's influence within it, mistaking influence for real power and privilege for real change. These limitations were not peculiar to Umeko: inherent in the contradictions of the domestic ideal itself, they appeared in the life and work of other proponents of domesticity in Japan and the West.

But to conclude by criticizing Tsuda Umeko for not being radical enough misrepresents her social and political situation. Only by maintaining the standards of the domestic ideal while resisting the more state-centered elements of ryōsai kemboshugi could gains be made. Women's higher education could be attempted only if the hierarchies of family and society remained unthreatened.

The centripetal pull of the official ryōsai kembo ideal finally, however, could be resisted no longer. Confined to the increasingly narrow bounds of the family, Japanese women were at last wholly absorbed by the family-state. The work done "in quiet places, in quiet ways" proved ineffective, even insubstantial, as all women of all classes were mobilized in the 1930s to work for the state under the aegis of government-administered mass organizations. These women's groups, begun in 1931 by the Ministry of Education and followed the next year by the army and navy, which amalgamated the Japan Women's Patriotic Association with other state-sponsored organizations, were not the interest groups of former years. They became the civilian wing of a mass conscript army when, in 1942, they were united into the Great Japan Women's Association (Dai Nihon Fujinkai).[1]

Nor did political rights come as a consequence of gradual peaceful change: constitutional and civil rights for women, not to mention educational equality, were granted by the occupying army of a foreign power only after the destruction of World War II. Significantly, General Douglas MacArthur justified his enfranchisement of Japanese women with appeals to the domestic ideal. Giving them the vote, he reasoned, would "bring to Japanese politics the spiritual influence of the Japanese home." Their "great and good influence is being progressively felt," he believed, and "is a continuing challenge to the men of Japan to reach an ever higher order of responsible statesmanship in service to the nation." The worth of Japanese women was once again seen in their role as the mothers of future men. "Practical experience in civic affairs and in the stewardship of their newly won civil rights," MacArthur said, "will materially broaden the field of home training, with its reflection to be found in the character, the wisdom and the vision of Japan's future leaders."[2]

Notes

Preface

1. Adrienne Rich, "Resisting Amnesia: History and Personal Life," in Rich, *Blood, Bread and Poetry* (London: Virago, 1986), p. 150.
2. Florence Howe, "Women's Studies and Social Change," in Howe, *Myths of Coeducation* (Bloomington: Indiana University Press, 1984), pp. 81–82.

Chapter 1: Introduction

1. The information presented here is taken from Joyce Ackroyd, "Women in Feudal Japan," *Transactions of the Asiatic Society of Japan* 7, no. 3 (November 1959): 31–68; W. G. Beasley, *The Modern History of Japan*, 3d rev. ed. (Rutland, Vt.: Charles E. Tuttle, 1985), pp. 38–97; Marius B. Jansen's introduction to *The Cambridge History of Japan: The Nineteenth Century*, vol. 5 (Cambridge: Cambridge University Press, 1989), pp. 1–49; and Richard Storry, *A History of Modern Japan* (Harmondsworth: Penguin, 1960), pp. 70–93.
2. The ages of the five have been given variously as seven to fifteen and eight to sixteen because of confusion due to the traditional

method of calculating a person's age. According to the old system, a baby was already a year old on its day of birth. Thereafter, years were added at each New Year rather than with each passing birthday. In this system Tsuda Ume's age is particularly puzzling: born on 31 December 1864, she was already two years old within twenty-four hours.

3. Hannah More is cited in Nancy Cott, *The Bonds of Womanhood: "Woman's Sphere" in New England, 1780–1835* (New Haven and London: Yale University Press, 1977), p. 74. *The Bonds of Womanhood* carefully dissects the contradictions of American notions of domesticity at the turn of the nineteenth century. This work and Cott's more recent *The Grounding of Modern Feminism* (New Haven and London: Yale University Press, 1987) are among the most important sources for my discussion. Other valuable studies of the Western cult of domesticity are Jeanne Boydston, Mary Kelley, and Anne Margolis, *The Limits of Sisterhood: The Beecher Sisters on Women's Rights and Woman's Sphere* (Chapel Hill: University of North Carolina Press, 1988); Joan N. Burstyn, *Victorian Education and the Ideal of Womanhood* (New Brunswick, N.J.: Rutgers University Press, 1984); Sara M. Evans, *Born for Liberty: A History of Women in America* (New York: Free Press, 1989); Mary Beth Norton, *Liberty's Daughters: The Revolutionary Experience of American Women, 1750–1800* (Boston: Little, Brown, 1980); Mary Poovey, *Uneven Developments: The Ideological Work of Gender in Mid-Victorian England* (London: Virago, 1989); and Kathryn Kish Sklar, *Catharine Beecher: A Study in American Domesticity* (New Haven and London: Yale University Press, 1973). Joan B. Landes's *Women and the Public Sphere in the Age of the French Revolution* (Ithaca: Cornell University Press, 1988), and Joan Wallach Scott's "Gender: A Useful Category of Historical Analysis," in Scott, *Gender and the Politics of History* (New York: Columbia University Press, 1988), pp. 28–50, also helped to clarify some of my ideas.

Chapter 2: To Study for the Good of Our Countrywomen

1. Charles Lanman, *Leaders of the Meiji Restoration in America* (Tokyo: Hokuseidō, 1931), p. 42. Lanman's book was originally published in New York and London in 1872 (in time for the Iwakura mission's arrival in England) under the title *The Japanese in America*. The contemporary American traveler to Japan, Maturin Murray Ballou, is cited in John Ashmead, *The Idea of Japan: 1853–1895* (New York: Garland, 1987), p. 431.
2. Marlene Mayo, "Rationality in the Meiji Restoration: The Iwakura

Embassy," in *Modern Japanese Leadership: Transition and Change*, ed. Bernard S. Silberman and H. D. Harootunian (Tucson: University of Arizona Press, 1966), pp. 348–49; Sharon L. Sievers, *Flowers in Salt: The Beginnings of Feminist Consciousness in Modern Japan* (Stanford: Stanford University Press, 1983), p. 13.

3. Lanman, *Leaders of the Meiji Restoration*, pp. 43–44.
4. *New York Times*, 20 May 1872; Adeline Lanman (hereafter AL) to Tsuda Ume (hereafter TU), 30 March 1889.
5. Cited in Ivan Parker Hall, *Mori Arinori* (Cambridge, Mass.: Harvard University Press, 1973), p. 185. Nineteenth-century Western racial theories (Social Darwinism) and eugenics were well known in Meiji Japan. Thirty-two translations of Herbert Spencer's works, for example, appeared between 1877 and 1900, and his theories of progress and civilization incorporating the evolutionary model were widely read. See Michio Nagai, "Herbert Spencer in Early Meiji Japan," *Far Eastern Quarterly* 14 (November 1954): 55–64.

The "woman question" also received the attention of Spencer and others. Evolutionary theory held that complexity, differentiation, and specialization of parts within organisms increased as one moved up the evolutionary scale. A civilized society also reflected this process in the heightened differences between the sexes and the specialization of their separate physical and social functions. Just as Victorian society was the zenith of civilization, they argued, so, too, were Victorian ideals of femininity the biological result of evolutionary progress. The white, Protestant, "Anglo-Saxon race" was the most advanced of all and achieved its apogee in its men. Any change in this "natural" development would therefore upset the precarious level of evolution, resulting in social decline and, ultimately, race suicide. See Lorna Duffin, "Prisoners of Progress: Women and Evolution," in *The Nineteenth-Century Woman: Her Cultural and Physical World*, ed. Sara Delamont and Lorna Duffin (London: Croom Helm; New York: Barnes and Noble, 1978), pp. 57–91, and Cynthia Eagle Russett, *Sexual Science: The Victorian Construction of Womanhood* (Cambridge, Mass.: Harvard University Press, 1989).

Such arguments were also used in Meiji Japan to justify the rigid control of both the state and the patriarchal family system. "We may conclude," wrote one Japanese scholar in 1883, "that it is our family system which maintains a balance and security in relationship between individuals and the Japanese society as a whole. . . . To mention but a few examples, there are many customs which are not written into our legal codes but are fundamental in the maintenance of social order. They are the establishment of branch families for sons other than the eldest, the system of subordination of branch families to the main family, the system of adoption for the succession of family headship, the system of succession of family headship, the system of the succession of ancestral occupation, and that of the observance of ancestral instructions. When we observe these facts, it becomes clear to us that the national characteristics of Japan can only be determined by her kinship systems" (cited in Nagai, "Herbert Spencer in Early Meiji Japan," pp. 62–63).

6. The imperial message is cited in Michio Nagai, "Westernization and Japanization: The Early Meiji Transformation of Education," in *Tradition and Modernization in Japanese Culture*, ed. Donald H. Shively (Princeton, N.J.: Princeton University Press, 1971), p. 47. Murray's report is reproduced in Herbert Passin, *Society and Education in Japan* (Tokyo: Kodansha, 1982), pp. 222–223.
7. Lanman, *Leaders of the Meiji Restoration*, p. 43.
8. Sievers (*Flowers in Salt*, p. 56) observes that the Meiji government viewed single young women as a "natural resource" to be exploited in the new industries, especially the spinning mills. This natural resource, however, was not merely an unlimited supply of cheap female labor: the government saw women's biological function of motherhood as another resource that could be used to the advantage of the state. The Hokkaido Colonization Board's recruitment, in fact, resembles the recruitment for the Tomioka spinning mill, another government-sponsored experiment in educating loyal samurai daughters in feminine skills with the view to their future employment as teachers of other females. See Thomas C. Smith, *Political Change and Industrial Development in Japan: Government Enterprise, 1868–1880* (Stanford: Stanford University Press, 1955), pp. 59–60.
9. The names of the five girls, like their ages, can be confusing. Along with a family name or names that could change because of adoption or promotion in rank, someone could also have several personal names: *yōshō* (childhood name), *gō* (literary name), *tsūshō* (common name), and *azana* (nickname). Ueda Teiko, for example, is also known as Ueda Sadako. I have used her childhood name, Teiko (or Tei), because Tsuda Ume refers to her that way. Similarly, Tsuda uses her own childhood name, Mume, when she writes of herself in her early compositions. She also does not use the "-ko" ending in such personal names as Ryōko and Shigeko.
10. Cited in James T. Conte, *Overseas Study in the Meiji Period: Japanese Students in America, 1867–1902* (Ph.D. diss., Princeton University, 1977), p. 45.

11. Except where noted otherwise, the information presented here about Yamakawa Sutematsu, Nagai Shigeko, and Tsuda Ume is taken from the two Japanese biographies of Tsuda Ume: Yoshikawa Riichi, *Tsuda Umeko den* (Tokyo: Tsuda Juku Dōsokai, 1931, reprint ed., 1956), and Yamazaki Takako, *Tsuda Umeko* (Tokyo: Yoshikawa Kobunkan, 1972); and from the biography of Tsuda Sen: Miyakoda Toyosaburō, *Tsuda Sen: Meiji no kirisutosha* (Tokyo: Nihon Kirisuto Kyōdan Kudan Kyōkai, 1972).
12. Sutematsu's older sister later taught at the Tokyo Women's Normal School, and the second eldest studied in Russia; her two brothers completed the customary samurai program of study within the domain school and then continued their education through the process known as *yūgaku*, schooling in various academies outside their domain. Like his brother Kenjirō, Yamakawa Hiroshi became head of an important school of higher learning, as director of the Higher Normal School in Tokyo. See the biography of Sutematsu by Kuno Akiko, *Rokumeikan no kifujin: Nihonhatsu no joshi ryūgakusei* (Tokyo: Chūō Kōron, 1988).
13. John G. Roberts, *Mitsui: Three Centuries of Japanese Business* (New York: Weatherhill, 1973), pp. 108–9. The quotation is from Oland D. Russell, *The House of Mitsui* (Westport, Conn.: Greenwood, 1970), p. 210.
14. Donald H. Shively, "Nishimura Shigeki: A Confucian View of Modernization," in *Changing Japanese Attitudes toward Modernization*, ed. Marius B. Jansen (Princeton, N.J.: Princeton University Press, 1965), p. 202; Kazutami Ukita, "Educationalists of the Past and Their Share in the Modernization of Japan," in *Fifty Years of New Japan*, comp. Shigenobu Ōkuma (London: Smith, Elder, 1910), pp. 145–46; Richard Rubinger, *Private Academies of Tokugawa Japan* (Princeton, N.J.: Princeton University Press, 1982), p. 133.
15. R. P. Dore, "The Legacy of Tokugawa Education," in *Changing Japanese Attitudes toward Modernization*, ed. Jansen, p. 126.
16. Rubinger, *Private Academies of Tokugawa Japan*, p. 149.
17. Gilbert Rozman, "Castle Towns in Transition," in *Japan in Transition*, ed. Jansen and Rozman, pp. 334–35.
18. Sen returned to Japan with a copy of the recently published *Essentials of the Principles and Practice of Medicine* by Henry Hartshorne, father of Ume's close friend, Anna Hartshorne, and an advocate of women's right to study and practice medicine. The work was soon translated by Kuwata Kōhei and became an immediate success with medical students. Because of the text's continued popularity, Henry and Anna Hartshorne were invited to Japan in 1893 by a group of Tokyo doctors, and the two returned again in 1897 as lay

missionaries, allowing Anna to renew an acquaintance with Ume begun at Bryn Mawr College.

19. Julia Meech-Pekarik, *The World of the Meiji Print: Impressions of a New Civilization* (New York: Weatherhill, 1986), pp. 77, 80.
20. Henry Faulds, *Nine Years in Nipon: Sketches of Japanese Life and Manners* (London: Alexander Gardner, 1887), p. 64.
21. Reproduced in *Tsuda Umeko monjo / Writings of Umeko Tsuda*, ed. Furuki Yoshiko et al., rev. ed. (Kodaira: Tsuda Juku Daigaku, 1984), p. 47.
22. TU, "Japanese Women Emancipated," *Tsuda Umeko monjo*, pp. 78–79.
23. Marlene Mayo, "The Iwakura Mission to the United States and Europe, 1871–1873," Columbia University East Asian Institute, *Researches in the Social Sciences on Japan* 2, no. 6 (June 1959): 30; Mayo, "Rationality in the Meiji Restoration: The Iwakura Embassy," *Modern Japanese Leadership*, ed. Silberman and Harootunian, p. 356.
24. TU, "Japanese Women Emancipated," p. 79.
25. Kuno, *Rokumeikan no kifujin*, p. 62.
26. TU, "Japanese Women Emancipated," pp. 81–82; Mayo, "Iwakura Mission," p. 32.
27. *New York Times*, 20 May 1872.
28. TU, "Japanese Women Emancipated," pp. 80–83.
29. Katharine McCook Knox, *Surprise Personalities in Georgetown, D.C.* (Washington, D.C.: privately printed, 1958), pp. 17–19. Kuroda revealed his scant understanding of what their American education entailed when, shortly after their return to Tokyo in November 1882, Ume and Sutematsu called to pay their respects to the statesman who had arranged for their American stay: after listening to the singing of one of the attendant geisha, Kuroda asked Ume to sing an English song (she obliged with "In the Gloaming" and "Jesus Lover of My Soul"), suggesting that he assumed their years in America had been devoted to the acquisition of ornamental accomplishments.
30. Arthur Sherburne Hardy, *Life and Letters of Joseph Hardy Neesima* (Boston: Houghton Mifflin, 1891), p. 122; TU, "Japanese Women Emancipated," p. 83.
31. Knox, *Surprise Personalities*, pp. 5–9. On Tsuda Hatsuko, according to Anna Hartshorne, "repression had done its work thoroughly; all her thoughts, expressions, forces were tucked away inside. She was kindness itself; I don't believe anyone ever saw her out of temper. But I don't think I ever saw her smile."
32. *Georgetown Courier*, 15 February 1873, 27 June 1874.
33. Kozo Yamamura, "The Meiji Land Tax Reform and Its Effects," in

Japan in Transition, ed. Jansen and Rozman, p. 383; Richard J. Smethurst, *Agricultural Development and Tenancy Disputes in Japan, 1870–1940* (Princeton, N.J.: Princeton University Press, 1986), pp. 48–52.

34. William Reynolds Braisted, *Meiroku Zasshi: Journal of the Japanese Enlightenment* (Tokyo: University of Tokyo Press, 1976), pp. xix–xx.
35. Braisted, *Meiroku Zasshi*, pp. xli–xliii.
36. Irwin Scheiner, *Christian Converts and Social Protest in Meiji Japan* (Berkeley: University of California Press, 1970), p. 22; John F. Howes, "Japanese Christians and American Missionaries," in *Changing Japanese Attitudes toward Modernization*, ed. Jansen, pp. 346–47. Uemura is cited in Irwin Scheiner, "Christian Samurai and Samurai Values," in *Modern Japanese Leadership*, ed. Silberman and Harootunian, p. 180.
37. Cited in Clara Whitney, *Clara's Diary: An American Girl in Meiji Japan*, ed. M. William Steele and Tamiko Ichimata (Tokyo: Kodansha, 1981), p. 280.
38. Cited in Masao Miyoshi, *As We Saw Them: The First Japanese Embassy to the United States* (1860) (Berkeley: University of California Press, 1979), pp. 65–66.
39. *The Autobiography of Fukuzawa Yukichi*, trans. Eiichi Kiyooka (Tokyo: Hokuseidō, 1981), p. 115. The examples from the American press are cited in Miyoshi, *As We Saw Them*, p. 67. The Iwakura mission was also favorably compared to the Chinese in both the American and the British press (Mayo, "Iwakura Mission," p. 41).
40. Lanman, *Leaders of the Meiji Restoration*, pp. 48, 52, 58. The form of racism that sees an entire group in terms of stereotypes was also present in the Lanman household. In 1892 when Annie, the Lanmans' cook, wanted to contribute to the scholarship fund for Japanese women Ume was organizing, Adeline Lanman warned: "As to the fund Annie may get for you, I fear it will not be much, as darkies are poor pay, & all are on the make, so you need not be disappointed in the amount" (AL to TU, 2 August 1892). Many years later, after one of Ume's employees stole two hundred yen, Adeline Lanman assumed that the thief must have been black but was puzzled because, as she wrote, "you have few negroes in Japan" (AL to TU, 7 December 1903).
41. Lanman, *Leaders of the Meiji Restoration*, p. 45.
42. Catharine Beecher, *A Treatise on Domestic Economy* (1841; reprint ed., New York: Schocken Books, 1977), p. 13.
43. Crocker and Lyon are cited in Evans, *Born for Liberty*, pp. 67, 72.
44. Sklar, *Catharine Beecher*, pp. 176, 187–92; *Dictionary of American Biography*, 1:22–23. Abbott is cited in Adrienne Rich, *Of Woman Born: Motherhood as Experience and Institution* (London: Virago, 1977), p. 44.

45. Earl H. Kinmonth, *The Self-Made Man in Meiji Japanese Thought: From Samurai to Salary Man* (Berkeley: University of California Press, 1981), pp. 10–11.
46. Samuel Smiles, *Self-Help* (London: John Murray, 1908), pp. 3, 424.
47. Nakamura Masanao, "Creating Good Mothers," *Meiroku Zasshi* 33 (March 1875), from a speech given on 16 March 1875 and reproduced in Braisted, *Meiroku Zasshi*, pp. 401–2. I do not mean to suggest that these ideas were imported to a Japan wholly devoid of similar indigenous views (nor, for that matter, that some monolithic feminism originated in the West and then spread throughout the world), thus espousing the assumption that Japanese feminism was born only when Western feminist works first reached the country's shores. Clearly, the impact of Nakamura's ideas suggests that they spoke to a native tradition.
48. Joyce Ackroyd, "Women in Feudal Japan," pp. 56–62; Sievers, *Flowers in Salt*, pp. 4–6. Kaibara is cited in Shidzue Ishimoto [Katō Shizue], *Facing Two Ways: The Story of My Life* (New York: Farrar and Rinehart, 1935; reprint ed., Stanford: Stanford University Press, 1984), p. 280.
49. Sievers, *Flowers in Salt*, pp. 15, 45.
50. Norton, *Liberty's Daughters*, pp. 156, 297.
51. Megan Baldridge Murray, "The Girl Thrown Away Forever: Memories of a Princess," *Vassar Quarterly* 79, no. 3 (Spring 1983): 10–14; Marian P. Whitney, "Stematz Yamakawa, Princess Oyama," *Vassar Quarterly* 4 (1918–19): 264–71.

Chapter 3: My Right, & My Place

1. Cited in Scheiner, *Christian Converts and Social Protest*, pp. 108, 115.
2. Cited in Whitney, *Clara's Diary*, p. 235.
3. Robert Lyons Danly, *In the Shade of Spring Leaves: The Life and Writings of Higuchi Ichiyō, a Woman of Letters in Meiji Japan* (New Haven and London: Yale University Press, 1981), p. 42. I thank Margaret Mitsutani for this reference.
4. Nor was this worldview limited to Japan. Victorian England, for example, often expressed its fascination with Japan by sentimentalizing it as an enchanted land of "wee folk." See Toshio Yokoyama, *Japan in the Victorian Mind: A Study of Stereotyped Images of a Nation, 1850–1880* (Basingstoke: Macmillan, 1987).
5. TU to AL, 14 December 1882, 23 November 1882, 7 December 1882.
6. TU to AL, 23 November 1882, 6 January 1883, 3 February 1883.

Ume nevertheless considered Japan the United States of Asia. "But I must & do remember that in no place in the world do women have the liberty & respect as in America," she wrote on 14 December 1882, "and our women are so much better treated than those of any other Asiatic nation, that one should not expect too much." Such people as Koreans she regarded as "worse than the savages of America in their ways" (TU to AL, 28 September 1883).

7. TU to AL, 9 June 1883, 12 August 1883, 7 December 1882, 16 March 1883, 19 March 1883, 3 September 1883. Holtham is cited in Bernard Cortazzi, *Victorians in Japan: In and around the Treaty Ports* (London: Athlone, 1987), p. 113.
8. TU to AL, 26 February 1883, 27 March 1883, 27 May 1883.
9. TU to AL, 7 December 1882, 23 May 1883, 5 November 1883, 19 September 1883. Ume's recollections are cited in Yoshikawa, *Tsuda Umeko den*, p. 149.
10. TU to AL, 23 December 1882, 31 March 1883, 12 August 1883.
11. TU to AL, 17 December 1882; Alice Mabel Bacon, *Japanese Girls and Women* (Boston: Houghton Mifflin, 1891), p. 197.
12. Ralph Wardlaw, one of the most popular nineteenth-century English writers on prostitution whose works were often cited as authoritative, said in his *Lectures on Female Prostitution: Its Nature, Extent, Effects, Guilt, Causes and Remedy* (1842): "The tendency is all downwards descent. . . . It is all down—down—down—rapidly down; down from stage to stage, till it terminates in some . . . scene of squalid wretchedness" (cited in Lynda Nead, *Myths of Sexuality: Representations of Women in Victorian Britain* [Oxford: Basil Blackwell, 1988], pp. 157–58).

    Ume's hostility toward geisha and concubines may have been motivated in part by personal reasons. In the years before she left for the United States she received dancing and singing lessons, suggesting that her father intended a future for her similar to her aunt Takeko's career as an attendant at Tokugawa Yoshiyori's residence, where she had two children by him.
13. Charlotte B. DeForest, *The Woman and the Leaven in Japan* (West Medford, Mass.: Central Committee on the United Study of Foreign Missions, 1923), pp. 191–92; Allen K. Faust, *The New Japanese Womanhood* (New York: George H. Doran, 1926), pp. 137–38.
14. TU to AL, 17 December 1882, 6 January 1883, 27 April 1883.
15. Margit Maria Nagy, *"How Shall We Live?": Social Change, the Family Institution, and Feminism in Prewar Japan* (Ph.D. diss., University of Washington, 1981), pp. 22–25. Kishida's speech is cited in Sievers, *Flowers in Salt*, pp. 40–41.

During the 1870s and 1880s numerous translations and original essays on woman's proper sphere were published. Katō (Ishimoto) Shizue (*Facing Two Ways*, p. 360) lists the following publications: Yumoto Kōkichi, *Women's Rights in the Western Countries* (1882); Fukama Naiki, *On Mill's Equality* (1884); Fukuzawa Yukichi, *On Japanese Women* (1885) and *On Social Intercourse of Man and Woman* (1886); Inoue Nao, *Japanese Women* (1886); Tatsumi Kojirō, *History of Women's Rights in the West and in Japan* (1887); Yoda Kō, *Monogamy* (1887); Nakayama Seiu, *Japanese Women of Tomorrow* (1888).

Also published in these years were translations of Herbert Spencer's writings on women, J. S. Mill's *Subjection of Women*, and some of Millicent Fawcett's speeches arguing women's right to political participation.

16. Sievers, *Flowers in Salt*, pp. 45–49. The Ministry of Education is cited in Shibukawa Hisako, "An Education for Making Good Wives and Wise Mothers (Ryosai Kenbo no Kyoiku)," *Education in Japan* 6 (1971), 51. The mission school is from DeForest, *Woman and Leaven in Japan*, p. 96.
17. Richard Rubinger, "Education: From One Room to One System," in *Japan in Transition*, ed. Jansen and Rozman, p. 223.
18. Cited in Donald H. Shively, "The Japanization of the Middle Meiji," in *Tradition and Modernization in Japanese Culture*, ed. Shively, pp. 102, 108; and Carol Gluck, *Japan's Modern Myths: Ideology in the Late Meiji Period* (Princeton, N.J.: Princeton University Press, 1985), p. 20.
19. Cited in Hall, *Mori Arinori*, p. 423.
20. Michio Nagai, "Westernization and Japanization: The Early Meiji Transformation of Education," in *Tradition and Modernization in Japanese Culture*, ed. Shively, p. 40n3. The *Kyōgaku Taishi* is reproduced in Passin, *Society and Education in Japan*, pp. 227–28.
21. Nagai, "Westernization and Japanization," in *Tradition and Education in Japan*, ed. Shively, pp. 41, 71.
22. Basil Hall Chamberlain, *Things Japanese* (London: John Murray, 1905), p. 504. Katō Shizue received a copy of the *Onna Daigaku* from her grandfather. "It was the epitome," she wrote, "of all I have had to struggle against—the moral code which has chained Japanese women to the past." The purpose of such texts, Katō noted, was "the perfection of the family system, [which] was the aim of every woman's education. For the tyranny of the family system, women had to be mentally killed—deprived of the strength with which to ward off the disgraces heaped upon them" (Ishimoto, *Facing Two Ways*, pp. 38, 281).
23. Ishimoto, *Facing Two Ways*, pp. 279–80.

24. Passin, *Society and Education in Japan*, pp. 97–98; Nagai, "Westernization and Japanization," pp. 55–56.
25. Cited in Gluck, *Japan's Modern Myths*, p. 168.
26. Burstyn, *Victorian Education and the Ideal of Womanhood*, pp. 85–89. Spencer and Clarke are cited in Russett, *Sexual Science*, pp. 120, 123. Maudsley is cited in Paul Atkinson, "Fitness, Feminism, and Schooling," in *Nineteenth-Century Woman*, ed. Delamont and Duffin, p. 101.
27. *Fukuzawa Yukichi on Japanese Women*, trans. and ed. Eiichi Kiyooka (Tokyo: University of Tokyo Press, 1988), pp. 7, 241. Pearson is cited in Lorna Duffin, "Prisoners of Progress: Women and Evolution," in *Nineteenth-Century Woman*, ed. Delamont and Duffin, p. 78.
28. Shively, "Japanization of the Middle Meiji," in *Tradition and Modernization in Japanese Culture*, ed. Shively, p. 113; Sievers, *Flowers in Salt*, pp. 14–15. The quotation is from Iwamoto Zenji's editorial describing the aims of his journal, *Jogaku Zasshi* (Women's education journal), and is cited in Kōsaka Masaaki, *Japanese Thought in the Meiji Era*, trans. David Abosch (Tokyo: Pan-Pacific Press, 1958), pp. 262–63. Fukuzawa Yukichi provides a good example of Meiji Japan's indecision regarding female education. Although he was a major advocate of women's education, making many radical suggestions in his writings about Japanese women, his daughters received little or no formal schooling beyond the ornamental accomplishments traditionally taught to samurai daughters.
29. Hartshorne, "Letters and Journals of Ume Tsuda"; Kuno, *Rokumeikan no kifujin*, p. 185.
30. TU to AL, 27 March 1883, 26 May 1883, 18 June 1883, 10 June 1883.
31. TU to AL, 11 April 1883, 6 January 1883, 31 October 1883. Inoue's words are cited in Shively, "Japanization of the Middle Meiji," in *Tradition and Modernization in Japanese Culture*, ed. Shively, p. 91.
32. TU to AL, 28 February 1884, 24 May 1884. Despite her praise for Itō, Ume was nevertheless frequently shocked by him. He, too, presented a challenge to her system of values, which equated the West with a superior civilization and Japan with degenerate decadence. Though "progressive and foreignized," Itō was "fond of the pleasures of Japanese life," she told Adeline Lanman. "Mr Itō, in spite of his foreign ideas, is far from being moral himself," she remarked. "I know *he spends nights out*" (TU to AL, 18 December 1883, 13 January 1884).
33. TU to AL, 18 September 1886. Similar impatience with the Women's Charity Society caused Ume to stay away from many of its activities: "The ladies bazaar is going on today, but I have nothing to

do with it today, and have not sent anything at all. I think they are over doing the thing, and we are having too much of it, so I have kept out of it today, & do not intend to go, & not help—as I give a yen a month to help the hospital, I think it is enough" (TU to AL, 6 December 1888).

34. Sumie Seo Mishima, *My Narrow Isle: The Story of a Modern Woman in Japan* (New York: John Day, 1941; reprint ed., Westport, Conn.: Hyperion, 1981), p. 63.
35. Sievers, *Flowers in Salt*, p. 93. Sievers argues that the women of Meiji Japan, far from being outside the scope of state action—as standard histories suggest—were actually the focus of much government policy. The authorities were especially concerned to get women out of politics and to keep them out. Certainly Inoue's presence, with his secretary, at the meetings of the Women's Charity Society supports Sievers's position that the Meiji authorities tried to redirect women's political energies away from politics and into government-sponsored activities and organizations.
36. Ishimoto, *Facing Two Ways*, pp. 44–45; Alice Bacon, *A Japanese Interior* (Boston: Houghton Mifflin, 1893), pp. 86–87.
37. Ishimoto, *Facing Two Ways*, pp. 53, 90, 281.
38. Ishimoto, *Facing Two Ways*, pp. 55–56; Sievers, *Flowers in Salt*, p. 106; Meech-Pekarik, *World of the Meiji Print*, p. 121. Nishimura is cited in Shively, "Nishimura Shigeki," in *Changing Japanese Attitudes toward Modernization*, ed. Jansen, p. 212.
39. Ishimoto, *Facing Two Ways*, p. 57. Of the similar training given to English girls, Joan Burstyn observes: "To make sure the ideal woman was content to cultivate domestic virtues, she had to be taught to accept physical boundaries to her activities, and her bodily movements had to be constrained by the conventions of ladylike behaviour" (*Victorian Education*, p. 36).
40. Ishimoto, *Facing Two Ways*, p. 63. School athletics and physical education were introduced in the 1880s as a means of discipline and control (Donald Roden, *Schooldays in Imperial Japan: A Study in the Culture of a Student Elite* [Berkeley: University of California Press, 1980], pp. 36–37).
41. Ishimoto, *Facing Two Ways*, pp. 45, 77; TU to AL, 28 November 1888.
42. TU to AL, 4 January 1884, 28 April 1885, 18 January 1884, 15 April 1885, 7 December 1887.
43. TU to AL, 22 July 1888. The emperor's words are cited in Nagai, "Westernization and Japanization," in *Tradition and Modernization in Japanese Culture*, ed. Shively, p. 45.

44. Alice Mabel Bacon, *Japanese Girls and Women*, rev. ed. (Boston: Houghton Mifflin, 1902), p. 434. Baelz ignored two major and well-publicized studies conducted only a few years earlier, which argued that higher education for women was not incompatible with marriage and motherhood. The Sidgwick report, compiled by a committee from the women's colleges at Cambridge and Oxford, offered evidence from a study conducted in 1887 of college-educated women, who reported better health than sisters or cousins who had not attended college. These two groups showed a similar rate of marriage, and the college-educated women, contrary to the dire warnings of medical authorities, had more children than the others. Two years earlier the American Association of Collegiate Alumnae published evidence that refuted the medical arguments against women's higher education made by such opponents as Clarke and Maudsley. This study reported that college-educated women were not less healthy than other women of their age, indicating that higher education did not incapacitate women for marriage or motherhood (Burstyn, *Victorian Education*, p. 150). Nishimura is cited in Shively, "Nishimura Shigeki," in *Changing Japanese Attitudes toward Modernization*, ed. Jansen, p. 229.
45. A good example of Ume's dual allegiance is her reaction to Gilbert and Sullivan's *Mikado*. "How does the opera the Mikado flourish," she wrote Adeline Lanman. "Items have appeared in the Japanese papers about it, as it has become little by little known, & the general feeling is quite a sore one. To make the government & the Emperor who name is taken as the title & to make them the subject of a ridiculous satire for the amusement of the English people is a shame & insult one of the papers says. Just suppose if on the Japanese stage in one of the Tokyo theatres Queen Victoria & the British royal family were made the subject of a ridiculous play, why the British representative would soon appeal for redress & make a great fuss. But Japan being the weaker side can't make a fuss. Just the costumes and manner would not be so much, but to make fun of the government, & to put such absurd things in the mouths of the officials & the Emperor especially when the mass of people are in ignorance of the true state of affair & believe it to be something like this—why it is an insult. If people ask you tell them this, & that it is an insult to every one, Japanese feel, & to a country as well & reasonably governed as Japan a farce." Despite her stance as the outraged patriot, Ume was curious about the operetta and had to invent excuses for her desire to read the libretto: "Can't you send

me the libretto of it just for fun? The costumes & all are very absurd I hear from Japanese and I should like to see & read it anyhow to judge of it." When, two months later, she had read it, Ume confessed to Adeline Lanman, "it is very amusing indeed" (TU to AL, 22 September 1886, 4 November 1886).

Chapter 4: Woman's Paramount Sphere

1. Barbara M. Cross, ed., *The Educated Woman in America* (New York: Teachers College Press, 1965,), pp. 36–37.
2. Cross, *Educated Woman in America*, pp. 37–42; Edith Finch, *Carey Thomas of Bryn Mawr* (New York: Harper and Brothers, 1947), pp. 161–257 *passim*; M. Carey Thomas's remark about failures is cited in Barbara Miller Solomon, *In the Company of Educated Women: A History of Women and Higher Education in America* (New Haven and London: Yale University Press, 1985), p. 84.
3. Cross, *Educated Woman in America*, p. 40.
4. Ashmead, in his study of nineteenth-century Western perceptions of Japan, notes that American women "felt themselves peculiarly called on to improve the status of women in Japan. They organized the first schools for girls in Japan, taught by such women as Mrs. [Julia D.] Carrothers and Mrs. [Mary Putnam] Pruyn, it was an American, Miss [Alice] Bacon, who wrote the first adequate description of the social life of the Japanese girl, and in the comments made by American travellers on the status of women in Japan, it is possible to detect, I believe, a greater intensity and desire to change the Japanese way of life than in the other writers on the subject examined here" (*Idea of Japan*, pp. 431–32).
5. Bacon, *Japanese Girls and Women*, 1891 ed., p. 55. Jean-Pierre Lehmann has written that *Japanese Girls and Women* "remains to this day the best account in English of Japanese women's status, life and customs in the nineteenth century" (*The Image of Japan: From Feudal Isolation to World Power, 1850–1905* [London: George Allen and Unwin, 1978], p. 196).
6. Bacon, *Japanese Girls and Women*, 1891 ed., p. 115.
7. Bacon, *Japanese Girls and Women*, 1891 ed., pp. 17–18, 35–36.
8. Bacon, *Japanese Girls and Women*, 1891 ed., p. 117. Many nineteenth-century feminists on both sides of the Atlantic began their careers as abolitionists and thus absorbed antislavery arguments into their discussions of women's rights. Elizabeth Cady Stanton and Susan B. Anthony, for example, frequently relied on the slave analogy to describe the victimization of women, presenting married women

fleeing their husbands' abuse as "fugitive wives" escaping to Indiana and Connecticut divorce mills "like slaves to their Canada, from marriages worse than plantation slavery." John Stuart Mill also used the analogy between slavery and marriage in his *Subjection of Women* (Elizabeth Pleck, "Feminist Responses to 'Crimes against Women,' 1868–1896," *Signs: Journal of Women in Culture and Society* 8, no. 3 [1983]: 454–55).

The slavery analogy was especially familiar to Alice Bacon. Her father, Leonard Bacon, a Congregational minister and professor at Yale Divinity School, was a noted abolitionist; his *Slavery Discussed in Occasional Essays* (1846) profoundly impressed Abraham Lincoln, who later echoed its words in his speeches (Theodore Davenport Bacon, *Leonard Bacon: A Statesman in the Church* [New Haven: Yale University Press, 1931], p. 269).

9. Bacon, *Japanese Girls and Women*, 1891 ed., pp. 107, 118. This criticism of the wife's traditional subservience is entirely Alice Bacon's. In a letter to Ume, Alice confirmed the emendations she made in the manuscript to soften some of the book's criticisms. She changed, for example, the characterization "slave and drudge," on the advice of Ume's brother-in-law, to "subordinate and servant." (Similarly, the word *foreignizing* became the more politically correct *nationalistic*.) But Alice Bacon balked at the suggestion that the criticism of this chapter's final paragraph be substantially diluted. "Have modified a little, the close of 'Wife and Mother,'" she wrote Ume, "but don't want to soften it too much, as it is still my opinion, & no one will be held responsible for it but me, if your name does not appear on the title-page" (Alice Bacon to TU, 26 September 1890).
10. Bacon, *Japanese Girls and Women*, 1891 ed., pp. 51–54, 78, 81.
11. Bacon, *Japanese Girls and Women*, 1891 ed., pp. 78, 224, 226–27.
12. Bacon, *Japanese Girls and Women*, 1891 ed., pp. 287–89.
13. TU, "The Education of Japanese Women (August 22, 1891)," *Tsuda Umeko monjo*, p. 32; TU, "The Education of Japanese Women," *Tsuda Umeko monjo*, pp. 19, 26; Solomon, *In the Company of Educated Women*, p. 73.
14. TU, "Education of Japanese Women," pp. 21–22, 24.
15. TU, "Education of Japanese Women (August 22, 1891)," p. 31.
16. TU, "Education of Japanese Women," pp. 22–23.
17. TU, "Education of Japanese Women," p. 26. The "gospel of gentility" is the phrase used by Jane Hunter to describe the Protestant middle-class ideal of "true womanhood" that American women missionaries tried to establish in China at the turn of the century, an effort very similar to Ume's program of bringing "civilization

and enlightenment" to Japanese women. (Hunter, *The Gospel of Gentility: American Women Missionaries in Turn-of-the-Century China* [New Haven and London: Yale University Press, 1984].)

18. TU, "Education of Japanese Women," p. 22; Patricia Hill, *The World Their Household: The American Woman's Foreign Mission Movement and Cultural Transformation* (Ann Arbor: University of Michigan Press, 1985), pp. 3–5.
19. Araki Noriko and Louise Ward Demakis, "The Scholarship for Japanese Women: 'A Free Gift from American Women,'" *Japan Christian Quarterly* 53, no. 1 (Winter 1987): 15–31. Commented M. Carey Thomas on the scholarship's administration: "Thus it will be out of the hands of the missionaries."
20. M. Carey Thomas seems to have been particularly insensitive to Ume. After she arrived at Bryn Mawr, Ume presented her with some of the silk she had received from the empress before leaving on the Iwakura mission. To Ume the silk was priceless—it was offered to Carey Thomas almost as a banner from one fighter in the struggle for women's education to another—but to M. Carey Thomas it was merely a square of pretty fabric. "I am very much pleased with the lovely Japanese stuff and the crepe of such an exalted history," she wrote Ume. "I shall use them for the two sides of a cushion" (M. Carey Thomas (hereafter MCT) to TU, 1 March 1891). Her callous treatment of Ume may be due to the fact that M. Carey Thomas, contemptuous of all nonwhite peoples, had a particular dislike of the Japanese (Finch, *Carey Thomas of Bryn Mawr*, p. 243).
21. *Biographical Dictionary of American Educators*, 1:51. Armstrong is cited in *Dictionary of American Biography*, 1:360.
22. Araki and Demakis, "Scholarship for Japanese Women," p. 18.
23. Cited in Araki and Demakis, "Scholarship for Japanese Women," pp. 18–19.
24. Kimura Akebono, "A Mirror for Womanhood," trans. Margaret Mitsutani, *The Magazine* 3, no. 5 (May 1988): 50. *A Mirror for Womanhood*, according to Mitsutani, is the first fictional work by a Japanese woman to use foreign settings and foreign characters. The story grew out of Kimura's longing to study in the West, a desire thwarted by her father, who put her to work in one of his chain of sukiyaki restaurants. After a brief, unsuccessful marriage, she wrote *A Mirror for Womanhood* and fulfilled her frustrated dreams in the brilliant career of her heroine. She died of tuberculosis the following year, at age eighteen. As Mitsutani notes, the meaning of Kimura's pen-name, Akebono (dawn), gives fitting expression to the hopes of many young Japanese women.

The title of Kimura's work, virtually the same as Nishimura Shigeki's *Fujo Kagami*, suggests the existence of a popular model of womanhood quite different from the Confucian ideal. That Kimura had to present her ideal of womanhood in a foreign setting, however, indicates how powerful the Confucian model was.

25. Gluck, *Japan's Modern Myths*, pp. 27–28.
26. Cited in Passin, *Society and Education in Japan*, p. 151.
27. Sievers, *Flowers in Salt*, pp. 104–5, 108–9; Katō is cited in Chieko Irie Mulhern, "Japan's First Newspaperwoman: Hani Motoko," *Japan Interpreter* 12 (Summer 1979): 317.
28. Nagy, "How Shall We Live?" p. 27; Roden, *Schooldays in Imperial Japan*, p. 160; Kōsaka, *Japanese Thought*, pp. 262–66.
29. Gluck, *Japan's Modern Myths*, pp. 109–10. Shimizu's article is summarized in Sievers, *Flowers in Salt*, p. 109.
30. TU, "The Future of Japanese Women," *Tsuda Umeko monjo*, p. 72.
31. TU, "Future of Japanese Women," pp. 72–73.
32. TU, "Future of Japanese Women," p. 73.
33. TU, "Future of Japanese Women," p. 75.
34. TU, "Future of Japanese Women," p. 76. Although Kishida Toshiko contributed frequently to the *Jogaku Zasshi* in the 1890s after her marriage and subsequent departure from the lecture platform, the journal was dismissive of such activists as Fukuda Hideko. Commenting on Fukuda's activities after her release from prison in 1889, the journal remarked: "A party of women headed by one Ei Kageyama [Fukuda] is to come together in Osaka, to deliberate on the subject of Women's Rights. Some of them are said to be of very vulgar origin and others to be of very rude and masculine manners" (cited in Sievers, *Flowers in Salt*, p. 51).
35. Sievers, *Flowers in Salt*, pp. 109–10. Although the extent of Ume's connection to Hatoyama Haruko is not clear, she was acquainted enough with her to write a letter of introduction to M. Carey Thomas for Hatoyama and her husband—"my friends Dr. and Mrs. Hatoyama of Tokyo"—when they visited the United States in 1901 (TU to MCT, 29 July 1901, Japanese Alumnae–Tsuda Papers, Bryn Mawr Archives, box 1, folder 2).
36. Cited in Sievers, *Flowers in Salt*, p. 87. Begun as an organization solely concerned with spreading the value of temperance, the WCTU soon became interested in other social problems after Frances Willard became its president in 1879. The largest women's organization of its time, the WCTU not only successfully campaigned for state laws to protect abused wives of drunkards but also advocated prison reform, the eight-hour workday, and publicly funded kindergartens. The organization established model shelters for neglected

and abused children, some even taking in the poverty-stricken mothers of such children, and offered day-care and kindergarten facilities for the children of working mothers (Pleck, "Feminist Responses to 'Crimes against Women,'" pp. 462–64).

37. Sievers, *Flowers in Salt*, pp. 98–102. The example of the WCTU is typical of the ways in which issues of social reform and women's advancement can gradually shift a women's organization to active involvement in politics and transform the question of temperance into an explicitly political set of concerns. Frances Willard wrote of the organization's forerunner, the Woman's Crusade: "Perhaps the most significant outcome of the movement was the knowledge of their own power gained by the conservative women of the Churches. They had never even seen a 'woman's rights convention,' and had been held aloof from the 'suffragists' by fears as to their orthodoxy; but now there were women prominent in all Church cares and duties eager to clasp hands for a more aggressive work than such women had ever before dreamed of undertaking" (cited in Barbara L. Epstein, *The Politics of Domesticity: Women, Evangelism, and Temperance in Nineteenth-Century America* [Middletown, Conn.: Wesleyan University Press, 1981], p. 103).
38. Cited in Yoshikawa, *Tsuda Umeko den*, pp. 199–203.
39. Sievers, *Flowers in Salt*, pp. 89, 103, 215–27.
40. Cited in Yoshikawa, *Tsuda Umeko den*, p. 202. Nead pays particular attention to the ways in which nineteenth-century philanthropy highlights the relation between class and sexual politics: "Social pity characterized the feminine ideal; it was a sign of class position and social status. So although philanthropy allowed middle-class women into the public sphere, it also perpetuated bourgeois definitions of the feminine ideal" (*Myths of Sexuality*, p. 201).
41. Furuki Yoshiko first drew my attention to the similarities between Ine's mother and Tsuda Hatsuko.
42. Miyakoda, *Tsuda Sen*, pp. 151–69.
43. Sen seems always to have been odd. Clara Whitney, perhaps maliciously, characterizes him throughout her diary as a bit of a buffoon, describing in an entry of 1879 his clownish appearance: "We rambled around until our delinquent friend came up, flushed and perspiring, dressed in foreign clothes—his ankles several inches out of his trousers, his diaphragm several inches below his waistcoat, showing to advantage an amount of linen quite astonishing. His collar, not being fastened properly, had slipped around to the side, and his cravat thus being tied under his left ear gave him quite a kittenish appearance. He arrived just in time to explain the dif-

ferent varieties of plants on exhibition with a great deal of panting and a great deal of perspiring" (*Clara's Diary*, p. 240).

44. A list compiled in 1884 in Tokyo of the most popular foods shows no evidence that any new foods were adopted. Not until the Taishō period (1912–1926) was there the beginning of a transition to a diet that included Western foods (Susan B. Hanley, "The Material Culture: Stability in Transition," in *Japan in Transition*, ed. Jansen and Rozman, pp. 458–60).
45. Yamagata is cited in Gluck, *Japan's Modern Myths*, p. 29.
46. Bacon, *Japanese Girls and Women*, rev. ed., p. 379. The Ministry of Education official is cited in Sievers, *Flowers in Salt*, p. 112.
47. Passin, *Society and Education in Japan*, pp. 97–98; Senju Katsumi, "The Development of Female Education in Private School[s]," *Education in Japan* 6 (1971): 39–40.
48. Cited in Baron [Dairoku] Kikuchi, "Female Education in Japan," *Transactions of the Japan Society of London* 7 (1907): 422.
49. Kikuchi, "Female Education in Japan," pp. 420, 429. The Diet resolution is cited in Gluck, *Japan's Modern Myths*, p. 147.

    The ethics textbook used in girls' middle schools taught the same lesson: the duty of a woman is "to get married, to help her husband, to bring up children, to attend to housekeeping. She is to welcome her husband home with a gentle look, and cheer him up for the following day's work" (cited in Faust, *New Japanese Womanhood*, p. 35).
50. Passin, *Society and Education in Japan*, p. 158; Nagy, *"How Shall We Live?"* pp. 38–40; Sievers, *Flowers in Salt*, p. 111.
51. Cited in Nagy, *"How Shall We Live?"* pp. 40–41. In her discussion of the relation between laws about women and the power of the state, Joan Scott notes that "emergent rulers have legitimized domination, strength, central authority, and ruling power as masculine (enemies, outsiders, subversives, weakness as feminine) and made that code literal in laws (forbidding women's political participation, outlawing abortion, prohibiting wage-earning by mothers, imposing female dress codes) that put women in their place. These actions and their timing make little sense in themselves; in most instances, the state had nothing immediate or material to gain from the control of women. The actions can only be made sense of as part of an analysis of the construction and consolidation of power. An assertion of control or strength was given form as a policy about women" ("Gender: A Useful Category of Historical Analysis," p. 47).
52. Mishima, *My Narrow Isle*, p. 65.

53. The Japanese Woman's Commission for the World's Columbian Exposition, *Japanese Women* (Chicago: privately printed for the Japanese Woman's Commission, 1893), p. 13.
54. TU, "Speech Given at the Denver Convention of the General Federation of Women's Clubs," *Tsuda Umeko monjo*, pp. 483–84; TU to AL, 16 December 1898. The close ties between the American woman's club movement and contemporary feminism, as well as the social and political clout many of these clubs wielded, is the subject of Karen Blair's *The Clubwoman as Feminist: True Womanhood Redefined, 1868–1914* (New York: Holmes and Meier, 1980).
55. TU, "Journal in London," *Tsuda Umeko monjo*, pp. 286–87.
56. Beale is cited in Josephine Kamm, *How Different from Us: A Biography of Miss Buss and Miss Beale* (London: Bodley Head, 1958), p. 82.
57. Poovey, *Uneven Developments*, p. 189.
58. Cited in Kamm, *How Different from Us*, p. 72.

Chapter 5: To Know the Contents of Life for Ourselves

1. Edward Seidensticker, *Low City, High City* (Rutland, Vt.: Charles E. Tuttle, 1983); Masao Maruyama, "Patterns of Individuation," in *Changing Japanese Attitudes toward Modernization*, ed. Jansen, p. 507.
2. Kinmonth, *Self-Made Man in Meiji Japanese Thought*, pp. 207–20; Roden, *Schooldays in Imperial Japan*, pp. 165–73.
3. Nagy, "*How Shall We Live?*" p. 97; Maruyama, "Patterns of Individuation," *Changing Japanese Attitudes*, ed. Jansen, p. 520.
4. TU to Abby and Emily Kirk, 6 August 1900, *Tsuda Umeko monjo*, pp. 375–77.
5. Kinmonth, *Self-Made Man in Meiji Japanese Thought*, pp. 157–59, 166, 176.
6. "Miss Tsuda's Address to the Graduates," *Alumnae Report of Joshi-Eigaku-Juku*, July 1915, *Tsuda Umeko monjo*, p. 150.
7. Report of the Committee on behalf of Miss Tsuda's School for Girls, Japanese Alumnae–Tsuda Papers, Bryn Mawr Archives, box 1, folder 3.
8. Roden, *Schooldays in Imperial Japan*, pp. 58, 103, 111, 139.
9. Roden, *Schooldays in Imperial Japan*, p. 50.
10. Mishima, *My Narrow Isle*, p. 60.
11. "Introductory," *Alumnae Report of the Joshi-Eigaku-Juku*, June 1915, *Tsuda Umeko monjo*, p. 106; TU, "Teaching in Japan," *Tsuda Umeko monjo*, pp. 96–97.
12. Mishima, *My Narrow Isle*, p. 60.
13. TU, "Introductory," *Tsuda Umeko monjo*, pp. 105–6.

14. Nagy, *"How Shall We Live?"* pp. 44–45.
15. Shoji Masako, "Women Educators Who Contributed to the Education of Women, 1," *Education in Japan* 6 (1971): 71; Shibukawa, "An Education for Making Good Wives and Wise Mothers," *Education in Japan* 6 (1971): 53; Nagy, *"How Shall We Live?"* p. 46.
16. TU to the Philadelphia and New York Committees of Miss Tsuda's School, 11 January 1912, *Tsuda Umeko monjo*, p. 417; Report of the Committee on behalf of Miss Tsuda's School for Girls.
17. Passin, *Society and Education in Japan*, pp. 77–78; Gluck, *Japan's Modern Myths*, pp. 151–52; Nagy, *"How Shall We Live?"* p. 137.
18. Cited in Gluck, *Japan's Modern Myths*, p. 268.
19. Mishima, *My Narrow Isle*, p. 56.
20. Sievers, *Flowers in Salt*, p. 166; Pauline C. Reich and Atsuko Fukuda, "Japan's Literary Feminists: The *Seitō* Group," *Signs: Journal of Women in Culture and Society* 2, no. 1 (1976): 289n11.
21. *Seitō*, 1, no. 1 (September 1911), translation from Reich and Fukuda, "*Seitō* Group," p. 287.
22. Hiratsuka Raichō, "Yo no Fujintachi ni," *Seitō*, 3, no. 4 (April 1913), translation from Reich and Fukuda, "*Seitō* Group," p. 291; Noriko Mizuta Lippit and Kyoko Iriye Selden, trans. and eds., *Stories by Contemporary Japanese Women Writers* (New York: M. E. Sharpe, 1982), p. xiii; Yukiko Tanaka, ed., *To Live and to Write: Selections by Japanese Women Writers, 1913–1938* (Seattle: Seal, 1987), p. x.
23. Cott, *Grounding of Modern Feminism*, p. 39.
24. Hiratsuka Raichō, "Yo no Fujintachi ni," in Reich and Fukuda, "*Seitō* Group," pp. 288–91; Sievers, *Flowers in Salt*, p. 180.
25. Sievers, *Flowers in Salt*, pp. 135, 184; Nagy, *"How Shall We Live?"* pp. 60–62.
26. Cited in Gluck, *Japan's Modern Myths*, pp. 169–70, and Roden, *Schooldays in Imperial Japan*, p. 195. Russian novels, Ibsen, and naturalism were specifically blamed for corrupting youth. Naturalism was cited as the cause of Raichō's failed double-suicide attempt. "CLIMAX OF NATURALISM," ran the headline in the *Asahi Shimbun*: "He: university degree holder, novelist. She: graduate of the women's college" (cited in Jay Rubin, *Injurious to Public Morals: Writers and the Meiji State* [Seattle: University of Washington Press, 1984], p. 89). I am grateful to Rebecca Copeland for this reference.
27. Sievers, *Flowers in Salt*, p. 180; Nagy, *"How Shall We Live?"* p. 226.
28. Sievers, *Flowers in Salt*, p. 172; *Alumnae Report of the Joshi-Eigaku-Juku*, July 1908, *Tsuda Umeko monjo*, p. 119. The prayer is cited in Dorothy Robins-Mowry, *The Hidden Sun: Women of Modern Japan* (Boulder, Colo.: Westview, 1983), p. 59.

29. Nagy, *"How Shall We Live?"* pp. 234–35. The commentator is cited in Miyamoto Ken, "Itō Noe and the Bluestockings," *Japan Interpreter* 10 (1975): 195.
30. TU to Nakamura Tsuya, 23 November 1916, *Tsuda Umeko monjo*, p. 461.
31. "Japanese Women of the Present Day," *Tsuda Umeko monjo*, pp. 503–4.
32. TU, "Japanese Women of the Present Day," pp. 504–6.
33. TU, "Woman Movement in Japan."
34. TU, "The Presentation of the Gospel in Japan," *Tsuda Umeko monjo*, p. 502.
35. Cited in Sievers, *Flowers in Salt*, p. 176. The New Woman was followed by the New Man Society (Shinjinkai), a leftist student organization begun at Tokyo Imperial University in 1918. Like the Seitōsha, the New Man Society spoke in images that emphasized newness and rebirth, brightness and dawn, universality and harmony, and popular revolution (Henry Dewitt Smith II, *Japan's First Student Radicals* [Cambridge, Mass.: Harvard University Press, 1972], pp. 53–55).
36. Itō Noe, although not a student at the Joshi Eigaku Juku, should also be mentioned here because her fate indicates the authorities' increasing use of violence to suppress dangerous thought. With Ōsugi Sakae and his seven-year-old nephew, she was strangled in a police cell on 16 September 1923 after the government had declared martial law in the days following the Great Kantō Earthquake.
37. Robins-Mowry, *Hidden Sun*, p. 51; Gluck, *Japan's Modern Myths*, p. 85.
38. Far from being undesirables, the two sisters were received at the White House during this tour, where they had an interview with Theodore Roosevelt and his family (Knox, *Surprise Personalities*, p. 28).
39. Minutes of the Japan Scholarship Committee, cited in Araki and Demakis, "Scholarship for Japanese Women," pp. 23–24.
40. TU to Abiko Yonako, 30 December 1910, *Tsuda Umeko monjo*, pp. 407–8.
41. "At the Onset of Illness," *Tsuda Umeko monjo*, p. 366; Mishima, *My Narrow Isle*, p. 63.
42. Mishima, *My Narrow Isle*, p. 70; Smith, *Japan's First Student Radicals*, p. 183.
43. My thinking here owes much to the conclusions drawn by Jeanne Boydston, Mary Kelley, and Anne Margolis in their discussion of the Beecher sisters and by Claudia Koonz in her analysis of the

German women's movement in the late 1920s (Boydston, Kelley, and Margolis, *Limits of Sisterhood*, and Koonz, "Some Political Implications of Separatism: German Women between Democracy and Nazism, 1928–1934," in *Women in Culture and Politics*, ed. Judith Friedlander et al. [Bloomington: Indiana University Press, 1986], pp. 269–85).

Umeko's faith in "influence" also characterized her attitude toward Japan's expansion in Asia. Because of Japan's rapid modernization—material proof of the nation's superiority—the Japanese had the capacity to influence their colonial subjects, she believed, and bring to them the inestimable benefits of their civilization. Writing her students from Hawaii in 1907, Umeko told them: "In such a place more than in any other, we see the difference between the activity, intelligence and character of the civilized man, and the indolence, ignorance and the feeble mind of the barbarian. Here we see the different races in all their different degrees of development, and the keen active mind of the educated white man a master over them all. Why speak of equal chances when intelligence, industry and character are bound to be the winners in any place and under any conditions? . . . Thus we Japanese too, not resting content with the easy work of developing the fertile spots on our own islands, should make the most of the opportunity which we best have to develop Formosa, Korea and Manchuria. What might these countries not become with their natural wealth and fine climate, if we Japanese used those natural resources to the greatest extent possible?" (*Alumnae Report of the Joshi-Eigaku-Juku*, June 1907, *Tsuda Umeko monjo*, pp. 113–14).

44. Robins-Mowry, *Hidden Sun*, p. 230.

Chapter 6: Conclusion: In Quiet Places, in Quiet Ways

1. Gregory J. Kasza, "The State and the Organization of Women in Prewar Japan," Research Report, *Japan Foundation Newsletter* 13, no. 2 (October 1990), 9–13.
2. Cited in Courtney Whitney, *MacArthur: His Rendezvous with History* (New York: Alfred A. Knopf, 1956), pp. 243, 292.

Bibliography

Manuscript Collections

The bulk of my source material is from the substantial collection at Tsuda College Library of unpublished letters written by Tsuda Umeko to Adeline Lanman—letters carefully saved by Adeline Lanman and returned to Tokyo after her death—as well as those from Adeline that were preserved by Umeko. Among Tsuda Umeko's papers are her earliest English compositions, articles she wrote for American publications, a journal kept during her stay in England, a diary written during the last two years of her life, and various letters to family, friends, and students. These items are found in *Tsuda Umeko monjo / The Writings of Umeko Tsuda*, a collection privately printed by the college in 1980 and revised in 1984. Related unpublished papers are letters to and from M. Carey Thomas and Mary Morris (two of whose letters to Umeko each contain a short letter to Mary Morris from James Rhoads, president of Bryn Mawr College, concerning Umeko's entrance into the college); letters from Alice Bacon and Anna Hartshorne; a journal Umeko kept during her first return voyage to Japan in 1882, "From Washington to Tokyo"; the typescript of her unfinished novel, *Ine, A Story of Modern Japan*; and the manuscript of "The Woman Movement in Japan," her 1915 speech to the Japanese YWCA.

Some time after 1913 Umeko planned to write an autobiography and left three pages of notes. Charles Lanman also planned a biography of Tsuda Umeko, "Ume Tsuda, or The Story of a Japanese Student," making preliminary notes for the project, which Adeline Lanman sent Umeko after his death. I have used both these notes and those made by Anna Hartshorne for *her* projected biography, "The Letters and Journals of Ume Tsuda."

At the Bryn Mawr College archives I have consulted letters from Tsuda Umeko to M. Carey Thomas, as well as materials related to the scholarship for Japanese women and the fundraising campaign for the Joshi Eigaku Juku and its rebuilding after the Great Kantō Earthquake in 1923.

Other Sources

Ackroyd, Joyce. "Women in Feudal Japan." *Transactions of the Asiatic Society of Japan* 7, no. 3 (November 1959).

Araki, Noriko, and Louise Ward Demakis. "The Scholarship for Japanese Women: 'A Free Gift from American Women.'" *Japan Christian Quarterly* 53, no. 1 (Winter 1987).

Ashmead, John. *The Idea of Japan: 1853–1895*. New York and London: Garland, 1987.

Atkinson, Paul. "Fitness, Feminism, and Schooling." In *The Nineteenth-Century Woman: Her Cultural and Physical World*, Sara Delamont and Lorna Duffin, eds. London: Croom Helm; New York: Barnes and Noble, 1978.

Bacon, Alice Mabel. *Japanese Girls and Women*. Boston and New York: Houghton Mifflin, 1891.

———. *Japanese Girls and Women*. Rev. ed. Boston: Houghton Mifflin, 1902.

———. *A Japanese Interior*. Boston: Houghton Mifflin, 1893.

Bacon, Theodore Davenport. *Leonard Bacon: A Statesman in the Church*. New Haven: Yale University Press, 1931.

Beecher, Catharine. *A Treatise on Domestic Economy*. 1841; reprint ed. New York: Schocken Books, 1977.

Blair, Karen J. *The Clubwoman as Feminist: True Womanhood Redefined, 1868–1914*. New York: Holmes and Meier, 1980.

Boydston, Jeanne, Mary Kelley, and Anne Margolis. *The Limits of Sisterhood: The Beecher Sisters on Women's Rights and Woman's Sphere*. Chapel Hill: University of North Carolina Press, 1988.

Braisted, William Reynolds. *Meiroku Zasshi: Journal of the Japanese Enlightenment*. Tokyo: University of Tokyo Press, 1976.

Burstyn, Joan N. *Victorian Education and the Ideal of Womanhood*. New Brunswick, N.J.: Rutgers University Press, 1984.

Chamberlain, Basil Hall. *Things Japanese*. London: John Murray, 1905.

Conte, James T. *Overseas Study in the Meiji Period: Japanese Students in America, 1867–1902*. Ph.D. diss., Princeton University, 1977.

Cortazzi, Bernard. *Victorians in Japan: In and around the Treaty Ports*. London: Athlone, 1987.

Cott, Nancy. *The Bonds of Womanhood: 'Woman's Sphere' in New England, 1780–1835*. New Haven and London: Yale University Press, 1977.

———. *The Grounding of Modern Feminism*. New Haven and London: Yale University Press, 1987.

Cross, Barbara M., ed. *The Educated Woman in America*. New York: Teachers College Press, 1965.

Danly, Robert Lyons. *In the Shade of Spring Leaves: The Life and Writings of Higuchi Ichiyō, a Woman of Letters in Meiji Japan*. New Haven and London: Yale University Press, 1981.

DeForest, Charlotte B. *The Woman and the Leaven in Japan*. West Medford, Mass.: Central Committee on the United Study of Foreign Missions, 1923.

Dore, R. P. *Education in Tokugawa Japan*. Berkeley: University of California Press, 1965.

———. "The Legacy of Tokugawa Education." In *Changing Japanese Attitudes toward Modernization*, Marius B. Jansen, ed. Princeton, N.J.: Princeton University Press, 1965.

Duffin, Lorna. "Prisoners of Progress: Women and Evolution." In *The Nineteenth-Century Woman: Her Cultural and Physical World*, Sara Delamont and Lorna Duffin, eds. London: Croom Helm; New York: Barnes and Noble, 1978.

Epstein, Barbara L. *The Politics of Domesticity: Women, Evangelism, and Temperance in Nineteenth-Century America*. Middletown, Conn.: Wesleyan University Press, 1981.

Faulds, Henry. *Nine Years in Nipon: Sketches of Japanese Life and Manners.* London: Alexander Gardner, 1887.

Faust, Allen K. *The New Japanese Womanhood.* New York: George H. Doran, 1926.

Finch, Edith. *Carey Thomas of Bryn Mawr.* New York: Harper and Brothers, 1947.

Fukuzawa, Yukichi. *The Autobiography of Fukuzawa Yukichi.* Eiichi Kiyooka, trans. Tokyo: Hokuseidō, 1981.

———. *Fukuzawa Yukichi on Japanese Women.* Eiichi Kiyooka, trans. and ed. Tokyo: University of Tokyo Press, 1988.

Gluck, Carol. *Japan's Modern Myths: Ideology in the Late Meiji Period.* Princeton, N.J.: Princeton University Press, 1985.

Hall, Ivan Parker. *Mori Arinori.* Cambridge, Mass.: Harvard University Press, 1973.

Hanley, Susan B. "The Material Culture: Stability in Transition." In *Japan in Transition: From Tokugawa to Meiji,* Marius Jansen and Gilbert Rozman, eds. Princeton, N.J.: Princeton University Press, 1986.

Hardy, Arthur Sherburne. *Life and Letters of Joseph Hardy Neesima.* Boston: Houghton Mifflin, 1891.

Hill, Patricia R. *The World Their Household: The American Woman's Foreign Mission Movement and Cultural Transformation.* Ann Arbor: University of Michigan Press, 1985.

Howe, Florence. "Women's Studies and Social Change." In her *Myths of Coeducation.* Bloomington: Indiana University Press, 1984.

Howes, John F. "Japanese Christians and American Missionaries." In *Changing Japanese Attitudes toward Modernization,* Marius B. Jansen, ed. Princeton, N.J.: Princeton University Press, 1965.

Hunter, Jane. *The Gospel of Gentility: American Women Missionaries in Turn-of-the-Century China.* New Haven and London: Yale University Press, 1984.

Ishimoto, Shidzue [Katō Shizue]. *Facing Two Ways: The Story of My Life.* New York: Farrar and Rinehart, 1935; reprint ed., Stanford: Stanford University Press, 1984.

Jansen, Marius. "The Ruling Class." In *Japan in Transition: From Tokugawa to Meiji,* Marius Jansen and Gilbert Rozman, eds. Princeton, N.J.: Princeton University Press, 1986.

The Japanese Woman's Commission for the World's Columbian Exposition. *Japanese Women.* Chicago: privately printed for the Japanese Woman's Commission, 1893.

Kamm, Josephine. *How Different from Us: A Biography of Miss Buss and Miss Beale*. London: Bodley Head, 1958.

Kasza, Gregory J. "The State and the Organization of Women in Prewar Japan." Research Report, *Japan Foundation Newsletter* 13, no. 2 (October 1990).

Katsumi, Senju. "The Development of Female Education in Private School[s]." *Education in Japan* 6 (1971).

Kawai, Michi. *My Lantern*. Tokyo: Kyō Bun Kwan, 1939.

Kikuchi, Baron [Dairoku]. "Female Education in Japan." *Transactions of the Japan Society of London* 7 (1907).

Kimura, Akebono. "A Mirror for Womanhood." Margaret Mitsutani, trans. *The Magazine* 3, no. 5 (May 1988).

Kinmonth, Earl H. *The Self-Made Man in Meiji Japanese Thought: From Samurai to Salary Man*. Berkeley: University of California Press, 1981.

Knox, Katharine McCook. *Surprise Personalities in Georgetown*. Washington, D.C.: privately printed, 1958.

Koonz, Claudia. "Some Political Implications of Separatism: German Women between Democracy and Nazism, 1928–1934." In *Women in Culture and Politics*, Judith Friedlander et al., eds. Bloomington: Indiana University Press, 1986.

Kōsaka, Masaaki. *Japanese Thought in the Meiji Era*. David Abosch, trans. Tokyo: Pan-Pacific Press, 1958.

Kuno, Akiko. *Rokumeikan no kifujin: Nihonhatsu no joshi ryūgakusei*. Tokyo: Chūō Kōron, 1988.

Lanman, Charles. *Leaders of the Meiji Restoration in America*. Tokyo: Hokuseidō, 1931.

Lippit, Noriko Mizuta, and Kyoko Iriye Selden, trans. and eds. *Stories by Contemporary Japanese Women Writers*. New York: M. E. Sharpe, 1982.

Maruyama, Masao, "Patterns of Individuation." In *Changing Japanese Attitudes toward Modernization*, Marius Jansen, ed. Princeton, N.J.: Princeton University Press, 1965.

Mayo, Marlene. "The Iwakura Mission to the United States and Europe, 1871–1873." Columbia University East Asian Institute, *Researches in the Social Sciences on Japan* 2, no. 6 (June 1959).

———. "Rationality in the Meiji Restoration: The Iwakura Embassy." In *Modern Japanese Leadership: Transition and Change*, Bernard S. Silberman and H. D. Harootunian, eds. Tucson: University of Arizona Press, 1966.

Meech-Pekarik, Julia. *The World of the Meiji Print: Impressions of a New Civilization.* New York: Weatherhill, 1986.

Mishima, Sumie Seo. *My Narrow Isle: The Story of a Modern Woman in Japan.* New York: John Day, 1941; reprint ed., Westport, Conn.: Hyperion, 1981.

Miyakoda, Toyosaburō. *Tsuda Sen: Meiji no kirisutosha.* Tokyo: Nihon Kirisuto Kyōdan Kudan Kyōkai, 1972.

Miyamoto Ken. "Itō Noe and the Bluestockings." *Japan Interpreter* 10 (1975).

Miyoshi, Masao. *As We Saw Them: The First Japanese Embassy to the United States (1860).* Berkeley: University of California Press, 1979.

Mulhern, Chieko Irie. "Japan's First Newspaperwoman: Hani Motoko." *Japan Interpreter* 12 (Summer 1979).

Murray, Megan Baldridge. "The Girl Thrown Away Forever: Memories of a Princess." *Vassar Quarterly* 79, no. 3 (Spring 1983).

Nagai, Michio. "Herbert Spencer in Early Meiji Japan." *Far Eastern Quarterly* 14 (November 1954).

———. "Westernization and Japanization: The Early Meiji Transformation of Education." In *Tradition and Modernization in Japanese Culture,* Donald H. Shively, ed. Princeton, N.J.: Princeton University Press, 1971.

Nagy, Margit Maria. *"How Shall We Live?": Social Change, the Family Institution and Feminism in Prewar Japan.* Ph.D. diss., University of Washington, 1981.

Nead, Lynda. *Myths of Sexuality: Representations of Women in Victorian Britain.* Oxford: Basil Blackwell, 1988.

Norton, Mary Beth. *Liberty's Daughters: The Revolutionary Experience of American Women, 1750–1800.* Boston: Little, Brown, 1980.

Passin, Herbert. *Society and Education in Japan.* Tokyo: Kodansha, 1982.

Pleck, Elizabeth. "Feminist Responses to 'Crimes against Women,' 1868–1896." *Signs: Journal of Women in Culture and Society* 8, no. 3 (1983).

Poovey, Mary. *Uneven Developments: The Ideological Work of Gender in Mid-Victorian England.* London: Virago, 1989.

Reich, Pauline C., and Atsuko Fukuda. "Japan's Literary Feminists: The *Seitō* Group." *Signs: Journal of Women in Culture and Society* 2, no. 1 (1976).

Rich, Adrienne, *Of Woman Born: Motherhood as Experience and Institution.* London: Virago, 1977.

———. "Resisting Amnesia: History and Personal Life." In her *Blood, Bread and Poetry*. London: Virago, 1986.

Roberts, John G. *Mitsui: Three Centuries of Japanese Business*. New York: Weatherhill, 1973.

Robins-Mowry, Dorothy. *The Hidden Sun: Women of Modern Japan*. Boulder, Colo.: Westview, 1983.

Roden, Donald. *Schooldays in Imperial Japan: A Study in the Culture of a Student Elite*. Berkeley: University of California Press, 1980.

Rozman, Gilbert. "Castle Towns in Transition." In *Japan in Transition: From Tokugawa to Meiji*, Marius Jansen and Gilbert Rozman, eds. Princeton, N.J.: Princeton University Press, 1986.

Rubin, Jay. *Injurious to Public Morals: Writers and the Meiji State*. Seattle: University of Washington Press, 1984.

Rubinger, Richard. "Education: From One Room to One System." In *Japan in Transition: From Tokugawa to Meiji*, Marius Jansen and Gilbert Rozman, eds. Princeton, N.J.: Princeton University Press, 1986.

———. *Private Academies of Tokugawa Japan*. Princeton, N.J.: Princeton University Press, 1982.

Russell, Oland D. *The House of Mitsui*. Westport, Conn.: Greenwood, 1970.

Russett, Cynthia Eagle. *Sexual Science: The Victorian Construction of Womanhood*. Cambridge, Mass.: Harvard University Press, 1989.

Scheiner, Irwin. *Christian Converts and Social Protest in Meiji Japan*. Berkeley: University of California Press, 1970.

———. "Christian Samurai and Samurai Values." In *Modern Japanese Leadership: Transition and Change*, Bernard S. Silberman and H. D. Harootunian, eds. Tucson: University of Arizona Press, 1966.

Scott, Joan Wallach. "Gender: A Useful Category of Historical Analysis." In her *Gender and the Politics of History*. New York: Columbia University Press, 1988.

Seidensticker, Edward. *Low City, High City*. Rutland, Vt.: Charles E. Tuttle, 1983.

Shibukawa, Hisako. "An Education for Making Good Wives and Wise Mothers (Ryosai Kenbo no Kyoiku)." *Education in Japan* 6 (1971).

Shively, Donald H. "The Japanization of the Middle Meiji." In *Tradition and Modernization in Japanese Culture*, Donald H. Shively, ed. Princeton, N.J.: Princeton University Press, 1971.

———. "Nishimura Shigeki: A Confucian View of Modernization."

In *Changing Japanese Attitudes toward Modernization*, Marius B. Jansen, ed. Princeton, N.J.: Princeton University Press, 1965.

Shoji, Masako. "Women Educators Who Contributed to the Education of Women, 1." *Education in Japan* 6 (1971).

Sievers, Sharon L. *Flowers in Salt: The Beginnings of Feminist Consciousness in Modern Japan*. Stanford: Stanford University Press, 1983.

Sklar, Kathryn Kish. *Catharine Beecher: A Study in American Domesticity*. New Haven and London: Yale University Press, 1973.

Smethurst, Richard J. *Agricultural Development and Tenancy Disputes in Japan, 1870–1940*. Princeton, N.J.: Princeton University Press, 1986.

Smiles, Samuel. *Self-Help*. London: John Murray, 1908.

Smith, Henry Dewitt, II. *Japan's First Student Radicals*. Cambridge, Mass.: Harvard University Press, 1972.

Smith, Thomas C. *Political Change and Industrial Development in Japan: Government Enterprise, 1868–1880*. Stanford: Stanford University Press, 1955.

Solomon, Barbara Miller. *In the Company of Educated Women: A History of Women and Higher Education in America*. New Haven and London: Yale University Press, 1985.

Tanaka, Yukiko, ed. and trans. *To Live and to Write: Selections by Japanese Women Writers 1913–1938*. Seattle: Seal, 1987.

Tsuda Umeko. *Tsuda Umeko monjo / The Writings of Umeko Tsuda*, Furuki Yoshiko et al., eds. Rev. ed. Kodaira: Tsuda Juku Daigaku, 1984.

Ukita, Kazutami. "Educationalists of the Past and Their Share in the Modernization of Japan." In *Fifty Years of New Japan*, Shigenobu Ōkuma, comp. London: Smith, Elder, 1910.

Umegaki, Michio. "From Domain to Prefecture." In *Japan in Transition: From Tokugawa to Meiji*, Marius Jansen and Gilbert Rozman, eds. Princeton, N.J.: Princeton University Press, 1986.

Whitney, Clara. *Clara's Diary: An American Girl in Meiji Japan*, M. William Steele and Tamiko Ichimata, eds. Tokyo: Kodansha, 1981.

Whitney, Courtney. *MacArthur: His Rendezvous with History*. New York: Alfred A. Knopf, 1956.

Whitney, Marian P. "Stematz Yamakawa, Princess Oyama." *Vassar Quarterly* 4 (1918–19).

Yamamura, Kozo. "The Meiji Land Tax Reform and Its Effects." In *Japan in Transition: From Tokugawa to Meiji*, Marius Jansen and Gilbert Rozman, eds. Princeton, N.J.: Princeton University Press, 1986.

Yamazaki, Takako. *Tsuda Umeko*. Tokyo: Yoshikawa Kobunkan, 1972.
Yokoyama, Toshio. *Japan in the Victorian Mind: A Study of Stereotyped Images of a Nation, 1850–1880*. Basingstoke: Macmillan, 1987.
Yoshikawa, Riichi. *Tsuda Umeko den*. Tokyo: Tsuda Juku Dōsoskai, 1931, reprint ed., 1956.

Index